THE FAMILY ON TRIAL

SPECIAL RELATIONSHIPS IN MODERN POLITICAL THOUGHT

THE FAMILY ON TRIAL

SPECIAL RELATIONSHIPS
IN
MODERN POLITICAL THOUGHT

PHILIP ABBOTT

THE PENNSYLVANIA STATE UNIVERSITY PRESS
UNIVERSITY PARK AND LONDON

Lines from "Perry Rouston" from *The New Spoon River* (Macmillan, 1968) by Edgar
Lee Masters are reprinted by permission of Mrs. Ellen C. Masters.

Lines from "Gravelly Run" from *Collected Poems 1951–1971*, by A.R. Ammons, are
reprinted by permission of W.W. Norton Co., Inc. © 1972 by A.R. Ammons.

Excerpt from "Four for Sir John Davies," © 1953 by Theodore Roethke, from the
book, *The Collected Poems of Theodore Roethke*, are reprinted by permission of
Doubleday & Co., Inc.

Library of Congress Cataloging in Publication Data

Abbott, Philip.
  The family on trial.

  Includes index.
  1. Family—Addresses, essays, lectures. 2. Children—Management—

I. Title.
HQ734.A173   306.8   80-26964
ISBN 0-271-00282-4

In Memory of Rachel Constance Abbott

CONTENTS

PREFACE

The biblical declaration that God "setteth the solitary in families" has been directly challenged in modern political and social thought. In some cases the solitary condition has been judged to be a morally superior one. In others the origin of families has been traced to much less benevolent sources. Sometimes the family is seen to be too rational, sometimes too emotional; sometimes too equalitarian, sometimes not equalitarian enough; sometimes too large, sometimes too small; sometimes too isolated, sometimes not isolated enough; sometimes too durable, sometimes too fragile; sometimes too violent, sometimes not violent enough. In nearly all cases, however, the concept of the family has remained a central item for reconstruction on the agenda of modern political thought.

Not all writers have called for the abolition of the family. And even among the "abolitionists" we find attempts to set the solitary into new and different units. The descriptions we offer suggest that these new resting places are often strange and awkward ones: Hobbes' family members tied in awful autistic knots of fear; Locke's rational couple who calmly join together to "propagate their species" and secure property rights; Rousseau's patriarchal idyll which attempts to overcome man's fear of female sexuality; Fourier's bureaucracies of panderers; Marx's romantic dyads floating atop his newly collectivized ensemble of children; Freud's ambivalent patriarchy in which every individual's eyes are pinned open to view each other's murderous impulses.

The fantastic nature of these models may cause the reader to wonder about the relevance of these great writers. A limited proof of their significance is that contemporary theorists have continued and expanded their agenda, now focusing upon childhood as a final solution to the political problem of the family. Here we are introduced to pleas for the "eroticization of children" and for freedom from the "tyranny of reproductive biology." Proposals for new bureaucratic support structures appear with great frequency: professional guardians, childrens' camps, cloning hospitals. But the complete proof is to be found in modern life itself. Who has not seen Hobbes's "empty shell family," suitably clothed in the remains of a bourgeois exterior, in his own neighborhood? Who has not heard Rousseau's outbursts against women offered with beery sincerity at the close of a party? Who has not met the Lockean professional couple earnestly pursuing the life of the free and rational? Who has not seen a Fourierist angelic couple in a pornographic movie "transformed" before one's eyes? Leon Trotsky's remark about history can indeed be paraphrased as "you may not care about political theory but it does care about you."

This book is designed to present a general and interpretive guide to thought about the family in modern life. It attempts to address the concerns of specialists in sociology, psychology, philosophy, history, and political science but it is also very much directed toward the general reader. Tocqueville observed that there seemed to be an American obsession with re-evaluating and remodeling the family. Those who offer guidelines for defining family relationships (from Judge Ben Lindsey to Margaret Mead, from John Noyes to Gay Talese and Nancy Friday, from the Grimké sisters to Betty Friedan) are earnestly discussed by the American public. Needless to say, all of us personally struggle with the families in our own lives.

Support for this book came from a National Endowment for the Humanities summer stipend and grants from the Earhart Foundation and the Wayne State University Institute of Gerontology. The entire manuscript was read by Larry D. Spence and Jean Bethke Elshtain. Their generous and constructive responses are very much appreciated. Helpful comments on portions of the manuscript were given by Mary Lyndon Shanley, Benjamin Barber, William Meyer, and Charles Parrish. A version of Chapter 10 appeared in Political Theory. *Permission to reproduce it here is gratefully acknowledged. John Pickering provided aid far beyond the requirements of an editor. Finally my wife, Patricia, and my children, Joshua and Megan, joyfully provided support. Appreciation for such acts can never be fully expressed with the formal language of debts.*

PART I

Between such animal and human heat
I find myself perplexed. What is desire?—
The impulse to make someone else complete?
That woman should set sodden straw on fire.
Was I the servant of a sovereign wish,
Or ladle rattling in an empty dish?

—Theodore Roethke, from "Four for Sir John Davies"

1

THE MODERN FAMILY
AS A
POLITICAL PROBLEM

Imagine this scene. Once upon a time people lived under horrible circumstances. Their movements were limited and closely watched. They were subjected to the whims of what we shall call "guardians" who were strategically placed among every four or five people. The guardians demanded both love and absolute obedience. Within these groups, scapegoats were often found to ease frustrations. Sometimes there were inchoate rebellions. There were beatings. Many fled; they appealed to a rigged legal order. But they were ostracized. Psychologically damaged, they often returned, sometimes to the same guardians and sometimes to new ones.

Always they labored under a three-tier class system. There was the guardian at the top. He was the only one with contacts to the outside world. Under the guardian was his supervisor, who was handpicked on the basis of complicated rituals. The supervisor did menial work and was subjected to the guardians' sexual demands. But the supervisor's main function was to control the third class. These people had absolutely no power. We shall call them "charges." They lived in a world of pure force. They were told when to rise, when and what and how much to eat, whom they could see and how to behave. If the supervisor could not deal with this class, the guardian was called in. Punishment was swift and harsh. As is the case with all oppression, the downtrodden and their supervisors developed close emotional ties. Even the guardians said they loved their supervisors and charges. Life under these distorted emotional conditions was fraught with danger. Sometimes the guardian would exchange one supervisor for another. Sexual rivalry comingled with jockeying for economic advancement or security. We almost forgot one thing. There were anonymous and strong powers who watched these little institutions very carefully. They plucked the charges from the supervisors at a young age and sent them to another institution. Later, half of the charges would become guardians themselves; the other half would become supervisors. A whole new set of little institutions would be started again and these higher powers would lean back to rest and watch the results of their efforts.

There are two endings to this story. One goes this way: One day a few supervisors and a few guardians rebelled. They refused responsibility for charges. They refused to be supervisors and guardians. They found freedom. The battle was a long one. It was difficult for people to see one another as other than guardian or supervisor. There were reverses; some fell back to the old ways. Another conclusion is this: The higher powers became disenchanted with the efficiency of the little institutions. Perhaps there were better ways of control than these units. They took on more and more responsibility for the charges and housed them in larger units. Guardians and supervisors were exchanged for keepers.

The above story is not a science fiction account of some strange tyranny. Nor is it an allegory of totalitarian administrative techniques. It is the work of modern political philosophers. The little institutions in the story are families, those seemingly innocuous structures in which we all grow up. The guardians are fathers; the supervisors, mothers; the charges, children.

The attack on the family in modern political thought has been sweeping and unremitting. Although the critiques vary in their intensity, dissatisfaction with the family is nearly universal in modern political thought — so much so that the family as an institutional form has come to be regarded as one of the central problems of political philosophy. Marx's view of the family is well known; it was an institution held together by the money relation and would be swept away by the revolution. But other forms of socialism have cast an even colder eye on the modern family; Fourier saw the family as modern society's most blatant form of egoism. More striking, however, is liberalism's disenchantment with the family; John Stuart Mill, a writer not generally given to overstatement, described the Victorian family as a "school of despotism" and compared arguments in its defense to the rationalizations of Southern slaveholders.

The treatment of the family in modern political thought is, nevertheless, still a complicated one and the issues on which this book will focus are contained in the above allegory. If we can finally be "freed" from families, do we face even greater restrictions?

Yet it is clear that we are now experiencing Hegel's Owl of Minerva phenomenon. Just as we begin to understand the nature of the modern family as an institution, it seems to be disappearing right before our eyes.

Dyadic relationships have assumed a new ephemerality. Ninety-six percent of the population will marry, thirty-eight percent of those will divorce, seventy-nine percent of those will remarry and forty-four percent of these will divorce again. The nidal climate of the modern family is disintegrating under the commitments of both spouses to work in the marketplace. More than half of all married women with school-age children hold jobs. Couples with no children under eighteen now make up forty-seven percent of all families. The lone dyad was once referred to as a childless family; it is now proclaimed to be "childfree." Truncated family forms have appeared in increasing numbers. Four children out of ten born in the 1970s will spend part of their childhood in a single-parent family.

One must be cautious in interpreting these developments. They are very recent and reflect changes over a period of less than twenty years. But most of these alterations have occurred with lightning quickness, some over a span of just five years, and at a drastic rate. Moreover, they do not appear to be precipitated by any such catastrophic events as war, revolution, and depression — the sort of phenomena that traditionally challenged family forms.

These observations lead us to one of the central questions of this book: How was the modern family received in political theory? Our general approach will be to attempt to determine how the modern family was conceived in political thought. Here are some of the questions we will try to answer:

1. What are the positions in regard to the family in modern thought?
2. How precisely are these positions related to the broader orientation of the political philosophy in question?
3. What roles does the writer assign the family and/or what roles would be transferred to other institutions?
4. What sort of political systems are consistent with the maintenance, revision, or abolition of the modern family, as seen by the political philosopher? How accurate and desirable are they?

We will focus in Part I upon six writers who, we will contend, are responsible for the initial formulation of the modern family and for the case that was to be built against it. Each represents a general approach to political and social theory. Here we will depart slightly from a conventional ideological analysis.

Hobbes and Locke offer us the first of five major orientations, one that we shall call a theory of *rational individualism*. This description is more narrow and probably more accurate than the standard application of the word "liberalism." Rational individualism sees the world composed of self-contained and autonomous units. The central task of political philosophy is to rationally devise means to contain these units without altering their essence. Hobbes and Locke offer positions that show some of the range that rational individualism can offer in respect to the family. Hobbes can accept neither the traditional partriarchalism that posits natural authority relationships nor an emotional bond as the basis for the family. Thus, as we shall attempt to show, he devises an "empty shell" contractual patriarchalism. The family still exists at a formal level for Hobbes but — since its relationships are no different in character from those of subject and sovereign, both emanate from raw fear and are resolved in contract — it is difficult to say that the family really survives at all.

We have then a far-reaching critique of the modern family before it is even in place. It is based upon a theory that was to become increasingly popular in political thought. But Locke is one of the first to present a political theory with the outlines of the modern family as a relatively equalitarian and child-centered institution. In this theory the family is given a crucial role: it is to be the sole socialization agency of citizens. But while Locke is anxious to demonstrate the uniqueness of familial as opposed to political authority, he is determined to paint the family in individualized terms. As it does with Hobbes, the family assumes an almost epiphenomenal status; politics and indeed family life are conceived in terms of "free and rational" persons. Locke introduces the concept of contractual marriage and divorce and even hints that the continuation of the family is problematic when children come of age.

Both Hobbes and Locke as the first and foremost representatives of rational individualism in political thought perceived that even this new model of the family was in important ways antithetical to their conception of politics and social life.

The second major orientation we shall examine offers an even more complicated position. This is the concept of *romantic individualism*. This theory, as does that of rational individualism, begins with the self as the center of analysis, but it is a much more complex self. The romantic individualist seeks personal awareness and perfection and his basic political problem is to find "authentic" bonds with others that somehow do not violate his search. Thus romantic individualism swings wildly between anarchic confrontations with society and the most severe submission to collective authority. As with his rational counterpart, the romantic individualist is not always the individualist that he claims to be.

The figure that we shall examine here — a towering figure — is Rousseau. Rousseau did much to complete the model of the modern family by introducing the idea of sentiment to the dyad, and he designed the family to stand in opposition to the demands of the polity. Rousseau drew a picture of the family that was based exclusively upon romantic love.

Grandparents, tutors, and servants were cast out of the family. Rousseau drew a clear distinction between home and household. His family as a small, intensely emotional, child-centered social unit stood as an island of virtue and displayed the equalitarian aspect of the modern family. In place of traditional patriarchy, Rousseau constructed a romantic version with the woman emotionally dependent upon the husband and "more isolated than a nun." However, Rousseau was not always content to recommend miniature models of romantic individualism. In other works, he treated the family as a suspect institution, a center of "particular will," that threatened the reign of virtue in an equalitarian republic.

Rousseau's ambivalence toward the family can be traced to the peculiar requirements of romanticism. But the romantic can devise institutions that are unabashedly collectivist. Thus we have devised another category, *romantic collectivism.* Our representative thinker here is Charles Fourier. Fourier begins the socialist tradition by placing his attack on the modern family at the center of his analysis. Thus begins the first in a long series of critiques which attempt to demystify the emotional basis of the modern family. In this case, the weapons of demystification are remarkably modern ones. The family as the apparent center of love and repose, an institution that seems to transcend the harsh realities of the larger society, is in fact an institution resting upon economic oppression and renunciation of instincts. To the romantic mind hypocrisy is the ultimate sin. For the family to be seen as a hypocritical institution is the basic argument for extinction. Fourier saw the bourgeois odes to family life and he saw the sexual exploits of the rich, the exploitation of working-class women, the pandering of peasant parents, the tragedies which poverty produced in children. He concluded that civilization was corrupt and the family was the seat of corruption.

The "new mode of domestic society" that Fourier offered in place of the family was a system of "amorous institutions" that allowed for the liberation of the instincts. His "regime of love" would guarantee a sexual minimum and as a consequence a social minimum to everyone. Thus Fourier outlines what more and more writers will attempt to offer: the creation of a climate of personal liberation within a collectivist order. In each case dyadic bonds, nidal climate, and special relationships will be attacked in order to find replacements.

The family is momentarily placed in the background in Marxist thought, the fourth of the major orientations. Here the motif is one of *rational collectivism.* The image of an agonizingly self-conscious self is rejected. Although he had some kind but patronizing words for both, Marx could not abide Fourier or Rousseau. Rational collectivism seeks to divine a principle that will objectively unite apparently disparate forces in history and society. Personal and collective existence is merged but on a rational basis, partially independent of individual will.

Marx and Engels never veered from their hostility to the family but remained convinced that it would vanish painlessly with the emergence of communism. But both Marx and Engels retained an odd and in some ways obscure commitment to the dyad itself, a point which we shall explore in Chapter 6.

Our final and fifth representative position in modern political thought in its treatment of the family is a bit more difficult to categorize. Sigmund Freud's revolutionary discoveries of the unconscious and its relation to instincts do not fit within the concepts of individualism, collectivism, rationalism, or romanticism. No one would accuse Freud of the slightest tinge of romanticism; but his rationalism always was superimposed upon an analysis of an intensely irrational world, a world that never could be entirely subsumed under an analytic framework. Furthermore, his collectivism was of the most cautious variety. There was only a small place for the ego (and larger places for the id and the super ego) in Freud's thought, even though it was still portrayed in friendly and sympathetic terms.

The social and political thought of Freud is conservative and it may be the only form of conservatism that modernity has as yet produced. But it is an especially weak conservatism not so much in terms of the force of Freud's arguments in themselves, but because the structural aspects of his theories always seem to undermine his recommendations. Thus Freud speaks of the family as the "germ cell" of civilization, but no one is more responsible than Freud for demystifying love or for laying open the murderous impulses within the family itself. While recognizing that Freud's political thought may be *sui generis,* we will call his work *psychological conservatism* and attempt to trace its relationships to traditional conservative responses.

These six writers and the forms of social and political thought they represent provide us with the basic approaches to the family in the modern era. But increments and important alterations have occurred. Part II attempts to record these changes. The rational individualist form of liberal thought has just about dispensed with the modern family. John Rawls' *A Theory of Justice,* which may be the last attempt to keep the family in a framework of political thought, betrays an open intolerance toward the family and toward the perceived demands of justice. Recent versions of romanticism have even discarded Rousseau's ambivalence and present a not very effectively disguised attack on the family in the name of pluralism. Marxism, by absorbing much of Freudian psychoanalysis, has added another weapon of demystification in the battle against the family. But most importantly, the attack upon the concept of childhood emerges as a centerpiece in recent studies of the family. The abolition of the child stands alongside the abolition of the family as part of the agenda of political thought.

Part III is our attempt to return the modern family to modern political thought. By treating the modern family sympathetically we shall try to outline a political theory which accommodates the family. Chapter 13 introduces the concept of special relationships in detail as a link between the family and the polity. Chapter 14 reviews political theories which might be able to successfully incorporate the concept and discusses a few policy alternatives that would move us toward our general framework. But before we begin, let us briefly review the historical changes in family structures and their relationship to political thought.

The family has not always been a problem in the history of Western political thought. There is the obvious exception of Plato, and a great exception it is indeed since the *Republic* stands as a model for a polity without the family. But for the most part the family was safely incorporated into political theory from Aristotle to Cicero and onward to Augustine and Aquinas. In all the works of these writers the family was conceived as a natural unit to which other human associations were added.

Three important characteristics highlight the traditional approach to the family. First, the family was seen as the first of a continuous series of institutions that evolved naturally and historically. The progression from family to household to village to state gave civil society in general both a theological and pluralistic foundation. The family was regarded as an important seat of authority but it was not the only one. Nor was the distinction between natural and civil society, so prominent in modern thought, a crucial benchmark. It is this point that so endeared Aristotle to Aquinas. Second, the family itself was conceived in patriarchal terms. In Aristotle's words, "every household has its father for king." Even in an age that sees patriarchy hidden in every pronoun, it is difficult to convey the exalted position of the male head of the household in ancient Greece and Rome. Here is the summary of Fustel de Coulanges:

> Nothing in modern society can give us an idea of this paternal authority. In primitive antiquity the father is not alone the strong man, the protector who has power to command obedience; he is the priest, he is heir to the hearth, the continuator of the ancestors, the parent stock of the descendants, the depository of the mysterious rites of worship and of the sacred formulas of prayer.[1]

The worst features of filial subjection were eliminated rather early in Athens. Yet the inferior position of women lasted much longer. The denial of the most elementary forms of public life to women remained one of the central features of family life for centuries. The Roman family until the age of Augustus was even more scrupulously patriarchal. The paterfamilias retained full legal authority over the son until his death. The father's power not only included property and marriage rights but also capital punishment.

Though the awesome character of Roman paternal power was never equaled in medieval society, the patriarchal family remained and was uniformly accepted in political thought. Aquinas casually noted the similarity between kings and fathers. The Fall provided an additional argument for male domination.

Finally, the family was conceived as an administrative, economic, and religious institution. Its procreative status was firmly immersed in these functions. The concept of "household" was the more accurate description of family life. Family and kin were encased in a larger institution that included servants or slaves.

The seventeenth century produced a flurry of patriarchal reaction but the very forces that were producing a dread of social and political change in many portions of the population were conspiring to release new views of the family and political authority in others.[2] The first inkling of religious toleration, the notion that the destruction of the feudal order held out the possibility of new forms of pluralism, the rise of a market economy and a new class with it — all of these changes — helped produce a new kind of family. Locke displaced Filmer and outlined a family form that was quite different from both the medieval arrangement and the starkly authoritarian version that briefly replaced it. Yet the more subtle but no less harsh patriarchy of Hobbes was not to be so easily defeated.

Marx said that one cannot speak of "the" family. The family as an institution admits to an enormous variety of arrangements. Nor is the change from one kind of family to another a linear one (a belief that Marx propounded). In some respects the ancient Greek family was closer to the early seventeenth-century family than to the medieval form. Malinowski argued that the tolerant father of forty thousand years ago or his South Sea remnant counterpart today bears a closer resemblance to the modern father than the patriarch of only four hundred years ago.[3]

Nevertheless, familial changes are not random. Beginning in the middle of the seventeenth century a new kind of family was born. By a distillation of several recent studies of the family and by adding a few notations of our own, we can outline what this new family looked like:

1. *New spouse relationships.* The relationship between husband and wife changed from one of paterfamilias and dependent to new patterns more equalitarian and intimate. The relative aloofness between spouses seems to have been a norm throughout all social classes, with the possible exception of the artisans. Here is Edward Shorter's summary of the "unbridgeable sentimental distance" between spouses:

... fragments of information about rustic sexuality fit into a larger
mosaic of silence and affectionlessness between husband and
wife. Each had his or her tasks to perform in the world, and each
would be judged by the community on the basis of how well these
work assignments were carried out.[4]

The rise of romantic love and the sheer increase in erotic activity in the
eighteenth century wreaked havoc on arranged marriages and familial
control over adolescents. Of course, intimacy does not automatically
require equality. But the notion that marriage was to be a love relationship
gradually pushed instrumental or rational inequality out of the picture. In
Daniel Defoe's words, "I don't take the state of matrimony to be designed
... that the wife is to be used as an upper servant in the house....Love
knows no superior or inferior, no imperious command on the one hand, no
reluctant subjection on the other."[5]

2. *New attitudes toward children.* Although there is some controversy on
this point, it appears that the family before the seventeenth century took
an extremely lax attitude toward children. Childhood was not seen as an
identifiable stage of human development. Ariès describes the medieval
attitude as one of "indifference," but to put the matter straightforwardly,
infants and children were treated alternately with neglect and brutality.
Infants were sent out to be nursed by overworked peasants and appren-
ticed to other households at the tender age of seven. This rapid absorption
of (surviving) children into the outside world was halted by a growing
awareness of the uniqueness of childhood, first expressed in patterns of
adult coddling and then with great determination, in a concern for the
child's moral and educational development culminating in the formal
institution of the "college." The concept of the family, which emerges in
the sixteenth and seventeenth centuries, so Ariès argues, "is inseparable
from the concept of childhood."[6]

3. *New structural basis.* The medieval family was organized on a lineage
basis. Again here is Ariès' interpretation:

> One has the impression that only the line was capable of exciting
> forces of feeling and imagination. That is why so many romances
> of chivalry treat it. The restricted family community, on the other
> hand, had an obscure life.... In the domain of feeling, the family
> did not count as much as the line.[7]

Thus the family as we know it was structurally nestled within a lineage
pattern. It was a knot, although a relatively insignificant one, in the
intersecting network that stretched across society.

The new family form drastically altered this arrangement. Linear and kinship ties became extensions of the family unit. It is as if the criss-cross of strings with tiny knots reversed its pattern. The knots became larger and the connecting strings less important. The family took on a "nuclear" pattern. In the process of assuming this new form, the domicile of the modern family gradually changed as well. The household, of which Aristotle and theorists after him had spoken, became "home." Guests would no longer move in and out at will; business would be transacted outside "living quarters"; the bedroom was invented.

Like all great social transformations, no one willed the new family into existence. It arose out of other pressures, but it is not clear in what ways the family was passively created and in what ways it shaped other new institutions. In any case, this new family form was an institution that was drastically different from previous forms. And it is this difference that in part creates difficulties in giving it a name. For some time now, many writers have been insisting that we call it the "bourgeois family." There is indeed a sense in which the new family form is a middle-class invention. But its emergence does not neatly fit the chronology of industrialization and besides, this kind of family had managed to send roots across many social classes. Parsons' description of the "isolated-nuclear family" may exaggerate the separation of the family from kinship units and the social structure. In any case, it is based on only one of the families' characteristics. The same criticism can be made against the idea of the "companionate marriage" suggested a number of years ago by Burgess, popularized by Judge Lindsey, and advanced more recently by Lawrence Stone. The "family of sentiment" comes closest to winning the name contest. If any characteristic deserves to be the basis for the new family, it is its emotional nature. But the concept of sentiment does not come close enough to describing the structural components of the new family (just as the structurally based names above fail to capture the *vie intime* of the new family). Therefore, I have taken another tack and suggest that we simply refer to this form as the "modern" family and then attempt to outline its most basic characteristics. All scholars agree that the new family — whatever we call it — is a modern development, being created in stages in Europe and North America between the seventeenth and eighteenth centuries. It is this period that is generally cited as one that sees the emergence of modernity in general. And the new family is very much a creature of modernity.

This leaves us with the task of delineating the basic characteristics of the modern family. For us there are three. We shall use them throughout this book as we survey the struggles of political theorists to come to terms with the modern family. One is the *dyad*; the couple is the basic unit of the modern family. It is a social structure based largely upon an intense emotional bond. Another is what we call the *nidal basis or climate* of the modern family. The modern family is not only a child-centered institution in the sense of nesting but it is an institution — perhaps the last surviving one — that functions as a home. In other times, the concept of home took other forms, a city or a neighborhood for instance, but it has always meant a spatial location for memories and spiritual nurture. Finally, and as we shall later show, there is the concept of the *special relationship,* closely related to the other two. If it were possible to construct a phrase describing the modern family that did not violate syntax or style, we could use this. We shall spend some time in a later chapter attempting to outline this concept. For now, let us be content with defining the special relationship as a complex emotional tie of some duration. With this concept we should be able to give the notion of sentiment in the modern family some cohesion and, be it hoped, some deeper appreciation.

2

THE THREE FAMILIES
OF
THOMAS HOBBES

The extreme rational individualism of Thomas Hobbes (1588–1679) has been the target of rebuttal since the publication of *Leviathan* in 1651. A good portion of the critiques of Hobbes have centered around his famous description of the state of nature as a condition of individualized warfare. Hobbes' contemporaries based their opposition to his individualism on the historical inadequacy of the state of nature. Filmer, for instance, complained that Hobbes' men seemed to spring from the earth as "mushrooms ... without any obligation to another."[1]

This chapter re-examines both the individualistic interpretation of the state of nature, one which apparently sees no familial ties, and a more recent notion that the Hobbesian state of nature consisted of patriarchal families.[2] Hobbes, in my view, not only conceives of family life in the state of nature but indeed introduces three conceptions of the family as an institution. Hobbes was apparently unable to settle upon any one conception of the family in the state of nature. Hobbes' reconstruction of the family is obscured by the fact that each Hobbesian family type is based upon contractual relationships. Most prominent in Hobbes' analysis is the patriarchal family, complete with Freudian adumbrations. Group marriage is another Hobbesian type, albeit one presented more cautiously than it was to be by Engels. Finally, one can provide a logical construction from the anarchic side of Hobbes' treatment of family life. This last is what I call the autistic family — a type actually found by an anthropological field worker.

We will offer some suggestions about why rational individualism is necessarily ambiguous about the structure of family life and briefly suggest the relevance of Hobbes for the family for contemporary political thought before we take it up again in Part II.

THE RECONSTRUCTION OF THE FAMILY

Before we are in a position to examine the types of families in the state of nature that Hobbes seems to offer the reader, it is necessary to present Hobbes' effort at the reconstruction of the concept of the family itself. For all of Hobbes' families have certain features in common. Each is based upon contractual relationships that justify inequality of power and are entered into by reluctant and fearful individuals. Moreover, the relationships among family members are never appreciably different than political relationships in general. Thus when de Jouvenel says that Hobbes' social edifice makes room for only two persons, "the individual, cut down to the measure of his essential characteristic of seeking pleasure and avoiding pain, and the sovereign, cut down to his essential characteristic of disposer of force,"[3] he could be describing family as well as political life. For what Hobbes did was take the family unit with its complex economic, emotional, and social bonds and break it up into individuals, re-explain its structure and relationships in terms of rational individualism, and put it back together again.

The structure of the family itself may *look* the same after being put back together, in the sense that the husband stands above the wife and the mother over the children. The function of the family may appear to be the same, and the pattern of relationships among family members is permitted to continue. But the family is transformed in several crucial respects. For a rational individualism presupposes a set of assumptions that provides an image of the family entirely different from the image of one held together by a social bond. That image is often strained and awkward when first applied. But to the extent that the image gains hold, largely owing to its credibility in other aspects of social existence, our view of the family is altered as well. What first appeared awkward and incongruous increasingly seems to fit tendencies in actual life, and the rational individualist approach to the family seems to fit both social reality and possibilities for the future. Thus when Hobbes tells us that the relationship between parent and child is to be explained in terms of inequality of power, we might complain of the application of his method to inappropriate areas. We may even wince a bit. In Hobbes' view, since the infant is at the mercy of the mother, she has two options: "She may either nourish, or expose it."[4] If power confers freedom, and freedom rights, why not lay out the choices available to the mother? But once we become accustomed to conceiving social life in terms of acting out choices made available by power relationships, the horror of conceiving parenthood in this manner subsides and one is left to deal with the problem of what rational considerations could move the mother to nourish the child rather than expose it. Parenthood in this version of the rational individualist perspective becomes a tactical problem not appreciably different from one that asks how one can be rationally motivated to obey the sovereign, or — to place it in terms of contemporary political problems — how one can be motivated to "freely" choose to buy a small car or to conserve energy.[5]

The family question for Hobbes becomes one of maintaining commitment to an association that if left to our own devices we might support only sporadically if at all. If such associations exist and appear to be stable, we must assume that they represent a uniform power relationship which leads to rational obedience. Hobbes explains paternal relationships as one of two forms of domination. The other is military conquest. Both involve attempts by the weaker party to "avoid the present stroke of death."[6] Commonwealth by acquisition, paternal or despotical, is no less binding than commonwealth by institution.

Despite the reconstruction we have been attending to, Hobbes does have some inherent difficulties with his task. In his decomposing of the family as a unit, if only to reconstruct it in the image of separate entities tied together now by rational consideration, Hobbes must deal with children. They are not rational and hence are strictly invisible in his system of politics. Children are placed in the same category as "naturall fooles," "mad-men," and "brute beasts."[7] All in this category have neither the power to make covenants nor the ability to understand them. In other words, without rationality they fail to be individuals. But Hobbes knows that children cannot be treated in the same way as fools and madmen, cast off from society without harm to the rational, or in the same way as beasts, to be killed and eaten. Therefore he must convince himself and the reader that (1) the parent-child relationship can be conceived as ultimately a contractual one; (2) there is sufficient motivation on the part of parents to enter into a contract with children. In dealing with these problems, Hobbes tells us much about his general views on the family as an institution. Grace and honor, two of the most important aspects of the traditional family, are thoroughly altered in accordance with his decomposition of the family as representing a unique feature of social life.

As to the first problem, Hobbes simply insists that there is a tacit covenant between parent and child:[8]

> For it ought to obey him by whom it is preserved; because preservation of life being the end, for which one man becomes subject to another, every man is supposed to promise obedience, to him, in whose power it is to save, or destroy him.

But this simply won't do. For if the child's submission is to be regarded as a contract, Hobbes clearly violates his own expressly stated restriction that the child is by his nature beyond covenants, that "law is no law to him." If the adult, having been spared by a parent, is to somehow recognize a covenant retroactively at a coming of age, Hobbes has created new problems. The period before adulthood must then be understood as domination without contracts and would make the parent-child relationship unique in Hobbes' system. Here it would seem that Hobbes would violate another rule of parental authority, that for a certain number of years the domination of parent over child was based on generation, not contract. In any case, if the rational calculation arising from fear is the motive for all contracts in Hobbes' work, the young adult, now rational and *equal,* would hardly have sufficient reason to recognize his alleged tacit consent.

Hobbes might have provided himself with a way out if he were to use gratitude, his fourth law of nature, as a basis for parental authority:[9]

> That a man which receiveth Benefit from another of meer Grace, Endeavor that he which giveth it, have no reasonable cause to repent him of his good will.

Presumably the child would still be unable to come under the obligation of gratitude. The advantage here, however, is that the recognition of a debt of gratitude has a backward cast to it. We are grateful for past actions and only after they have been performed can we recognize our obligation. While we can indicate that we *would* be grateful if certain actions were undertaken, our gratitude must be withheld until the deed is done. Yet a promise of our future gratitude in some ways violates the whole basis of the gift relationship. For Hobbes reduces the notion of gratitude to a model of exchange just one step removed from contract. The contract model presupposes an exchange of promises on the spot, so to speak. There is, of course, the fear of nonperformance "on either part," a condition that makes contractual relationships in the state of nature so difficult. The difference with the gratitude relationship is that the initial performance is technically based only on "grace" or "free gift" and therefore does not call for any *quid pro quo.* But Hobbes insists that there really can be no such thing as grace: "For no man giveth, but with the intention of good to himself...."[10] Therefore the recipient owes a debt of gratitude not as a result of independent appreciation of kindness or of supererogation but a simple payment for performance rendered. Thus Hobbes is able to say that breach of gratitude "hath the same relation to grace, that Injustice hath to Obligation by Covenant."[11] The gratitude relationship is extremely close to a contractual one. Both are exchanges of goods and in some form both are motivated by individual hope of gain; the difference is that the second party is not required to indicate his payment explicitly and at the moment of the first person's actions.

This reconstruction of the gratitude relationship and the virtual destruction of the notion of grace associated with it effectively eliminate judging familial relationships in any terms other than rational individualism. Patterns of affection and mutual sacrifice between husband and wife and between children and parent are to be seen as a tangle of exchanges designed to promote the interest of each party in a contest of unequal power.

But still Hobbes is not content to rely heavily upon the reconstructed gratitude relationship. Emasculated in the service of rational individualism, the notion of gratitude is nevertheless regarded with suspicion. The question of honoring parents discussed in *De Cive* was dropped in *Leviathan*. In the former, Hobbes shows his discomfort with the gratitude model. The young man coming of age now stands "in less fear" of his father and "if regard he had to true and inward honour, do honour him less than before."[12] Note that Hobbes is not speaking of the attainment of moral autonomy on the part of the son and of the impact this might have on father-son relationships. Power determines inward honour, and the power of the father has now lessened. "For honour . . . is nothing else but the estimation of another's power: and therefore he that hath least power, hath always least honour."[13] But the father is still not without resources at his disposal. As the liberator of his son he cannot be expected "to match the enfranchised with himself."[14] Therefore, as a condition of his freedom, the young man "doth promise all those external signs at least, whereby superiors used to be honoured by their inferiors."[15] Thus the father is never again the object of "true" honor but is able to extract a formal reverence from his son. As if to be glad the whole exercise is over, Hobbes concludes: "from whence it follows, that the precept of honouring our parents, belongs to the law of nature, not only under the title of gratitude, but also of agreement."[16] The contract concept must be picked up and thrown down firmly over parent-child relationship much as one would hurriedly drop a makeshift cage over some set of predatory animals. The gratitude relationship, reconstructed as it is, is not reliable enough to secure a foundation for domestic relationships in an order based upon rational individualism.[17]

But why would the parent run the risk of dishonor on the part of his grown child? In fact, is it not a very good bet that the son would rationally be moved to commit parricide? We are here dealing with a pre-Freudian world; but the desire, particularly in the state of nature, to dethrone and destroy the father in order to take possession of the goods of the family (including the mother) fits all too well in Hobbes' system. The significance of the primal crime for Freud in terms of the problem of social order parallels Hobbes' concerns. After the murder of the father, the relative equality of the sons prevented any one of them from successfully assuming the role of the patriarch: "Thus there was nothing left for the brothers, if they wanted to live together, but to erect the incest prohibition — perhaps after many difficult experiences — through which they all equally renounced the women whom they desired, and on account of whom they had removed the father in the first place."[18] This reconstruction of the family, that is, the family after the primal crime, served to strengthen it drastically as a unit. Now the family was not based only upon the "necessities of society," but also upon the sense of guilt and remorse from complicity in the common crime. Of course, the son's defiance continually reappears, often in disguised forms, but under normal conditions this serves only to strengthen the blood bond. Thus the most momentous advance in social order can be said, at least in this version of Hobbes' presentation, to occur surreptitiously within the state of nature.

The father can guard against this threat; and indeed Hobbes sees him as so doing. Paternal dominion is discussed in terms of commonwealth by acquisition and the son is treated along the same lines as the servant and the prisoner of war. Because of both opportunity and motive, the threat of murder is much more likely within the household than from without at the hands of a marauding stranger.

This is indeed a frightful state of nature, more horrifying than the general insecurity that drives us to lock our doors, because it emanates from within the household. Hobbes was not unaware of the implications and attempted to reach a resolution:[19]

> It hath been objected by some: if a son kill his father, doth he do him no injury? I have answered, that a son cannot be understood to be at any time in the state of nature, as being under the power and command of them to whom he owed his protection, as soon as ever he is born. . . .

Thus the son is never in the state of nature; and Hobbes, for all his willingness to look unblinkingly at the consequences of social disintegration, refuses to extend his model fully into the household. The right of self-preservation and the sources of war, competition, diffidence, and glory never intrude into the family although Hobbes is quite willing to apply the motivations of the rational individualist to family life. The child is the first citizen, despite his existence beyond contract.

THE EMPTY-SHELL PATRIARCHAL FAMILY

In discussing Hobbes' general image of the family, we have gone far in describing what is the most prominent type of family organization in the state of nature. Certainly it is a patriarchal family and Hobbes at points is clear that the state of nature is composed of tightly organized household units that face one another in a condition of war:[20]

> ... a great Family if it be not part of some Commonwealth is of it self, as to the Rights of Sovereignty, a Monarchy; whether that Family consist of a man and his children; or of a man and his servants together: wherein the Father or Master is the Sovereign.

While Hobbes was anxious to conceive of politics as a solution to the anarchical consequences of rational individualism, he was not willing to carry anarchy into the household, let alone into the inner recesses of family life. His revised patriarchal model enabled him to avoid this position. It afforded him all the stability of the traditional patriarchalism of Filmer while it still allowed him to explore the origins of the state on an individualistic basis. His image of the household was one of subdued individuals. At best the form of organization represents what Goode has called the "empty-shell" family:[21]

> Its members no longer feel any strong commitment to many of the mutual role obligations, but for various reasons the husband and wife do not separate or divorce. Violent, open quarrels are not common in this family, but the atmosphere is without laughter or fun. Members do not discuss their problems or experiences with each other, and communication is kept to a minimum. Parents and children fulfill their *instrumental* obligations but not *expressive* ones.

This description portrays the American middle-class version of the empty-shell family. In the state of nature the family is governed much like a conquered territory with its members performing their respective tasks. No special relationships are formed; in fact, the family takes on the characteristics of a bureaucratic institution. There is more than enough evidence in Hobbes' work for this description of family life. Recall Hobbes' axiom that "all society ... is either for gain, or for glory; that is, not so much for love of our fellows, as for the love of ourselves."[22] Hobbes intended to carry this individualism deep into social life in order to eliminate a conflict between duties and nature in the life of family and the life of the state. Biological parenthood is dismissed as a foundation for any unique set of duties and replaced by a power relationship. Children are easily subdued. The position of the head of the household is decided by contract. Hobbes is adamant, despite later language, in his refusal to trace the origin of the family to patriarchy: "There be always two that are equally

Parents."[23] But while God ordained equal authority in both parents, he left it to them to determine the locus of authority for "no man can obey two Masters." At this point the reasoning becomes confused. States normally recognized paternal authority as resting in the father "because for the most part Commonwealths have been erected by the Fathers, not by the Mothers of families."[24] This would make internal sense if Hobbes had argued that men were the heads of households in the state of nature by virtue of their brute power. But he is quite clear in asserting the opposite:[25]

> And whereas some have attributed the Dominion to the Man only, as being of the more excellent Sex; they misreckon in it. For there is not always that difference of strength or prudence between the man and the woman, as that the right can be determined without war.

The disposition of the child appears to allow for the following alternatives: A voluntary decision between both parents leads to a contract concerning who should care for the child. In the absence of contract, dominion is in the mother. In the event of war between the parents, Hobbes seems to suggest, dominion is likely to go to the father.

If the patriarchal family is the result of a contract between husband and wife, that is, if the wife regularly relinquishes her authority over an infant, Hobbes makes a case that fits his larger model well. The family is already a well-established social unit in the state of nature. It is voluntarily created from contracts between parent and child and between husband and wife, it is based entirely on rational calculations of gain or mutual fear, and it thus exhibits the same character of relationships that constitute intercourse among citizens and between the citizen and the state. Accordingly, Hobbes is able to say that it is the "Fathers of families" who constitute Commonwealths and thus come quite close to the intent of the patriarchal thesis held by Bramhall, Filmer, and others. But then we must read the description "warre of every man against every man" in the state of nature as "warre of every father against every father."

Let us leave aside the anthropological question of whether family warfare is likely to have been muted by growing networks of kinship ties. For Hobbes is not quite willing to let the reader accept his own version of the patriarchal model. The relationship between men and women rests solely upon the "naturall inclinations of the Sexes" and Hobbes seems to suggest the institution of marriage is absent or in its nascent stages: "For in the condition of meer Nature, where there are no Matrimoniall lawes, it cannot be known who is the Father, unless it be declared by the Mother."[26]

If human relationships in general are as transitory and limited as Hobbes tells us they are in the state of nature, he is now reminding us that

family organization consistent with primitive communism. Group marriage in a period of relative economic equality would expose the bourgeois family for what it was, a creation of the system of commodity production. This earlier form of family provided for common defense and cooperation without jealousy and competition. Moreover, there appears to be no system of authority in group marriage. Only in the transition to the pairing family does force begin in the form of marriage by capture.

Without judging the historical plausibility of group marriage we can begin to see by Engels' use of it, Hobbes' caution. Competition is one of Hobbes' "principal causes of quarrell" and his example is taken from familial force. Men "use violence, to make themselves Masters of other men's persons, wives, children and cattel."[32] Compare the image Engels is desirous of conveying:[33]

> ... group marriage, seen close at hand, does not look so terrible as the philistines, whose minds cannot get beyond brothels, imagine it to be.... It takes years ... to discover beneath these marriage customs ... their controlling law: the law by which the Australian aborigine, wandering hundreds of miles from his home among people whose language he does not understand, nevertheless often finds in every camp and in every tribe women who give themselves to him without resistance and without resentment....

It is difficult to imagine Hobbes' human beings giving up anything without resistance and resentment. But we can still see the reasons for Hobbes' limited commitment to the notion of group marriage. In his model no special relationships are formed; with social bonds absent, Hobbes is still able to focus upon the implication of rational individualism for the political order without having either to destroy or protect established personal relationships. In Freud's terms, as long as genital satisfaction makes its appearance like a "guest who drops in suddenly, and, after his departure, is heard of no more for a long time,"[34] the problem of the family as a social unit which somehow must be superseded by larger forms of organization does not arise. Thus Hobbes is not averse to describing relationships in the state of nature in terms that suggest this model: "No lawes of Matrimony; no lawes for the Education of Children; but the law of Nature, and the natural inclination of the Sexes."[35] And as we have seen, he is not even concerned that this model should leave us with the mild suggestion of polygyny.

The other form of family structure that fits Hobbes' description is quite different from group marriage. In order to construct a picture of it we only need to focus upon the principal elements in the state of nature that Hobbes himself emphasizes: radical individualism and scarcity. These give rise to what we might call the autistic family. I realize that the term "autistic family" appears contradictory. Autism suggests a withdrawal into the self through fantasy construction. Yet the term can be useful if it serves to focus upon the basis for autistic behavior. For instance, Bettelheim has examined the similarities between autistic children and concentration-camp inmates.[36] The link between the behavior of persons in both groups is the extreme situation. Bettelheim is careful to point out that the autistic withdrawal pattern is the result of the need to pay the "minutest attention" to a mortally threatening environment. Life under conditions of imminent death is so debilitating that the very inner maneuvers designed to protect us debilitate us further. The reactions are progressive and dialectical. The eventual presence of what Bettelheim calls "moslem" behavior, an indication of withdrawal of *all* interest in the external world, represents a closing stage, the "true watershed" between those apt to survive and those apt to die. Therefore an autistic family organization might involve the most minimal interaction — living in proximity to one another and recognizing each other's presence. Its existence is indeed fragile. Moreover, there can be no doubt that Hobbes intended the state of nature to be an extreme situation, and that, in fact, he believed that an analysis of the extreme situation was the appropriate basis for constructing a political philosophy. There is merit then in Leo Strauss' contention that Hobbes had constructed a "completely defective state of mankind" from which the most basic human associations were threatened.[37]

Until recently, we have not had evidence of changes in human relationships that extreme scarcity and individualism produce in the context of primitive societies. The centrality of kinship and community widely observed in these societies would appear to make the anthropological basis of Hobbes' state of nature quite implausible. But Colin Turnbull's discovery of the Ik, a displaced East African tribe, provides striking parallels to one possible family structure in Hobbes' system. Driven by a nearly permanent state of starvation, the Ik have developed a form of social organization that truly fits Hobbes' belief that men enter society only for love of themselves. "Goetes" (to take) and "nyeg" (hunger) are the principal words of the Ik vocabulary and self-preservation is the only shared social value.

What happens to the family in these circumstances? The Ik continued to have children; husband and wife continued to share the same hut; kinship was still formally recognized. But a horrible familial autism emerged from the Ik's situation.

Children are cared for until the age of three. The character of that care is made clear in Turnbull's description below:[38]

I imagine the child must be rather relieved to be thrown out, for in the process of being cared for he or she is carried about in a hide sling wherever the mother goes, and since the mother is not strong herself this is done grudgingly. Whenever the mother finds a spot in which to gather, or if she is at a water hole or in her fields, she loosens the sling and lets the baby to the ground none too slowly, and of course laughs if it is hurt. I have seen Bila and Matsui do this many a time. Then she goes about her business, leaving the child there, almost hoping that some predator will come along and carry it off. This happened once while I was there — once that I know of anyway — and the mother was delighted. She was rid of the child and no longer had to carry it about and feed it, and still further this meant that a leopard was in the vicinity and would be sleeping the child off and thus be an easy kill. The men set off and found the leopard, which had consumed all of the child except part of the skull; they killed the leopard and cooked it and ate it, child and all. That is Icien economy, and it makes sense in its own way. It does not, however, endear children to their parents or parents to their children.

Why do the Ik have children? Why do they not engage in open infanticide? Turnbull surmises that Ik parents calculate that there is always a chance of a good year in the fields and children can be used to send off animals and birds.

Sex has also succumbed to the requirements of an extreme individualism. Naturally the sex drive is weakened by hunger and young girls find that their bodies are a valuable commodity with neighboring tribes. But the impact of the Ik social code went deeper. When Turnbull argued that copulation was different from masturbation, the Ik reply was "who knows what the other is feeling? In each you only know your own feeling."[39] Thus sex lost its capacity to be a source of cohesion or disruption in the Ik state of nature.

Turnbull argues that the family does not exist in Ik society. There are husbands and wives, parents and children, grandparents and extended kin. But since the basic principle of interaction is one of "natural exploitation," it is fair to say that the Ik have successfully abandoned the family as a useless appendage. Yet in Hobbes' terms it is not possible to say that such arrangements cannot be regarded as familial. His most complete model, the patriarchal family, is based on the same absence of affection and love that characterizes the Ik. One model represents an image of Hobbesian human beings subjected to certain centrifugal forces. While it is correct to say that the model of the autistic family is construed more from Hobbes' general premises than from his other descriptions, we still can contend that this model reflects his general outlook more accurately than does the model of group marriage. We need only ask if Turnbull's description of the Ik is consistent with Hobbes' general treatment of the family. Our answer is yes with one important qualification. The "natural" condition of the Ik does not force them to create "convenient Articles of Peace, upon which men may be drawn to agreement." Turnbull notes that the Ik (and perhaps our "advanced" societies as well) have abolished desire and "consequently that ever present and vital gap between desire and achievement, treating us, in a word, as individuals with one basic individual right, the right to survive."[40] A family that is autistic means, of course, that it has very few remnants of a social bond. Life within it is indeed incommodious. But the autistic family has managed to deal with the trauma of existence in a way that has removed Hobbes' "desire" for "commodious living." Each individual has moved to an arena of emotional space within himself. Hobbes' first law of nature has eliminated intra- and interfamilial conflict. There is no inexorable pressure to create civil society. Men in the state of nature have indeed discovered that "Desires . . . are in themselves no sin," but they have found a way to suppress them without society. Of course Hobbes would not have been happy to learn that his natural condition could be interpreted in this fashion. But only his own form of rational individualism could lead to this result.

If the state of nature is still best understood as a logical construct, especially in terms of its relevance to the preoccupations of modern political thought, our treatment suggests a useful lesson. For if the importance of Hobbes rests with his ability to fully draw the consequences of an extreme rational individualism, the sorts of families he described as consistent with his vision can tell us much about the position of the family today and our attitude toward it. It has already become fashionable to regard the internal intimacy of the family as a myth that rests upon brute power of husband over wife, parent over child, child over grandparent.[41] In this sense, we cay say that Hobbes' reconstruction of the family has been quite successful. For if human beings are conceived as aggressive and self-contained organisms, relationships of love and affection as well as any dependency or hierarchy must represent a hidden power component.[42] But on Hobbes' terms, liberation from the family hardly implies the construction of other more genuine forms of solidarity. The Hobbesian state assumes the role of the new pater familias. But it is not in the image of a strong, demanding, and benevolent father that the sovereign is created. He is rather a rational creation of our own actions, an insurance agent with a gun.

3

JOHN LOCKE: FAMILY LIFE FOR THE FREE AND RATIONAL

The Hobbesian contract originated in terror. As such, it could be forced into a patriarchal conception of the family. The father could be seen as all of us see him at certain points in our lives: aloof, independent, and omnipotent. But as we just argued, the fit was less than perfect. Hobbes offered no psychic glue that could internalize our terror and transform it into awe and reverence. Two other models of family life thus stood in the background: the anarchy of group marriage and the system of immobilized terror that we described as the autistic family.

It was the contract that was the source of Hobbes' failure to successfully construct a single new family form. However much Hobbes might try to reinterpret the concept of the contract, he never wished to completely erase the element of voluntarism implied by even the most abject submission. The Hobbesian contract emphasized necessity but it was a necessity arranged by "free" men and women. In this context John Locke's political theory is more bold than Hobbes'. The submission of the "free and rational" is never morally justified. The family must be conceived in contractual terms but without terror. This is a contract theory at a purer level. Locke (1632–1704) is not always able to keep to it but he is able to show the main outlines of such a theory. Needless to say, it has been completed by others.

John Locke's *Two Treatises* is concerned with two topics: the family and political power. Of course, the latter is the topic that the twentieth century has most recognized. But the former, Locke's treatment and reorganization of the family, is as significant to political thought as is his contribution to politics proper. Locke, though not unmindful of the anarchic implications of his theory, never willingly entertains a Hobbesian solution: he treats both topics in the context of a rational individualism. For Locke, men are all "Free and Rational"; in their rational condition they may "order their Action . . . as they think fit . . . without asking leave or depending upon the will of any other Man."[1]

Locke never departed from his belief that men were free and rational, and that political order must somehow be constructed upon premises which respected this assumption. Locke's achievement in this regard is well known. A constitutional order based upon consent is "the only way whereby any one divests himself of his Natural Liberty."[2] But if the patriarchal thesis that political power is an extension of fatherhood is rejected and replaced by the doctrine of consent, how is the family then reconstituted? Locke's answer reflects all the ambivalence that modern liberal thought shows toward the family. This, despite the fact that the family is rearranged after his own image of free and rational men.

If we are free, rational, equal, and independent, how can we explain relationships of emotion and dependency separate from consent?

Hobbes too was preoccupied with this question and confronted the patriarchal thesis. As we have seen, Hobbes' solution was not a perfect one. He rested most of his case upon an empty-shell patriarchal family with authority based upon consent motivated by fear. Thus Hobbes came close to achieving his desire of destroying the family while maintaining a major portion of patriarchal symbolism. Locke has somewhat different purposes when he attempts to answer the same question. For he is concerned with the fragility of ethics in the absence of the authority, not with its irrelevance. Where Hobbes is eager to draw the collectivist implications from rational individualism, Locke flinches. "Our state here in this world is a state of mediocrity," he wrote in his journal. "It is a state wherein we are not capable of living together exactly by a rule, nor altogether without it."[3] This tension characterizes all of Locke's political thought and forms the basis for his liberalism. Since it is "unreasonable for Men to be Judges in their own cases," civil government is the "proper remedy for the Inconveniences of the State of Nature."[4] Yet the rulers "are but men"; they too can be corrupted by "Passion and Revenge."[5] Civil society can become a state of war, in which case it is better to live without a common judge. At least there "men are not bound to the unjust will of another."[6] In either civil society or the state of nature, war means that justice is no longer within human reach. Every man must "judge" in his "own conscience" and "appeal to Heaven."[7]

The book of *Judges* is Locke's main source of scriptural authority on this point. In some ways it is a curious choice. The story of Jephtha is the centerpiece of his effort: "Had there been any such Court, any superior

Jurisdiction on Earth, to determine the right between Jephtha and the Ammonites, they had never come to a State of War, but we see he was forced to appeal to Heaven. Where there is no Judge on Earth, the Appeal lies to God in Heaven."[8] The question of "Who shall Judge?" is raised again and again in the *Second Treatise*. Locke attempts to construct models of routinized politics that will prevent this question from being asked. For in the state of war there is "no Judge on Earth." Thus Locke's heady individualism is always threatened by "vain Ambition" and "evil Concupiscence" even as he struggles to push his individualist premises toward constitutionalism. As many commentators have noted, the Hobbesian solution is never too far removed from Locke's formulation with all the implications for the family that it entails.

All this makes Locke's heavy reliance upon *Judges* even more intriguing. For *Judges* provides many more precedents for the view Locke is attacking. It is a theological account of the founding of a nation and Locke even admits that this is a case "where God himself immediately interpos'd."[9] "The Lord raised up judges" to deliver the Israelis. Presumably without divine intervention the Israeli nation would never have been founded. After each judge the children of Israel "did evil in the sight of the Lord." If we are to accept the moral of *Judges,* individual autonomy, the very basis of liberal doctrine, always led to corruption. *Judges* concludes with this lesson: "In those days there was no king in Israel: every man did that which was right in his own eyes."[10] As a description of the state of nature it was hardly a "State of Peace, Good Will, Mutual Assistance and Preservation." There was widespread child sacrifice and treachery (Abimelech's murder of his brothers, Delilah's betrayal of Samson), civil war (Ephraimites and Gileadites), gang rape and mutilation (the Benjamites) and mass carnage. Moreover, *Judges* is a set of stories firmly related to a patriarchal conception of society. Not only is it an account of the origin of a state from patriarchal clans, but it ends with the eventual creation of a kingdom and an imperial Israel.

Force and violence, not consent, appear to be the origin of civil society. Locke admits that without "the Judges and First Kings," military leaders all, young societies "could not have subsisted": "All Governments would have sunk under the Weakness and Infirmities of their Infancy; and the Prince and the People had soon perished together."[11] But for Locke the moral of *Judges* is not simply the general depravity brought on when "every man did that which was right in his own eyes" but the inability of men to find justice under conditions of severe conflict. In *Judges* justice could only be dispensed by God.[12] Thus the Israelis never really had kings in *Judges,* only "Captains in War"; the only question the people had in mind was "How shall this Man save us?" The authority of the judge was primarily external: "Though they command absolutely in War, yet at home and in time of Peace they exercise very little Dominion, and have but a very moderate Sovereignty."[13] But while conditions of the founding require only military leadership, the very martial spirit of early societies makes constitutional restrictions on power unnecessary. In this "Golden Age" there are no separate interests between ruler and ruled. Only "when Ambition and Luxury, in future ages taught Princes to stretch Prerogative and produce "vicious subjects, did Men find it necessary" to find out ways "to restrain the Exorbitances and prevent the Abuses" of monarchies.[14] Thus *Judges* established for Locke not the need for monarchy, but only the need for some authority.

Locke does not mention the reneging of the Ephraimites or the gangster rule of Abimelech, both of which are hardly examples of republican virtue on the part of citizenry and rulers. In any case, there is a definite anticipation of Rousseau in Locke's reliance upon the alleged irrational untaught inhabitants of the "Woods and Forests," who "keep right by following Nature."[15] Monarchy is the child of "Cities and Palaces" and for Locke it constitutes a second Fall.

But the concessions to patriarchal history go farther than the admission of the origin of government in one-man rule even though the judges were not to be regarded as kings. ". . . Government commonly began in the Father."[16] There are reservations, of course. Cruel or incompetent fathers are by-passed or overthrown; men have withdrawn from their families of birth to create new governments. Nevertheless, Locke admits early government was predominantly based upon an autocratic familialism.

If the uncorrupted life of people in primitive socieites bred benevolent patriarchs, Locke does not draw explicit parallels with family structure in modern societies, monarchical or republican. Yet the inferences are there. They are supplemented by an economic history that stands alongside the political interpretation. For, as we shall see, while Locke relies upon *Judges* to confront the patriarchal conception of the origin of the state on its own terms, he uses the earlier patriarchs, from Adam to Abraham, to link the family to economic development.

THE FREE AND RATIONAL FAMILY

What sort of family does Locke construct? He approaches the family carrying two burdens. Not only must he explain how the free and rational come to live together under terms of emotion and hierarchy, but he must construct a family that reflects a balance between authority and submission. No tyrannies can exist in Locke's system, no matter how small. We find then that Locke tells us that the "two Powers, Political and Paternal" are "perfectly distinct and separate" while he goes about his task of making them quite similar.

There are some remarkable parallels in the treatment of the family in

Locke and Hobbes. Locke denies that "begetting produces authority." "What Father of a Thousand," Locke asks, "when he begets a child, thinks further than satisfying his present Appetite?"[17] But he denies the supremacy of the father in the household. When God discovered the taking of the forbidden fruit, Adam could hardly "expect any Favors, any grant of Priviledge."[18] And Locke denies that the duty of obedience to the parent extends beyond adulthood. "The Bonds of this subjection are like swaddling cloths, that loosen till at length they drop off, and leave a Man at his own Disposal."[19] Obedience to a parent is dependent upon parental care. A father can forfeit paternal authority. The family as a social institution arises from the simple but "strong desires of Copulation."[20] God has placed in the "Constitution of Man" as well an extended period of infant helplessness and the consequent dependency of the female.

Locke attempts to accomplish several basic tasks in his account of the family. He tries to show that it is at once natural *and* individualistic and distinct *and* separate from political authority. Hobbes wanted only the individualistic base and Filmer, of course, only the natural one. The basis for family life is described in theocentric terms. Locke is answering Filmer, but the response is appropriate to Hobbes as well. Children are the property not of parents but of God: "They who say the Father gives Life to his Children are so dazzled with the thought of Monarchy, that they do not, as they ought, remember God, who is the Author and giver of Life: 'Tis in him alone we live, move and have our Being."[21] Recent commentators have emphasized the strong theocentric basis in Locke's writings.[22] Nowhere is this more prominent than in his justification of the family.[23] But the emphasis upon God as the "Author and giver of Life" served broadly political purposes for Locke. It permits him to date the origin of the family with society as well as to design the family on an individualistic basis. The desire for sex is conjoined with the desire to care for one's offspring. The length of time the human infant is helpless makes the conjugal bond "more firm and lasting in Man than the other Species of Animals."[24] The formation of the family is a given that arises well before the institution of civil society. There is no talk of constructing ties of legitimacy or forging an incest taboo. The first family is a secure, stable, monogamous unit. In fact, in Locke's scheme the family precedes the system of private property. The latter occurs only with the scarcity of land brought on by the invention of money.

Much attention has been paid to Locke's contention that God gave property for the use of the "Industrious and the Rational." But we must note Locke's antecedent argument. God made the family necessary "so their Industry might be encouraged, and their interest better united...."[25] But if the family is natural in a way that even property is not, how does Locke merge this position with his belief that every person is free and rational?

We saw the difficulties Hobbes was confronted with when he faced the problem of children and covenants. Locke begins with similar suppositions. We are "born Free as we are born Rational; not that we have actually the Exercise of either: Age that brings one, brings with it the other too."[26] Rather than to resort to the Hobbesian fiction of infant consent, Locke reaches back to God's command to men "to preserve their offspring." But parental authority is temporary and designed by its very nature to end. The task of the parent is to bring the child under the "Law of Reason" so that he may be free. Locke presents us with one of his few justifications for positive freedom:[27]

> The Freedom then of Man and Liberty of acting according to his own Will, is grounded on his having reason.... To turn him loose to an unrestrain'd liberty, before he has Reason to guide him, is not the allowing him the priviledge of his Nature, to be free....

Thus Locke is confident enough to tell us that "we see how natural Freedom and Subjection to Parents may consist together, and are both founded on the same Principle."[28] Parents produce miniatures of themselves: free and rational men are "not to be subject to the arbitrary will of another."[29] Parental authority is based neither upon consent nor on inevitable hierarchy in nature. But Locke's image of parental attachment is based on a single premise: God's command to care for one's offspring. This is a slender thread to restrain a rational individualism, especially when theology was to lose its rhetorical force. The importance of this command basis becomes even more evident when Locke looks at relationships between men and women. Here the contract model is forthrightly employed. "Conjugal Society" is made by "voluntary Compact between Men and Women." Following the liberal model in politics, Locke tells us that the contract is limited to the "things of their common Interest and Property."[30] While marriage confers sexual rights, they are a means to procreation. Locke guardedly hints that divorce is acceptable when children can "shift for themselves."[31] The purpose of marriage is birth of children and their support and education. When they enter the larger society of the free and rational, the maintenance of each marriage is problematical.

The significance of Locke's reorganization of the family in his pursuit of a rational individualistic order now becomes clearer. Let us look at what he has done. When Locke insists that paternal and political power are "perfectly distinct," he comes close to suggesting that despite its existence in the earliest stages of the state of nature the family is less than a "little society." For the family has a limited function — the socialization of citizens. To fulfill this function in the state of nature is no doubt difficult, for the free and rational lack a common judge to settle disputes. But the family still attempts to perform its tasks much like a clock that, missing a crucial part, still runs but does not keep time reliably. Of course, in some ways this analogy does not quite fit, since Locke seems to suggest that the family was in part a conduit for the increasing instability in the state of nature.

Commentators have always had difficulty in determining the relative general stability of the state of nature. Was it a "state of peace, good will, natural assistance and preservation?" Or was it a state of "anarchy and confusion"? Locke's reliance upon *Judges* only seems to confuse the issue. But part of the answer to this question lies in exploring the conjecture that there are two states of nature for Locke — or more properly, two tendencies in the state of nature. Although, as we suggested, *Judges* is hardly an ideal example for Locke to use to illustrate this point, he does use it as an approximation of primitive society. It contains Locke's picture of a Golden Age. It is characterized by relative homogeneity. Status differences are minimal and when they exist they are based upon easily identifiable talent. Locke speaks of the "great confidence the Innocence and Sincerity of that poor but virtuous Age ... gave of one another."[32] Needs were uniform and simple: "their Possessions, or way of living ... afforded little matter of Covetousness or Ambition...."[33]

It was the command of God Himself to subdue the earth. This undertaking gave rise to private possession. But "private possession" meant little under nomadic conditions. In "the first ages of the world, when Men were more in danger to be lost," the availability of land made it "impossible for any Man ... to entrench upon the right of another."[34] Only "as Families increased and Industry enlarged their states" did a system of private property emerge. It is at this point that Locke suggests that complaints about the size and wealth of property holdings begin, despite his insistence that private possession was the result of consent.

Thus "the partage of things" and the "inequality of private possessions" occur by consent "out of the Bonds of Society." They also seem to be partly the result of family organization. Contrary to the chapter outlining the state of nature, Chapter 5 of the *Second Treatise* is concerned only with family units. When "Man" labors he is the head of the household. Examples in Locke's account of private property move freely from the nomadic communism of the Indians and ancient Israelis to the estate of the squire but in each the family is both the consumption unit and the labor unit. There is no direct discussion in Locke of a change in family structure occurring with the institution of money. But the use of money is an event of enormous significance for Locke. Before it, he asks "What would a Man Value Ten Thousand or an Hundred Thousand Acres of excellent land, richly cultivated, and well stocked too with Cattle in the middle of the inland Parts of America, where he had no hopes of Commerce with other Parts of the World, to draw Money to him by the Sale of the Product?"[35] He answers that the labor would not be worth the effort and "we should see him give up again to the wild Common of Nature, whatever was more than would supply the Convenience of Life to be had there for him and his Family."[36]

Did the parent's duty to "preserve, nourish and educate" his children lead to "the desire to have more than [was] needed"; that is, did the existence of the family itself lead to the invention of money and to the "inequality of private possessions"? On Locke's terms, the answer is yes and no. One must remember God created the earth under conditions that would benefit the rational and industrious. The family itself was so designed as to encourage industry and rationality.

The movement from the Golden Age to a system of private property did give rise to conditions that made it impossible for the benevolent patriarch to govern. The "Ambition and Luxury, in future Ages" forced men "to examine more carefully the Original and Right of Government; and to find out ways to restrain Exorbitances, and prevent the Abuses of that Power which they having intrusted in another's hands only for their own good, they find was made use of to hurt them."[37]

One must be careful not to draw too many inferences from Locke on this point. The Golden Age is contrasted with the monarchy, not with capitalism. Nevertheless, private property and money, even in Locke's terms, gave an outlet for those desires to have more than was needed. The patriarch became the monarch who could not be trusted. Men must come to see that the father was monarch only by consent. The rejection of monarchy thus implied the rejection of the patriarchal family. The connection between polity and family, never readily accepted by Locke, had to be severed completely. Trust must be directed toward a constitutional order derived from consent individually given.

The Family as a Specialized Institution

On these terms, we can see the family become what Locke intended it to be, a unique but limited institution encased in a society based upon different premises. Wherever he could, Locke attempted to sustain a structural resemblance between the family and the political order: marriage was a contract among equals; children owed honor only to parents who deserved it. But Locke was most intent upon insuring that the family bond remain separate from the political order. A good part of that separateness was managed by Locke's insistence that parenthood carries no "regal authority." Not only is parental power not absolute or arbitrary but moreover it is temporary.

But this very preoccupation with the distinctiveness of the family makes it very much an adjunct institution to the political order. Locke has seen to it, albeit in a fashion very different from Hobbes', that the family does not pose a threat to the political order. Its major function is the socialization of the child to the world of free and rational individuals. The free and rational may have more limited obligations to the family than other personality types. But, as a producer of a personality type, the family insures the continuance of the constitutional order. Locke insists that inheritance of land and consequent obedience to the state are not a "natural tye" between father and son but a "voluntary submission," and the insistence is designed to emphasize that citizenship is separate from the family. The free and rational must give their consent "separately in their turns, as each comes to be of Age."[38] They must not conclude "they are naturally subject, as they are men."[39] The family's task is to create the free and rational, but the free and rational must recognize their obedience as separate individuals.

In order to appreciate how modern is the family that Locke has constructed, one can briefly review Talcott Parsons' account of the "new" nuclear family. Parsons noted that nonkinship units have assumed most of the functions of the economic and social order. As a result, the family has become a highly specialized institution, "probably more specialized than it has been in any previously known society."[40] At a macroscopic level the family has become almost completely functionless:

> It does not itself, except here and there, engage in much economic production; it is not a major direct agency of integration of the larger society. Its individual members participate in all these functions, but they do so "as individuals," not in their roles as family members.[41]

Parsons went on to note that this nonkinship organization of society and the decline of the family as a multifunction unit produced a paradox. Society became dependent more exclusively on the family for the performance of certain of its vital functions. Despite extreme social differentiation and individualization, "the human personality is not born but must be made through the socialization process."[42] We are reminded of Locke's analysis: "We are born Free as we are born Rational; not that we have actually the Exercise of either. . . ."

The brief presentation of Parsons illustrates how much Locke was able to anticipate the modern family. Locke's family was no doubt as specialized as Parsons', particularly in regard to economic production. But the claim that parental and political power are distinct clearly produced the family of specialized function. As important as the function is, however, it is to be regarded as a supporting one. Nurturing the free and rational without economic or political power is a task to be completed in the interest not of the family but of society.

The history of the treatment of the family from a rational individualist perspective is a long and complicated one. We should avoid the temptation to lay all the problems it creates upon Locke. Yet several points can be made regarding his effort. Locke can hardly be singled out for making the family over in his own image of politics. Nearly every writer we will examine is unable to avoid this temptation. But the consequences of this effort are different political theories. In his effort to remake existing political order Locke found it necessary to remake the family as well. A part of this effort was to so design the family as to make it clearly separable from the political order. That separation was achieved in part by conceiving the family as a natural unit in society, in some ways not as much subject to contrivance as the efforts of the free and rational men in politics. Yet Locke never really attempted to examine the natural aspects of the family. Being concerned with producing individuals who would people the new politics of liberal constitutionalism, Locke simply equated the natural with the free and rational. Later liberal theorists would ask why the family should be charged with such a task. This question would be raised with more urgency as social and economic change makes it appear that the family is not producing the type of people it was assigned to do. Other writers would complain about the excessive privatism of family life. But what outlook can we expect from an institution whose major or only function is itself internal? Still others would raise questions about the motives for assigning women equality in an institution that is natural when the business of society is carried on in institutions that are managed by men and governed by the rules of convention.

If in responding to these questions one were to base his answer on Locke, one would be left to rely on his maxim that next to self-preservation "God planted in Men a strong desire also of propagating their kind."[43] But Locke is never clear about the status of the rule. Sometimes it is an instinct entirely separate from self-preservation, sometimes it is a mere extension of it. Sometimes the desire to propagate is not presented as an instinct at all but as a duty. God "ordered" it and men have an obligation "to preserve what they have begotten."[44] Locke makes it clear at several points that the "inclinations of tenderness and concern" are not strictly instinctual. Fathers do neglect their children. Garcilaso de la Vega's account of the Peruvians who begot children on purpose to "fat and eat them" greatly impressed Locke. He heaped scorn on Filmer for even mentioning similar practices:

> Let it be, that they exposed them; Add to it, if you please, for this is still greater Power, that they begot them for their Tables to fat and

> eat them: If this proves a right to do so, we may, by the same Argument, justifie Adultry, Incest and Sodomy, for there are examples of these too, both Ancient and Modern; Sins, which I suppose, have their Principal Aggravation from this, that they cross the main intention of Nature, which willeth the increase of Mankind, and the continuation of the Species in the highest perfection, and the distinction of Families, with the Security of the Marriage Bed, as necessary unto.[45]

Men could indeed "cross the main intention of Nature." Locke concludes that man can sink to a "Brutality below the level of Beasts" because "the imagination is always restless and suggests variety of thoughts."[46] When "Fashion hath once established, what Folly or craft began, Custom makes it Sacred, and 'twill be thought impudence or madness, to contradict or question it."[47] Reason is the "only star and compass" to guide men toward the main intention of nature. Yet Locke suggests that the primitive is less likely to be beguiled by the power of this horrific imagination. But Locke never relies on a Rousseauean natural man in his political thought. The constitutional order is designed for the free and rational. It houses no general will. The authority accorded the "nursing fathers" was natural, even unimaginative, yet men still "found it necessary to examine more carefully" the basis of government. If the simplicity of primitive life prevented imagination, individual reason must now perform this function.

But if the *Two Treatises* offers us any one caution, it is the theme that human reason is a magnificient but very fallible guide. It may be our only compass but life is still mediocre; men cannot live exactly by rules or altogether without them. It is in this context that Locke's failure to examine the natural in regard to the family is so unfortunate. In politics the mediocre nature of the human condition is confronted. In the family, power is diffused and submitted to the contract, but the very basis of family life is left untouched. It is encapsuled only in the maxim "Propagate your kind," standing somewhere between an instinct and a duty with only reason to guard against the imagination.

4

JEAN-JACQUES ROUSSEAU: ROMANTIC PATRIARCHY

Jean-Jacques Rousseau's legacy to the twentieth century would appear to be anything but helpful in our exploration of the family and its relationship to politics. His work seems to represent beliefs that spell the destruction of the family so that room can be made for a truly just political order.[1]

Thus Rousseau (1712–1788) would seem to represent the negative arm of a large dialectic formed by modern political thought as it approaches the family. But we have seen that Locke's portrayal of the modern family is a mixed one, one that has its own internal dialectic. Much the same can be said about Rousseau. One critic has emphasized that Rousseau could conceal a point by making it simultaneously obvious and (for most readers) invisible.[2] Rousseau will describe the first family as giving rise to the "sweetest sentiments known to men."[3] But he would still speak of the family in terms of man's loss of innocence.[4] There are in his works many adulatory remarks about motherhood but there are also vicious asides on the depravity of women in general.[5] Then there is *Emile*. Indeed, *Emile* was seen by Rousseau's contemporaries as a didactic tract on education and on the promotion of the family. It enjoyed an enormous popularity, despite attempts to suppress it. If the *Social Contract* titillated the imagination of the revolutionary, *Emile* did the same for the parent as pedagogue.[6]

If Rousseau sought to restore political authority to its pristine form in the *Social Contract,* he also believed that the family was an institution equally fit for rejuvenation. *Emile* was his answer to a second alternative. In one approach Rousseau gives us a picture of the family surrounded by a corrupt society. Here education must be private and designed to protect the family as an independent unit that challenges society. In the other model, the family is blessed by a true citizenry. Here education can afford to be public because "men are free."[7] Familial and political authority, in a sense man and citizen, are treated differently. But the key to Rousseau's equivocal treatment of the family lies in the manner in which he regarded women. Romantic individualism, as we shall see in Chapter 11, submits the family to unbearable centrifugal forces. Rousseau held these pressures in check by refusing to allow the woman to pursue the romantic's quest for the authentic self. For Rousseau was an obsessive woman hater. A sexual contract, antecedent to the famous social contract, explains Rousseau's approach to the family. The result is a new family model: romantic patriarchy.

SEX AND LOVE IN THE STATE OF NATURE

In order to see more clearly Rousseau's effort, let us look at the *Second Discourse*. Here he offers us his famous description of man's departure from his natural condition. The *Discourse on the Origin of Inequality* begins and closes on discussions of two kinds of inequality. One is natural or physical and "consists in the difference of ages, health, bodily strength, and qualities of mind or soul."[8] The other is moral or political and rests upon convention authorized by consent. What role does the family play in Rousseau's account of the progress of moral inequality? The earliest account Rousseau offers of man's natural condition shows almost no familial organization. Rousseau asks if sexual desire would disrupt the life of natural man: "What would become of men, tormented by this unrestrained and brutal rage, without chastity, without modesty, daily fighting over their loves at the price of their blood?"[9] He concludes that sex has no disruptive capacity in the state of nature because the moral aspect of love is absent. There is no fixation on any particular object of male desire. The natural man has no "abstract ideas of regularity and proportion"; "any woman is good for him."[10]

It is this moral aspect of love that irritates the imagination and leads to "cruel disputes." If we are to imagine only the physical in love, we find that desire is felt "less frequently and less vividly": "Everyone peaceably waits for the impulsion of nature, yields to it without choice with more pleasure than frenzy; and the need satisfied, all desire is extinguished."[11] Without moral love there are no laws of continence; without continence, no debauchery, no shame, no abortion.

Thus Rousseau concludes that after digging back to the true state of nature, even natural inequality has less "reality and influence" than other writers claim. In the earliest reaches of the state of nature the relationship between the sexes was peaceful but sporadic, limited to brief sexual encounters. There was no cohabitation. Since natural man's intelligence made no more progress than his vanity, he did not recognize even his own children. Rousseau is careful to remind his reader that sex for natural man lacks brutality and the basis for conflict. Independence does not create the conditions for insecurity. Men do not need women, nor do women need men, save for the impulse of sex which can always be "conveniently satisfied." But if Rousseau exposes "Hobbes' error," he is equally intent upon refuting Locke. The discussion of the sexes in the *Second Treatise* is criticized for being designed to give "rather a reason for existing facts than to prove the real existence of these facts."[12] While the male-female bond is advantageous, "it does not follow that it was thus established by nature; otherwise it would be necessary to say that nature also instituted civil society, arts, commerce, and all that is claimed to be useful to men."[13] Thus both Hobbes and Locke fail to truly explore the natural. Each in his own way attributes convention to nature in his treatment of the sexes, Hobbes by positing a strong libido and Locke by positing familial dependence.

The very first developments in prehistory related to survival. Natural man found that he must do more than profit from the "gifts of nature": "It was necessary to become agile, fleet in running, vigorous in combat."[14] Weapons were fashioned and fire was tamed. This struggle produced the first awareness of relationships between man and the environment. Rousseau refers to this new consciousness as a "mechanical prudence" related only to safety. But prudence also gave rise to the first indication of self-esteem. Superiority over other animals produced "the first stirring of pride." Awareness of fellow men was more constant and on those few occasions when cooperation was necessary, ad hoc groups were formed. The notion of a contract emerged from these "free associations."

Rousseau stops at this point to remind the reader that he is covering "multitudes of centuries like a flash": "the more slowly events followed upon one another the more quickly they can be described."[15] More rapid advances follow. Natural man sheds his indolence. "The more the mind was enlightened, the more industry was perfected."[16] The savage no longer sleeps under a tree or in a cave; hatchets are discovered and huts are made. Here the family is born. Rousseau's account becomes confusing at exactly this point. The family seems to appear full-blown with "husbands and wives, fathers and children," united by "conjugal love and paternal love."[17] This, despite Rousseau's criticism of Locke and his promise that events will now be described in more detail. We are told about the effects of family life: the differentiation of the sex, the origin of language, the loss of "ferocity and vigor," the new taste for commodities. We are not told, however, how the "habit of living together" in villages altered natural man's promiscuity and for that matter, produced a paternal love. How precisely did moral love become attached to physical love and how did this attachment produce the family? If we look back at Rousseau's description of natural man, we might suppose that the end of his wanderings brought people into more constant view. Comparisons might develop in the mind and a preference for a single sexual partner emerge. Rousseau's only example of natural inequality occurs after the establishment of families:

> A permanent proximity cannot fail to engender at length some contact between different families. Young people of different sexes live in neighboring huts; the passing intercourse demanded by nature soon leads to another kind no less sweet and more permanent through mutual frequentation. People grow accustomed to consider different objects and to make comparisons: imperceptibly they acquire ideas of merit and beauty which produce sentiments of preference. By dint of seeing one another, they can no longer do without seeing one another again.[18]

This is all Rousseau tells us about the origin of the family. The remainder of the discussion is a reflection upon primitive society in general and the alteration in sentiments it produces. Despite pages devoted to prefamilial life and Rousseau's promise to describe later development in detail, the reader has only a very sketchy image of the origin of the family. It arises as a result of a more sedentary life after men have attained mechanical prudence but before they have achieved language, after the rise of free association but before property or government. It means the first division of labor ("Women . . . grew accustomed to tend the hut and the children, while the man went to seek their common subsistence"),[19] but is based upon neither economic nor political necessity. Rousseau insists "reciprocal affection and freedom were its only bonds."[20]

Part of Rousseau's problem in explaining the creation of the family lies in the vigor with which he denied anything resembling familial ties in the original state of nature. If indeed children could fend for themselves at a very early age, if a woman's survival is not threatened by pregnancy and nursing, if sex has such an anonymous quality to it, how could the family be born by mere "mutual frequentation"? In this respect, Rousseau has not advanced beyond Locke. Locke's family exists from time immemorial. Rousseau rejects that notion but ends up with two accounts, one which allows no relationship between the sexes and one which pictures the family fully developed. There is not much in the *Second Discourse* that connects the two. Natural man and natural woman stumble upon one another in the forest, have sex, and wander off in different directions. The next image we are presented with is a Romeo and Juliet, oblivious to the crushing necessities of primitive society, driven by an "impetuous fury" for sexual exclusivity.

But if there is independence for natural man, there is "sweetness" for his counterpart. Sex is now connected with love. Yet this "tender and gentle sentiment" is nevertheless the most dangerous of all: "Jealousy awakens with love; discord triumphs, and the gentlest of the passions receives sacrifices of human blood."[21] Violence becomes a problem in Rousseau's state of nature long before private property and civil law. His first admission of its existence is precisely at the point of the first revolution, the rise of the family.

While Rousseau would rail against the "insane" and "dreadful" system of Hobbes for understanding only what it was like to be a bourgeois of London and Paris, his account of the origin of the family is as bourgeois as any other. The sexual exclusivity of the family is traced to romantic love of the most idealized sort. The first male-female bond is formed solely from "reciprocal affection." Partners cannot "do without seeing one another." Their attraction is based upon a sense of beauty that tears the heart apart. In criticizing Hobbes, Rousseau had mentioned that nothing is so miserable as a savage "tormented by passions." But what is this new form of attraction, this "impetuous fury" that arises at "the least obstacle" to affection, but a transference of modern passion to primitive life?

Thus conjugal love poses problems. Its intensity is so great that it "seems fitted to destroy the human race it is destined to preserve." It torments men and leads them to an "unrestrained and brutal rage." Ways must be found to restrain and guide this passion. On the other hand, Rousseau (unlike later romantics) was adamant that the promiscuity of natural man and natural woman ought not be carried over to society. Women of Paris and London become Rousseau's examples of decadence. Not one of them is "really pure in heart": "There is modesty in the brow, but vice in the heart."[22] Once in society, moral love must be protected and nurtured. While Rousseau gives natural man every liberty he can imagine; he is a stern teacher of morality in civil society. Love may be an artificial sentiment and beauty a corruption of civilization, but once they are established Rousseau proscribes no return to the sexual life of natural man.

THE ISOLATED FAMILY

It may be useful at this point to compare Rousseau's treatment of the origins of the family to Locke's. Despite Rousseau's long rebuttal to Locke's efforts, the accounts are similar. It is true that Rousseau insisted upon the existence of a long prefamilial life for natural man. But at the point of origin of the family, both accounts converge. The family is somehow connected to a more active life and the emergence of private property. For Locke, property arose "as Families increased and Industry enlarged their states." For Rousseau, when "industry was perfected" and produced the "establishment of families," this in turn introduced a "kind of property" (*"une sorte de propriété"*). In both, nascent family life represented a "golden age." Rousseau made this idyllic period central to his political philosophy; but as we noted, Locke also protested affection for that "poor but virtuous age." In both writers, however, the golden age is marred by the first instances of violence. Force is related in both accounts to a new scarcity produced by increased needs. Locke focuses upon the invention of money, Rousseau upon love; both place great emphasis upon the end of man's nomadic life as a necessary cause of discord.

In opposition to Hobbes, both Locke and Rousseau reject an explanation of the origin of the family in patriarchal terms. Both describe a relatively equalitarian family. For Rousseau it is based upon "reciprocal bonds of affection and freedom," for Locke upon contract. Both also base the parental bond upon love rather than force.

The difference between the two accounts, and it is a major difference, is Rousseau's emphasis upon the social bond between male and female and the implication this bond has for the human condition. Despite his unwillingness to explore it, Locke insisted upon the natural aspect of this bond. Rousseau is obsessed with exploring this relationship; in fact, all of his political thought centers around the concept of a social bond and its maintenance. This concept is the heart of Rousseau's thought and it delineates the difference between a rational and a romantic individualism.

In Chapter 3 we discussed the problems that face the rational individualist when he approaches the family. Both Hobbes and Locke were forced to explain how free and rational men could find themselves in institutions based upon emotion and hierarchy. The rational individualist must see the value of the family as an institution and he must be made loyal to it in terms consistent with his own calculations. For Rousseau, as a romantic individualist, the family poses a somewhat different problem. The rational individualist need only break up the current social order to be aware of his basic freedom and independence. For Hobbes this implied revealing the role of force in human relations and the consequences it entailed. For Locke, this meant re-examining the basis of authority in order to discover the basis of our original rights. For both Hobbes and Locke, the rational individual perspective lies just beneath the conventions of society. This is not the case for Rousseau. Man's nature, his individualism, is buried very deep in the psyche. In fact, it is only in his mind, dim and distorted, that his true nature is revealed. In his *Confessions* Rousseau writes of the difficulties of disentangling "the true feeling of nature" among so many prejudices and unnatural passions. Both Rousseau's obsession with corruption and his effort to show how far back in history one must go to find the original state of nature and the golden age reveal the difficulty. He found out that he had to "dig down to the root" to show the true human condition.

But the extent of the departure from man's original individualism was only half of Rousseau's problem. The rest has to do with the nature of the individualism he seeks. Rousseau's individual may not merely consult his reason to find himself. Reason is, in good part, his affliction.

Although Rousseau would surely protest, his conception of true liberation is an ethereal thing. It is based upon self-love, but not selfishness; upon reason, but only reason connected to the heart; upon passion tender and gentle, not passion unbridled and impetuous; upon love of strength but not love of power; upon self-affirmation but not vanity; upon pleasure but not debauchery; upon pursuit of excellence but not competition. There are really only two signposts in this search: self-preservation (which "is always good" — "we must love ourselves above everything") and empathy.

If this is the task Rousseau sets before each person, how does the family fit into the plan? Only under the conditions of true liberation is it possible for individuals to fashion the social bonds for family life. Should these bonds be weakened or broken, the family becomes "little more than a group of secret enemies."[23] For the rational individualist, the family is maintained, at least ultimately, by rational education. For Rousseau, the family can continue to exist only when individuals find their true selves. If they do find their selves, "there is no more charming picture than that of family life." But "when one feature is lacking the whole is marred."[24] It should not be surprising that in many of Rousseau's works the family is rejected as the major social bond of the liberated individual. A more certain and permanent link is offered. The family is passed over as one of the "false notions of the social bond."[25] But let us first examine Rousseau's attempt to save the family.

We noted Locke's achievements in conceiving the modern family — the relative equality of the spouses, the child-centered nature of the institution, its specialization of function. Rousseau fills out portions of Locke's concept, rejects certain aspects of it, and perhaps most significantly, carries the concept of the family and its relation to the political order in a different direction.

The most prominent feature of Rousseau's view of family life is its isolated and inward-looking character. Rousseau chastises both men and women for leaving the home and directing their attention to society at large. The strongest words of *Emile* are reserved for women who seek the "worldly pleasures" of the town. Since the real nurse is the mother and the real teacher is the father, servants must not be given these functions.

The household is reduced to individuals tied together by nature. Where shall they live? Rousseau is equally concerned with Emile's relationships with society as a whole and those with his own family. The tutor selects the country, far from "the vile morals of the city, whose gilded surface make them seductive and contagious to children.[26] Rural life teaches Emile respect for the land and simplicity but its most significant value lies in the fact that it allows the family to exist in independence and isolation. Family members will not be drawn into the social whirlpool of city life.

The choice of Emile's occupation receives an extended treatment by the tutor. Rousseau insists that complete independence is not possible: "When we leave the state of nature we compel others to do the same." Once a member of society, one is "bound to work." "Every idler is a thief."[27] But within this context, the question of independence is paramount. While farming is the "earliest, the most honest of trades," it is too dependent upon the actions of others to be recommended for Emile. The occupation of artist is adamantly rejected: "I would rather have him a shoemaker than a poet, I would rather he paved streets than painted flowers on china."[28] As to the policeman, spy, and hangman: some occupations develop "detestable qualities of the mind, qualities incompatible with humanity." Emile must have a useful honest trade; a trade will make him independent within society. Rousseau sums up his purpose when he notes that the trade must be of use to Robinson Crusoe on his island. Rousseau chooses carpentry for Emile: "It is clean and useful; it may be carried on at home; it gives enough exercise; it calls for skill and industry, and while fashioning articles for everyday use, there is scope for elegance and taste."[29]

The education of Emile reveals Rousseau's attempt to emphasize the necessarily inward character of the family in modern society. The mother is urged to "raise a wall round your child's soul." *Robinson Crusoe* is the first book Emile will read. It will always "retain an honored place" and "serve to test our progress toward a right judgment."[30] Crusoe is valued not only for his rustic life but also for his self-sufficiency. The worth of material objects will be gauged according to the needs of Defoe's hero. "Every substance in nature and every work of man must be judged in relation to his own use, his own safety, his own preservation, his own comfort."[31] Emile will learn to value iron more than gold, glass more than diamonds, a shoemaker more than a jeweller. Goldsmiths, engravers, and embroiderers may fit Locke's idea of gentlemanly worth but for Emile they are "lazy people who play at useless games."[32]

Thus through his adolescence, Emile's knowledge is confined to nature and things. He knows no history, no metaphysic or morals. And most importantly, Rousseau would have Emile ignorant of sex as long as possible. The onset of sexual desire is like a second birth and uncontrollable passions emerge. Henceforth no human passion will be a stranger to Emile and the tutor must be prepared to assert even stronger control. Special skill and care need to be "devoted to guarding the human heart against the depravity which springs from those fresh needs."[33] Rousseau recommends measures designed to produce late puberty and insure abstinence before marriage. The tutor must "establish law and order among the rising passions, prolong the period of their development" so that "they are controlled by nature herself, not by man."[34] The tutor will go so far as to reply to a child's question, "Where do babies come from?", thus: "Women pass them with pains that sometimes cost their life."[35] The associated ideas of pain and death will cover the child's question with "a veil of sadness which deadens the imagination and suppresses curiosity; everything leads the mind to the results, not the causes of childbirth."[36] Sex will have no titillating association for Rousseau's child. On the contrary, if his curiosity is not quelled, at least it will be "turned to the infirmities of human nature, disgusting things, images of pain."[37]

The preparations Rousseau has his tutor go through in selecting Emile's wife are again designed to keep the young man's passions in control. Rousseau insists that the young must be permitted to choose their own mates and afterwards parents be consulted. But neither Emile nor Sophy meet one another by chance. The tutor arranges their first meeting, he insists upon determining when, where, and how often they shall meet, and at one point he forces them to separate for a year. Somehow Emile must forge a bond that spares him from being ruled by another.

Rousseau is not averse to praising mediocrity if it is deemed necessary for preserving restraint in social life. Emile's profession is selected for its capacity to maintain independence. The ability to produce "some elegance" in carpentry is a consideration, but a secondary one. The career of great talent and brilliance can be pursued only through the help of others. Artists need commissions, civil servants need the ears of ministers, teachers need sponsors. Emile's independence is gained at the price of anonymity. Even his history lessons are arranged to support this view. "Only the wicked become famous," the tutor reminds his pupil.[38] Control of our passions will lead to a life of sedate mediocrity.

THE FEMALE PROBLEM AND THE SEXUAL CONTRACT

But Rousseau reserves the real target of his campaign of restraint and mediocrity for women. It is they who bear most of the price for the rejection of modern society's self-esteem. The submission of women to men and of women to the requirements of the family forms a major portion of Rousseau's image of the family as a solution to our discontents. The position of a woman can only be described as one of surrender. Not only are women "specially made for man's delight" but in addition they are required to "endure even injustice at his hands."[39] We noted Rousseau's concerns with controlling human passion in the education of Emile. They assume nearly an obsessive character. If Emile is to be taught self-control so that he may obtain self-mastery, Sophy must be taught self-control so that she will accept submission. If Emile must learn to accept the authority of his tutor as natural, Sophy must learn to accept all authority as natural. If

Emile's knowledge of abstraction is delayed, Sophy's is postponed forever. If Emile is to be taught that cleanliness has value, Sophy is taught it should "absorb one half of her time and control the other."[40]

All of these differences in the education of Emile and Sophy are justified by the assertion that a "woman has the same needs as a man but without the same right to make them known."[41] The concern for appearance governs Sophy's life. Rousseau tells us that one should check a boy's prattle by asking "What is the use of that?" A girl is admonished by inquiring, "What effect will that have?"[42] A woman's conduct is to be controlled by "public opinion." Female adultery, Rousseau's cardinal sin against the family as an institution, must be avoided not only in fact but in inference: ". . . it is not enough that the woman should be chaste, she must preserve her reputation and her good name."[43] Girls must be kept busy but their work should have a passive aspect. Rousseau has Sophy liking needlework best; lacemaking is her favorite occupation because "there is nothing which calls for such a pleasing attitude." All women are to be docile. Boys want "movement and noise, drums, tops, toy-carts; girls prefer things with appeal to the eye and can be used for dressing-up — mirrors, jewelry, finery and specially dolls."[44] Each of Sophy's characteristics reflects this attribute. While Emile must sacrifice ambition and fame to be independent and free, Sophy must cultivate a deeper mediocrity. Her singing voice is never trained too much; her piano playing has taste rather than talent, her clothes are simple; her mind is "pleasing but not brilliant, and thorough but not deep"; if punished, she is gentle and submissive, more ashamed of the fault than the punishment. In short, for Sophy to be free she must learn to be an ideal wife:

> . . . in submission to man's judgment she should deserve his es-
> teem; above all she should obtain the esteem of her husband; she
> should not only make him love her person, she should make him
> approve her conduct; she should justify his choice before the
> world, and do honour to her husband through the honour given to
> the wife.[45]

This special education assigned to women is expressly designed to protect the family. As with all of Rousseau's social thought, the proposals are severe. A real mother is no woman of the world, "she is almost as much of a recluse as the nun in her convent."[46] Plato, who receives a sympathetic review early in *Emile,* is now chastised: Having got rid of the family he has no place for women in his system of government, so he is forced to turn them into men.[47]

The woman as mother and wife is an exclusive role. Rousseau asks, "Can she be a nursing mother today and a soldier tomorrow? Will she change her tastes and her feelings as a chameleon changes his colour?"[48] The husband and father can, of course, make such transitions. But for Rousseau the temptations of the world outside the family are simply too great for women. Here again Rousseau applies the same general standards in his search for virtue in a corrupt society. The depravity of urban life is threat enough to Emile's character, but additional precautions must be taken to protect women.

Our depiction of Rousseau's vision of the family is nearly complete: inward-looking, as self-sufficient as possible, child-oriented, and above all, patriarchal. To name these specifics is not to say that the ambiance of the family is at all formal or distant in its relationship with the man as father and husband. Love is indeed the sentiment that pervades family life. Emile and Sophy are madly in love and the tutor reminds them that the secret of marriage "consists in remaining lovers when you are husband and wife."[49] Children add to dyadic sentiment: they "form a bond between their parents, a bond no less tender and a bond which is sometimes stronger than love itself."[50] If love is maintained in marriage, "we should find a paradise upon earth."[51]

But why must Emile's Sophy assume the manner, and indeed, the tactic of the "total woman" for marriage and family life to succeed? An answer to this question can provide us with the key to Rousseau's treatment of the family. One of the most intriguing aspects of all of Rousseau's thought is fear and hatred of the free woman. This theme runs through all of his work, but is especially prominent in *Emile*. In some respects the free woman epitomizes Rousseau's fear of modern society. She is vain and greedy; she is without scruple and without restraint. The tutor is willing to selectively expose his pupil to all the follies of modern life in order to inculcate humility. He will let flatterers take advantage of him, "pluck him," "rob him" and even later "mock him." "I will even thank them to his face for the lessons they have been good enough to give him." But he will never permit Emile to fall to the "wiles of wanton women."[52]

It is not that sex itself is the problem. Sexuality was of no concern for the natural man of the state of nature. It is at least manageable within the confines of the properly contracted marriage. It is women who are the problem. Let us return for a moment to the *Second Discourse* at the point in which Rousseau makes the distinction between moral and physical love:

> The physical is that general desire which inclines one sex to unite with the other. The moral is that which determines this desire and fixes it exclusively on a single object, or which at least gives it a greater degree of energy for this object. Now it is easy to see that the moral element of love is an artificial sentiment born of the usage of society, and extolled with much skill and care by women

in order to establish their ascendancy and make dominant the sex that ought to obey.[53]

Now just a few pages later Rousseau, as we have already noted, traces the rise of moral love to toolmaking and sedentary life. He insisted, also as we noted, that this new form of love formed "the sweetest sentiments known to man," in part because it was a bond based upon "reciprocal affection and freedom." Thus it cannot be that moral love is simply a woman's trick. But women apparently have the power to corrupt this sort of love, turn it to *their* advantage and enslave the male sex.

> Women so easily stir a man's senses ... that if philosophy ever succeeded in introducing this custom [female sexual aggressiveness] into any unlucky country, especially if it were a warm country where more women are born than men, the men, tyrannised over by the women, would at last become their victims, and would be dragged to their death without the least chance of escape.[54]

Only the modesty that God gave women restrains their "boundless passions" and by inference allows men to escape their torment: "For nature has endowed women with a power of stimulating man's passions in excess of man's power of satisfying those passions...."[55] The male realization and fear of woman's capacity for multiple orgasms, now alleged by some commentators to be a product of late capitalism, appears to exist in the eighteenth century. Rousseau suggests a bargain, a contract of sorts, that is the beginning of the resolution to the female problem. If the vagina is the man's enemy, the major threat to his independence, it is also the resource for his escape. "The woman's mind exactly resembles her body," Rousseau tells us. She knows that her "boundless passion" is related to her role as a receptacle in the sex act. Her weakness is in fact her strength:

> She is ashamed to be strong. And why? Not only to gain an appearance of refinement; she is too clever for that; she is providing herself beforehand with excuses, with the right to be weak if she chooses.[56]

Rousseau bemoans "how skillfully" a woman can stimulate the efforts of the aggressor. Female animals are different. Their desire speaks of necessity: "when the need is satisfied, the desire ceases; they no longer make a feint of repulsing the male, they do it in earnest."[57]

At one level Rousseau knows that rape is an injustice. But look at the way he condemns it:

The freest and most delightful of activities does not permit of any real violence: reason and nature are alike against it; nature, in that she has given the weaker party strength enough to resist if she chooses; reason, in that actual violence is not only most brutal in itself, but it defeats its own ends, not only because the man thus declares war against his companion and thus gives her a right to defend her person and her liberty even at the cost of the enemy's life, but also because the woman alone is the judge of her condition, and a child would have no father if any man might usurp a father's rights.[58]

All the classic condemnations of rape are in that passage: rape is an act of violence against a person; a woman has a right to determine when, where, and with whom she shall have sex, rape is an extreme violation of human dignity. But resting next to these statements is the assertion that a man's patrimony is damaged. Sandwiched between the portrayal of rape as a basic wrong is Rousseau's observation that nature has given the victim strength enough to resist if she chooses. Rousseau has drawn such attention to woman's alleged capacity for stimulation by feigned submission that the whole question of rape becomes definitionally blurred. If all sex is characterized by female resistance and then submission of some sort, and if her weakness is a form of excuse, a tactic related to her "unbounded passions," when does conventional sex become rape? How do we tell exactly when that "freest and most delightful of activities" becomes "real violence"? Rousseau tells us that a woman always repulses the pursuer and defends herself, whether she desires sex or not. The difference from case to case is that the protests do "not always have the same vigour."[59] Indeed, Rousseau continues by asserting that men will never know if their sexual success is won by force or by voluntary surrender. This is the "charm of the man's victory" and the "woman is usually cunning enough to leave him in doubt."[60] Now all of this would not be so damaging to Rousseau if his account were couched in terms of examples from debutante balls or, more to his liking, from rustic spring festivals. But he himself moved beyond the conventional dalliances of the sexes to the subject of rape.

In the next part of this discussion there is a remarkably cruel aside on the law found in *Deuteronomy* that punished both the rapist and the victim if the offense was committed in the town. If the rape occurred in the country, only the assailant was punished. Rousseau notes that "if fewer deeds of violence are quoted in our days, it is not that men are more temperate, but because they are less credulous, and a complaint which would have been believed among a simple people would only excite laughter among ourselves."[61]

The presentation of the material here is also quite complex. He tells us that the cry of rape is more likely to be believed by those close to "the simplicty of nature." We moderns are less credulous and presumably can see rape for the ambiguous activity that it is, given the peculiar nature of the relationship between the sexes. But then Rousseau reminds the careful reader that that is not what he is saying. No, quite the contrary; after all, we, who would laugh at such a cry, have been "uprooted by our profligacy." So now it seems the simple people were after all right in heeding the cry of rape. But wait, we are again treated to another slight turnabout. The example that he offers for which the ancients are to be commended is the law in *Deuteronomy* that is notorious for making the assumption that *both* parties are responsible in an apparent rape unless in an environment of isolation.

Thus for Rousseau a woman's weakness is a tool of her real strength and that strength is her "boundless passion." But that strength, since it is based upon an ostensible passivity, can be turned to man's advantage. Rousseau suggests modesty as a learned attribute for women. Modesty is broadly consistent with woman's nature in that it mimics her weakness (her real strength) but it serves to restrain her boundless passions. A genuine modesty makes her weakness a real weakness and not a cover for her strength. Thus Rousseau is finally able to say that a woman has the same needs as a man, but without the same right to make them known.

Modesty will constrain women in the company of men. Every man will know that he is safe, that his home harbors no "secret" enemy. But the woman's commitment to modesty is always in danger of crumbling. Philosophers attack it as a form of insincerity. Rousseau knows quite well that for women modesty may have its hypocritical edge. But, he contends that "If I were tempted to steal, and in confessing it I tempted another to become my accomplice, the very confession of my temptation would amount to a yielding to that temptation."[62] Besides, strip a woman of modesty and she again becomes the victor:

> When the natural curb is removed from their sex, what is there left to restrain them? What honour will they prize when they have rejected the honour of their sex? Having once given the rein to passion they have no longer any reason for self-control.[63]

Modesty assures a measure of sexual exclusivity on the part of women. Since "a male is only a male now and again" and "the female is always a female," at least her sexuality can be directed to the needs of men.[64] Rousseau is able to connect the constraint of the female to family life and both to the purity of the country:

Vague assertions as to the quality of the sexes and the similarity of their duties are only empty words. . . . It is a poor sort of logic to quote isolated exceptions against laws so firmly established. Women, you say, are not always bearing children. Granted; yet that is their proper business. Because there are a hundred or so of large towns in the world where women live licentiously and have few children, will you maintain that it is their business to have few children? And what would become of your towns if the remote country districts, with their simpler and purer women, did not make up for the barrenness of your fine ladies? There are plenty of country places where women with only four or five children are reckoned unfruitful. In conclusion, although here and there a woman may have few children, what difference does it make? Is it any less a woman's business to be a mother?[65]

Rousseau tells us that "it is only fair that woman should bear her share of the ills she has brought upon man."[66] The punishment is a romantic patriarchalism: a family based upon sentiment with the woman "almost as much a recluse as the nun in her convent."

MATERNAL AUTHORITY

In the beginning of *Emile*, Rousseau explores some of the differences between man and citizen. A man lives for himself; a citizen is "but the numerator of a fraction." The latter "no longer regards himself as one, but as part of a whole, and is conscious only of the common life."[67] *Emile* shows how a man "can live with others if he is educated for himself alone."[68] Emile may be good, he may even be virtuous, but he is not a citizen. The natural man in society is able to function through the social bond of the family. The woman, as we have just seen, must withdraw even deeper into the family and away from society in order to remain "good." But the family is an institution which by its very nature assumes greater importance when surrounded by a corrupt society. Rousseau was not content to recommend just little islands of goodness in the social order. The social bond of citizenship as a means by which human nature could be transformed and purified was indeed Rousseau's grand vision.

When Rousseau pursues his vision, his commitment to the family must of necessity be loosened. It is interesting to see how he manages to transfer his allegiance to this very different kind of social bond. The bond of citizenship, however antithetical it appears to be in relation to the familial bond, is rarely seen as directly replacing the family or as the basis for an attack on it.

But before we look at Rousseau's treatment, let us look at the manner in which he conceives of the social bond of citizenship. The best concise statement can be found in his discussion of Lycurgus:

> ...he undertook to legislate for a people already debased by servitude and by the vices the latter brings in its train. He fixed them a yoke of iron, the like of which no other people has ever borne; but he tied them to that yoke, made them, so to speak, one with it, by filling up every moment of their lives. He saw to it that the image of the fatherland was constantly before their eyes — in their laws, in their games, in their homes, in their mating, in their feasts. He saw to it that they never had a free instant or free time that they could call their own. And out of this ceaseless constraint, made noble by the purpose it served, was born that burning love of country which was always the strongest — or rather the only — passion of the Spartans, and which transformed them into beings more than merely human.[69]

With the duties of state "filling up every moment" of the citizen's lives, how will the parent possibly have time to build a wall around the child's soul? In fact, the demands of citizenship appear to be so great — meetings, games, military duty — that they resemble the whirlpool of urban life that Rousseau so detested. The difference, of course, is that the political activity of citizenship promotes solidarity instead of egoism, and spiritual vigor instead of the enervation that comes from the pursuit of women and money.

The fanaticism that characterized Rousseau's demands for correct family life is reflected in his portrayal of citizenship as well. Let the social bond be weakened ever so slightly and citizenship assumed only a "vain, illusory, and formal existence."[70] Citizenship, like family life, is an affair of the heart; it responds to the same passions and is capable of the same degeneration. In fact, the *Social Contract* contains a distinction between natural and moral liberty that corresponds directly to that distinction between physical and moral love. Natural liberty, with the "right to everything," is replaced by moral liberty, with "true mastery" of the self. Once a person attains the latter as a citizen he has risen above quality of a "stupid unimaginative animal" to that of "an intelligent being and a man."[71] Of course, the risks of corruption confront the citizen as they do Emile. His moral liberty, like his moral love, is sweet and ennobling, but is always challenged by those with "secret motives": "iniquitous decrees directed solely to private interests [can] get passed under the name of laws." Eternal vigilance is required else "in every heart the social bond is broken."[72]

Rousseau appears to have two general views on the place of the family in a revitalized political community. One can be found in *The Government of Poland,* the other in the *Discourse on Political Economy. The Government of*

Poland is Rousseau's most conservative work. Part of the reason for this conservatism may be that he felt Poland had traveled less far down the road to corruption than other European powers and hence still had traditions to conserve. In any case, the chapter on education begins with this radical demand upon the family:

> The newly born infant, upon first opening his eyes, must gaze upon the fatherland, and until his dying day should behold nothing else. Your true republican is a man who imbibed love of the fatherland, which is to say love of the laws and of liberty, with his mother's milk. That love makes up his entire existence: he has eyes only for the fatherland, lives only for his fatherland; the moment he is alone, he is a mere cipher; the moment he has no fatherland, he is no more; if not dead he is worse off than if he were dead.[73]

Obviously, the family alone is not up to the task of producing individuals who imbibe laws and liberty along with mother's milk. Rousseau recommends a system of public education to complete the task. He does allow parents to educate their children if they wish. There is no restriction. Private education must be supplemented by participation in the games of the public gymnasium. Children must get accustomed at the earliest possible moment "to rules, to equity, to fraternity, to competitions," and most important of all, "to living with the eyes of their fellow citizens upon them, and to seeking public approbation."[74]

The family then is incapable of training the citizen. The social bond of citizenship requires constant supervision. Success lies "in seeing to it that every citizen shall feel the eyes of his fellow-countrymen upon him every moment of the day."[75] Then everyone is dependent upon the rest for individual achievement. The "resulting emulation" will produce a patriotic fervor that "raises men — as nothing else can raise them — above themselves."[76] The life within the family must constitute some kind of withdrawal, as Rousseau discussed so clearly in *Emile*. The eyes of the public cannot see within the home. In *Emile*, Plato was vigorously criticized for drawing the conclusions toward whch Rousseau now seems to be moving. He had asked, "Can devotion to the state exist apart from the love of those near and dear to us? Can patriotism thrive except in the soil of that miniature fatherland, the home? Is it not the good son, the good husband, the good father who makes the good citizen?"[77] Yet *The Government of Poland* never continues the lines of argument with which it begins. Patriotic fervor would seem to be threatened by the family but Rousseau never allows the issue to be opened. In fact, when the family is used for the needs of the state, it serves explicitly inequalitarian purposes. The criterion for freedom for peasants is their devotion to their families. One incentive for a soldier's skill with weapons is the distinction it will bring his family. Titles of distinction are conferred upon the families of heroes. Scholarships are given to the children of virtuous families.

The family then is a servant of the state; a powerful but limited socializing agent and an example of emulation for citizens.

Near the end of *Political Economy* a resolution is openly offered. After detailing the corruption endemic in modern life and asking, "How can patriotism germinate in the midst of so many other passions which smother it?"[78] Rousseau takes on the family. The family is now judged an unreliable institution. It cannot be counted upon to educate its children. Fathers die and deprive the child of the final fruits of education, and the country sooner or later suffers: "Families dissolve, but the State remains."[79] A republic cannot rely upon the prejudices of fathers in the education of children inasmuch as "that education is of still greater importance to the state than to the fathers."[80] Why should a father object to the state "charging itself" with the "important function" of education? For the first time a note of real suspicion creeps into Rousseau's view of the family as an institution:

> Should the public authority, by taking the place of the father, and charging itself with that important function, acquire his rights by discharging his duties, he would have the less cause to complain, as he would only be changing his title, and would have in common, under the name of *citizen,* the same authority over his children, as he was exercising under the name of *father,* and would not be less obeyed when speaking in the name of the law, than when he spoke in that of nature. . . .[81]

There is more in this important paragraph and we will quote the continuation in a moment. But note the character of the argument so far. One who considers resisting the state's authority over his children is evincing a certain egoism and most importantly an opposition to the authority of the state itself. If relinquishing the child to the state does not change the character of the child's relationship to the parent, what is the nature of the complaint? Could it be that the father has educational designs other than the creation of a citizen? What has happened to Rousseau's commitment to the nidal climate and the uniqueness of the natural in childrearing that characterized his argument in *Emile*? In that essay Rousseau insisted that a father who realized the value of a good tutor would do without one. Now Rousseau insists upon broader horizons for virtue than the family and he perceives that the family will violate the major condition of the citizenship bond, equality:

> If children are brought up in common in the bosom of equality; if they are imbued with the laws of the State and the precepts of the general will; if they are taught to respect these above all things; if they are surrounded by examples and objects which constantly remind them of the tender mother who nourishes them, of the love she bears them, of the inestimable benefits they receive from her, and of the return they owe her, we cannot doubt that they will learn to cherish one another mutually as brothers, to will nothing contrary to the will of society, to substitute the actions of men and citizens for the futile and vain babbling of sophists. . . .[82]

Identical patterns of childrearing will produce attitudes that do not challenge the citizen bond; each person wills "nothing contrary to the will of society."

But the structure of the family is also presented in a different manner in the *Discourse of Political Economy*. We saw how in *Emile* and in the *Second Discourse* Rousseau drew a picture of the family based largely upon sentiment. In marriage sexual attraction would lose its frenetic and tormented character; reciprocal affection would be the basis of the family. In *Political Economy* the family is portrayed in terms more closely fitting the rational individualist model. Thus fathers' authority is "established in nature" but it is based upon his physical strength and the child's need for protection. Rousseau emphasizes the transitory aspects of the family: "In a word, the little family is destined to be exstinguished, and to resolve itself some day into several families of a similar nature. . . ."[83] But most significantly, there is the absence of the discussion of love. Children should be obedient to the father first from necessity, then from gratitude. Rousseau is demanding in regard to filial duty ("after having had their wants satisfied by him during one half of their lives, they ought to consecrate the other half to providing for his")[84] but avoids recourse to sentiment. Maternal affection for children, the plea that rings out from the first pages of *Emile,* is left undiscussed. Of love between man and wife, Rousseau is also silent.

What is emphasized is the difference between the family and the political order. Rousseau insists upon attacking Filmer's "detestable system" by adopting the principle of distinctiveness of the family. What he seems to be doing is contrasting a democratic political order with a patriarchal family. Citizens are "naturally equal," family members are not. The economic task of the state is to keep individuals in "peace and plenty," the object of the family is to "increase the patrimony of the father."[85]

Yet in the tract that contains the most direct attack on the family, Rousseau gives the institution a highly rational and individualistic character. The whole discussion is curious. *Gemeinschaft* and *Gesellschaft* seem to describe one of the major distinctions between household and political economy. Yet Rousseau has portrayed the family in the most formal terms. One might dismiss the contradiction by keeping in mind that Rousseau is dealing with family and state as economic institutions. The exploration of intimacy might be considered beyond the scope of the essay. But we just saw how eloquently Rousseau spoke of the general will. The state is discussed in anything but formal terms. Now the danger lies in citizens, not family members, becoming strangers. The state is a "great family," and any reduction of its purpose to economic function is explicitly rejected. Rousseau will not reduce "public esteem" to a "cash value" or have "virtue rated at a price." The mother as the fount of affection who had disappeared in the discussion of the family reappears as a metaphor of the state. The state is our "common mother" to whom we are grateful for the "inestimable benefits" we receive.

With the image of the state as the domesticated female, Rousseau is able to portray lesser associations in society in terms of those free and wild women he so despises. Citizens are only men and we cannot expect to expunge all the passions from them. But, as citizens they can be taught "to prefer that which is truly beautiful to that which is deformed."[86] Such education must begin with children but Rousseau continues the analogy for all citizens regardless of age. All citizens must "voluntarily will what is willed by those whom we love."[87] Patriotism is a "fine and lively feeling" that appears fanciful to any who have not experienced it. At one point Rousseau suggests that love of one's country is "a hundred times more lively and delightful than the love of a mistress."[88] It is a "warm" and "sublime ardour" — a nearly exact description of both Emile's love for Sophy, and a child's love for his mother. As wife or mother, the restrained but loving domesticated female, the state is hardly a threat to virtue. Lesser interests are dangerous, however. "Other passions" can "smother" patriotism. Avarice is described as a "mistress." Personal interests increase as an association within the state becomes narrower and "the engagement less sacred."[89]

We are now able to see Rousseau in some perspective. The common theme that links his reconstruction of the family and his attack upon it is his preoccupation with the sexual bond and the problems that it poses. The domesticated female — loving and stable but above all controlled — is the stuff from which the social bond is made, in the form either of the maternal state or of the family. But most importantly this new form of patriarchy, with the woman symbolically triumphant and effectively restrained, provided a release from the frenetic search for the authentic self that so characterizes this form of individualism. Once other images of the family grew, Rousseau's solution to the "problem" of the family, which was a solution to the female problem as well, would be seen in a different light.

5

CHARLES FOURIER AND THE REGIME OF LOVE

We began our discussion of the formulation of the modern family with Hobbes. We noted how "advanced" Hobbes' thought was in terms of the family; how he was willing to strip the sentimental veil from family life even before it was fully in place, how deeply he carried his individualistic principles into the social order, how he painted a picture of autistic family life. Another writer who anticipated the conclusions of a tradition of political thought is Charles Fourier (1772–1837). True, Fourier is not usually treated in this fashion. He is regarded as an eccentric, or even a madman. He was an early socialist reformer who threw the first salvos of criticism against the new industrial order, but Marx and Engels complained about his lack of an economic theory and his naiveté in regard to the revolutionary transformation of society. Liberal writers point to Fourier's fantasies as proof of the delusional basis of socialism.

But Fourier (vital statistics notwithstanding) was a post-Freudian and a post-Marxist — the most modern political philosopher than can be read today. In fact, nearly all the major strands of modern political thought — especially the search for personal liberation within a collectivist order — are explored and carried to their logical conclusion in Fourier. Only one element is lacking, and that is Fourier's total commitment to order: not the order derived from Spartan virtue or from revolutionary asceticism or from the rule of law — all of these notions are rejected by Fourier — but the order derived from a catalogical approach to social life. Fourier called for and explored a society based upon the glorification and release of emotion. Happiness was to be obtained by the flowering of all the passions and

Fourier knew every one of them. There were twelve passions derived from three groupings with specified gradations in each. Precisely 810 personality types were possible. Even Fourier's manias, his passions gone berserk, were catalogued:

> ... all manias must be classified and divided into series. The first problem will be to determine the numerical [incidences] of every mania. We will know, for example, that a certain mania appears only once in ten phalanxes and that another will have only one representative in 100 phalanxes. Some particularly rare manias will be represented only once in 10,000 or even 100,000. The mania with only one devotee in 100,000 phalanxes will be in just about the last 40 representatives on the whole face of the earth. Nonetheless it will constitute a part of the omnigamous series and we must include it in our calculations. In Harmony great efforts will be made to bring together the devotees of such extremely rare manias.[1]

Fourier himself confessed to a mania, sapphianism (love of lesbians), and concluded that "in the whole world there are only 26,400 people like me."[2] Charts, lists, category upon category, and a neologism for each characterize Fourier's works. He was truly the Bentham of the left. Sympathetic commentators are anxious to overlook this aspect of Fourier and seek to explain it in personal terms. But, as we shall see, the cataloging impulse is essential to a system based upon the exaltation of every conceivable passion. It forms the basis for the replacement of the institutions Fourier seeks to abolish. Fourier insisted that "morality is impotent without the bayonet, that this is the pivot around which all legislation revolves."[3] The only real alternative was for morality to be replaced by a total encouragement of the multiplicity of passions. The rational organization of work, the polity, and of course, the family, would be replaced with natural "amorous institutions." Only the most precise organization of the passions, many of which Fourier admits are under the wrong conditions dangerous, can produce Harmony, the final stage of human development. Thus if Fourier appears to be a Benthamite sexologist and his new institutions take on the appearance (to bourgeois sensibility, of course) of pandering, it is because no one had more faith in the capacities of bureaucracy than Fourier. That faith was deeper and greater than Marx's, who used it only to collectivize labor.

THE ANGELIC COUPLE
Our acceptance of Marx's and Engels' dismissal of early socialism may be a grudging one, but it is so complete that we often lose sight of the origins of

socialism itself. Socialism began without a theory of revolution or economic transformation or even a theory of history, but it did start with a particular vision of love and friendship. Early socialism had a theoretical critique of the family long before its critique of capitalism. The "duodecimal Jerusalems" upon which Engels heaped scorn were designed as escapes from industrialism as much as from the family, the form of love and friendship that capitalism was seen as sponsoring. In fact, except for Proudhon — whose support of the family was derived in part from his romance with the French peasantry — those socialists with the widest view of social transformation were those likely to leave the family untouched. Cabetism envisaged socialism on a large scale replete with five-year plans and consumer asceticism. Equality between the sexes was accepted but the father was recognized as the head of the family. The moving rationale of Saint-Simon's system was technocratic competence. The rationalization of production by the *industries généraux* would naturally eliminate the family as an economic institution, but on the subject in general Saint-Simon had little to say. However, when his followers began to emotionalize his system, the critique of the family emerged soon enough.

Those socialists motivated by the same desire to promote love and brotherhood were those who dared to look at society in microcosm. They saw the family as an enemy institution. Fourier certainly saw it as such; so did the founders of the nineteenth-century American Bible communist societies and the precursors of the kibbutzim. Even later, Sorel, dissatisfied with the rationalism of Marx, would return to the family in fascination as a breeding ground for intense emotion.[4] The very absence of a sense of grand historical momentum forced these socialists to return to the family as the key to the transformation of the political order. Writers in the Marxist tradition would later be forced to turn their attention from the panorama of terror and economic transformation to those tiny centers of affection and differential award. Whether the family were conceived as the last bastion of inequality or as a long-hidden secret betrayer of the Revolution, socialists would eventually re-examine the family.

But Fourier was the first to present this critique. His critique of the family forms the basis of his general critique of civilization, Fourier's term for industrial society. Much of his discussion is an exposé of the hypocrisy of society: the sexual adventures of the rich, the exploitation of working-class girls in the city, the pandering of young daughters by "respectable" peasant parents, and the sheer tortures of raising children in an environment of poverty. His treatment of this material is powerful and is a testament of Fourier's genius in sketching everyday life.

Let me present just one example of Fourier's efforts. After insisting that one must look behind the odes to the family as a "gentle moral household that raises tender children," Fourier asks his reader to look at the family of the poor. Here is the conversation that he asks us to overhear:

> Four men sat down at a table near my own. They were artisans, a little above the poorest class. One of them was saying, "I'm asking that girl in marriage because she'll have money; the family is comfortably set. You can be sure I don't want to be a sucker again. Take a wife who hasn't a penny, then the children come; it's the devil to take care of them, it's hell."
>
> "Then you had a lot of them?" said one of them.
>
> "I had six — feed all that and the wife!!!"
>
> "What, six? Good heavens! A worker who hardly earns a thing, to feed six children!"
>
> "Yes, six; but they all died, fortunately for me. And the mother's dead too."[5]

And here is Fourier's reaction to it:

> Notice the words *fortunately for me!* This exclamation surprised me little because I know the frightful position of a worker without fortune reduced to feeding six children and a mother who is unable to work. She is obliged to comfort an urchin who cries, wipe up another, spank this one, whip that one. These wretched children ask for bread as if it were to be had. They are given the whip when they are hungry. The interest of this conversation lies in the unanimity of the three companions in regard to the father's exclamation, "fortunately for me they are all dead, and the mother too." All three expressed agreement that it was indeed very fortunate for him. This then is the paternal and conjugal statement of the people that philosophers depict so movingly on stage. They do not see that the poverty of lowly households transforms fathers into brutes worse than ferocious animals. Even a lioness grieves if she loses her young; she is furious if they are taken from her. Then as soon as you wish, gentlemen of progress, elevate moral man to the moral height of wild beasts![6]

For me this is a moving passage. It reaches the heart. It exposes the vanity of unreflective philosophy and it shows the extent to which necessity can alter both natural sentiment and conventional morality. The phrase "fortunately for me" and the casual agreement that it elicits force Fourier to examine the role of familial sentiment in the current social order. Later on in the same discussion Fourier speculates upon the fate of the six dead children had they lived: the sons would have become cannon fodder, the daughters prostitutes.

But Fourier was no romantic familialist. The purpose of the alleviation of poverty would not be to resurrect the family. The middle and upper classes exhibit the "same depravity but in different forms. "All family relations are corrupt."[7] Sons still rejoice at their father's death. The peasant expression *père vit trop,* father who lives too long, is reflected in the very nature of any institution that bestows benefits on survivors. The solution that Marx would offer, the collectivization of labor, is not enough to eliminate the woes of the fathers. The family itself is a problem. Great attention must be paid to creating new institutions to replace it. All philosophers preach fatalism in regard to family strife but what is needed is a "new mode of domestic society."

A brief look at Fourier's treatment of the bourgeois family can help us make our point. The best way to begin is to present the reader with one of Fourier's innumerable lists, this one on the "perils of married life." Two features stand out in this presentation. One is related to the emphasis upon matters unrelated to love and the negative impact they have on the family. Running the household, coping with in-laws, dealing with finance, preparing for the economic catastrophe of death — all of these disrupt and poison the bond between spouses. The other, and the most important, has to do with the bond of sentiment itself between spouses and between parent and child. If any theme runs through all Fourier's critique of the family, it is the absurdity and waste associated with monogamy. In one list, Fourier focuses upon the monotony of marriage and the impossibility of fashioning a lifelong bond. We noted Rousseau's obsession with adultery. For Fourier adultery was actually an integral part of the institution of marriage itself. It was a shadowy institution to be sure; in fact, it was a sort of permanent revolution against the family itself. For Rousseau adultery was such a threat that it must be guarded against at all costs lest the family become nothing more than secret enemies. Fourier saw the family as by nature an institution containing secret enemies. "Civilized society, in all concerns of love" is in fact a system of "secret insurrection."[8] There was purpose to the proliferation of adultery in modern society. Naturally, the family itself created it. Previous societies had "permanent and compulsive" seraglios. Monogamy forced a system that was actually more advanced. Seraglios were "vague and free" now. Urban shopgirls formed a class "in actual fact as emancipated as if full liberty in love existed."[9] The growth of mercantile and fiscal systems, the loosening of "religious reins," and the decline of venereal disease were also causes of "amorous license."

To attach the raising of children to the enforced bond of monogamy was to create even more hatred and disruption. The parent, troubled and tormented by enforced monogamy, must save for the child's future, act as a disciplinarian, and be a friend as well as an educator. Even the love of parent for child, should it not be corrupted, is by its nature unjust. The child cannot return the mature love of an adult, the parent gives so much more, and frustration, the hallmark of all civilization, characterizes the relationship.

The family, then, is a state of war. But even the sentiment that does exist among family members is an enemy of justice: "Civilizees concentrate all their affection upon one woman and a few children, and are encouraged in this vile egoism...."[10] Fourier, the pluralist that he was, was unable to deny that monogamy was not suitable for *some* individuals. His attitude toward "monogenes" is especially instructive. For here, Fourier was forced to present a critique of monogamy itself and we arrive at the real heart of his critique, the rejection of dyadic relationships themselves.

The most striking and informative instance of his presentation is the case of the "angelic couple." Fourier begins with a situation which nearly everyone has experienced: "Almost every town and village has at least one extraordinarily handsome man and one extraordinarily beautiful woman." He calls them Narcisse and Psyche, and he observes that this couple excites everyone's desires and passions. But "civilized law" requires that they bestow affection only upon one another; in fact, the angelic couple are literally possessed by one another. But the pair really are "sublime" only to each other; they are "laughable and insipid egoists in the eyes of others":

> The world rightly regards a civilized love affair as a caricature, a travesty of the generous spirit which it is supposed to represent. It is a league based on pure interest from which the two lovers take all the profit with sharing the pleasures which they continually flaunt. In this respect civilized lovers are comparable to ignoble gluttons who go bragging about their fine dinners in front of wretched people who are deprived of what they need.[11]

This is an extraordinary passage even for so audacious a writer as Fourier. Dyadic lovers are subsumed under the language of socialism and portrayed as minicorporations. The angelic couple greedily rake in profits; natural talent should not bestow such riches. Like the hated capitalist who flaunts his wealth, the angelic couple insist upon parading themselves before society. Signs of affection are conspicuous consumption designed to establish status superiority. The system of dyadic love is indeed an open conspiracy. The decadence of modern society is easily exposed by illustrating how open is the display of such crass egoism. Even the gastronomic analogy is instructive; exclusivity is seen as the denial of what any objective observer would call a universal need. Oh, the injustice of it all! If God intended us all to share the beauty of nature, "He must have prepared some means" for our satisfaction.[12]

As Fourier outlined the transformation of everyday life for the poor in Harmony, he now shows us how these "selfish lovers" can be made into the angelic couple. For Psyche and Narcisse to share their favors with only two other people would be a "double infidelity," and "infamous and degrading passion." If sexual fellowship there must be, our couple must "surrender themselves to a mass of suitors."[13] Only by constantly expanding the benefits of their natural beauty can they "contribute to the progress of wisdom and virtue." Each partner must "minister to the sensual pleasures of the other by seeking out and providing suitors."[14] Each will consider "the procurement of pleasures for his or her angelic partner as a service of high friendship."[15] Twenty suitors apiece is the number Fourier assigns for the angelic couple to meet their social obligations. Each affair must last long enough to "satisfy the most ardent suitors." Two or three months should suffice. Naturally the angelic couple are denied a physical relationship with one another; the destruction of the dyad must be complete.

The angelic couple is aptly named. Fourier sees them in openly religious terms. Their activities are described as "pious works." They "religiously offer ... their favors"; partners receive them "with a holy respect which resembles that of Christians taking communion."[16] Sex with one of the angelic couple is a "balm of saintliness" so attractive that the example will inspire "selfish and jealous" lovers everywhere "to return to the path of virtue, to call a halt to fidelity."[17]

THE SEXUAL MINIMUM

Fourier's plans for the couple are only part of his attempt to replace conventional social arrangements with "harmonious" ones. The dyad represents only one of his so-called twelve passions of mankind. There were the luxurious passions, corresponding to the five senses, the affective or group passions (love, friendship, ambition, parenthood or "familism") and the serial or mechanizing passions (the cabalist or intriguing, the butterfly or variety, and the contrast and the composite; the latter was a kind of heavenly appreciation of physical and spiritual pleasures). Then there were manias, those rare and peculiar passions. Fourier insisted that no passion, not even the most obscure mania, could be repressed: "As soon as we wish to repress a single passion we are engaged in an act of insurrection against God. By that very act we accuse Him of stupidity in having created it."[18] He avoided the charge that he was repressing an important passion like familism or an important manifestation of the passion of love in dyadic form by claiming that both these forms were pursued to the detriment of others. A significant alteration had to occur. The family could exist in Harmony but not as "the pivot of the social mechanism" that it was.[19] For the family was the "enemy of the social state"; it refused to be absorbed into "the collective solidarity."[20] The same charge was leveled against the dyad. Fourier contended that the dyadic relationship simply could not last very long even among monogenes (those who, by nature preferred dyadic relations). Thus the apparent reasons for the tenacity of the family as an institution must rest elsewhere.

In reality then, dyads were serial; that is, monogenes moved from one lover as a sole object of affection to another as sole object. Fourier regarded this as a vicious form of behavior and despite his promise of neutrality toward all personality types, could scarcely control his anger:

> It is exclusive cohabitation with a single object; it has the very infamous property of successive forgetfulness. Men and women are accustomed to forgetting all preceding lovers in favor of the dominant one ... they boast of a rigorous fidelity and truly observe it for as long as the amorous bond lasts, after which they fall into perfect indifference toward those whom they love. This behavior, simple fidelity, is disdainful in that it leaves no trace of a bond.[21]

The polygene who loved many individuals at the same time was much preferable. Affection was cumulative and more in fitting with the goals of Harmony. Here I think, lies the key to Fourier's system. Like Rousseau, Fourier's philosophy centered upon the social bond. Fourier thought he had found the solution to maintaining social bonds by multiplying and extending their number. This solution, in part, formed his critique of the family and of dyadic relationships. Fourier's favorite biblical lesson was the story of Cain and Abel. Cain could not dismiss Abel because he was his brother. Had they been merely friends, they could have parted; the horror of fratricide would never exist. The three group passions — friendship, love, and ambition — were free bonds; the bond of the family was not. "God would be an enemy of freedom if he had chosen as the base and pivot of social mechanism the only group which is not free."[22] Similarly, the dyad limited love and friendship. It created outsiders, narrowed a vision of others, and was so intense that its closeness created enemies not friends. So friendship was to be the pivot of social order and love its attendant. In this respect Fourier's efforts are extremely important, though I believe this to be a disastrously misplaced use of friendship.

For the basis of the regime of love Fourier employs the socialist concept of the social minimum. Harmony is known for its emphasis on the variations of work tasks and hours, and for the absence of utilitarian standards in jobs. For instance, Fourier has his workers tend fields of flowers as well as wheat and barley. But all these attempts to guarantee "industrial attraction" are cast in the context of a social minimum:

> ... in this new order the common people must enjoy a guarantee of well-being, a minimum income sufficient for present and future needs. This guarantee must free them from all anxiety either for their own welfare or that of their dependents.[23]

Marx and Engels were quick to point out that Harmony was anything but an equalitarian paradise. Its production may have been socialized but dividends were parceled out according to investment. Nevertheless, Fourier did not stop with the concept of social minimum:

> Let us take note of the supreme injustice of our civilized legislators and the noxious spirit which inspires their secret policies. They are not unaware that the sense of taste, the need for subsistence, is the guiding force in the lives of the common people. They know that when food is lacking, the common people and simple soldiers will rebel and overthrow their government. Yet the law provides no guarantee of a minimum of subsistence.... Oblivious of their obligation to provide a minimum of subsistence, the lawmakers are even less willing to grant a minimum of sexual gratification. They suppose that the sexual needs are less urgent than the need for food. This is an error. Even though a person can do without sexual intercourse but not without food, it is certain that the need for tactile or sensual pleasures causes as many social disorders as does the need for subsistence.[24]

Sexual deprivation, as well as hunger, destroys an individual's sense of honor. It drives people to commit "crimes and misdeeds." The disorders "caused by the fear of amorous deprivation are not ... as obvious as those caused by hunger riots."[25] But the results are similar. The "fear of doing without physical love" leads people to "ridicule sentimental love" and makes deceit the underlying character of relations between men and women. Parents allow their unmarried daughters "to suffer and die for want of sexual satisfaction." Elderly women, "whose charms have withered with age," demean themselves before lovers to protect their sexual appetites. We saw how Fourier sketched out his approach with the case of the angelic couple. In the discussion of the sexual minimum, he carries his idea one step further. This very important example is an illustration:

> In 1816 a young man was prosecuted in the French courts for having raped six women whose ages ranged from sixty to eighty. ... His trial was discussed in all the journals.... The man was

found guilty and sentenced. Yet it might have been wiser to distribute pieces of his clothing as religious relics to inspire imitation of his fine example. It is evident that this young paragon was *acting out of need*; and it is also evident that the sexual needs of men and women can become just as urgent as their need for food.[26]

An odd example indeed for a writer who is granted by the left to be a champion of woman's rights. Fourier's point, however, is that rape is a response to a form of hunger, a deprivation of touch. But the "means of escape has been discovered." It lies in the formation of "groups intended to provide everyone with a minimum of physical satisfaction in love."[27]

AMOROUS INSTITUTIONS AND SENTIMENTAL SOUVENIRS

Fourier is never a more complete cataloguer than when he is constructing his "amorous institutions." For he recommends anything but a sexual laissez-faire in Harmony. It discriminates against the old, the unattractive, the poor, and those with rare sexual desires. Moreover, it is unable to free need or instinct. To do so would mean that "love become the essential concern of everyone in Harmony...." There must be confessors, strategically placed around the globe to link up the most appropriate couples or, better yet, to preside over orgies. There must be Courts of Love run by an elaborate bureaucracy — high priests, pontiffs, matrons, fairies, fakirs, genies. There must be world wars, "amorous" wars to be sure, since the exchange or "redemption" of "amorous prisoners" can form the basis for a sexual redistribution between old and young, rich and poor, attractive and unattractive. As this passage indicates, the negotiations of these affairs are dizzying in their complexity:

> Isaum, the son of the caliph of Baghdad, is twenty-one years old. He is the fifth captive. Too young to be a knight-errant, he has accompanied the horde as an adventuring seraphim. He has already distinguished himself for his virtue, however, and at the Phalanx of Scamander he was promoted to the rank of angelic candidate for having bestowed his favors upon the whole choir of venerable ladies of Scamander.
>
> Discussion opens concerning the redemption of Isaum. The paladin Orythia pays court to him. He is willing to become her captive; but Leucothea, a young girl with whom Orythia is in love, also wishes to redeem him. Orythia does not wish to displease the charming girl and concedes Isaum to her, begging her to re-member the sacrifice. Isaum intervenes to conciliate the two and declares that he will not give himself to either of them unless they

promise to enjoy each other's favors. He pledges to collaborate with them as a lesbianist, or a lover at the service of the two ladies and participating only on their orders and to activate their pleasures. Leucothea, urged on by Isaum and Orythia, accepts the proposition. The agreement is sealed with a lesbian kiss and Isaum receives the unanimous applause of the assembly for his generosity. . . .[28]

But amorous institutions, however complicated they may be, are designed to achieve more than the release of sexual needs. Fourier believed that sex, in civilization constrained by dyadic relationships and the inequality of physical attraction, grotesquely separated physical from romantic love. Only in Harmony could sensual and physical love coexist. But it is on precisely this point that Fourier lapses into his own grotesqueness. Since dyadic relationships are to be discouraged in Harmony, Fourier was forced to find another way to construct social bonds. The intensity of dyadic love was in part derived by the amount of time couples spent with one another and the consequent range of experiences that only they shared together. This sort of relationship is largely unavailable in Harmony. It is replaced by the highly organized but limited encounters arranged by the Courts of Love or by the system of what Fourier called "composed fidelity." The latter, the natural behavior of polygenes, involved affairs with several people at once. Thus a trigene loved three men simultaneously in periodic alternation. Imagine then a relatively simple case. Two trigenes have a love affair; each is also likely to be having two other affairs at the same time. Thus we have six affairs at one moment in time. If we accept Fourier's usual estimate of an affair at about three months, over a period of a year two trigenes will have formed bonds of affection with 24 individuals. Multiply this over a lifetime and add the factor that there are pentagenes and omnigenes and one has a complex melange of amorous bonds. But all polygenes, unlike monogenes, leave behind traces of friendship, "sentimental souvenirs," when they end their affairs. Here is Fourier's conclusion to much more complicated mathematical calculations of an omnigene named Artémise:

> Thus there are 1800 people who have modest legacies to inherit from the affluent Artémise. Today her colossal fortune would be prey of a half-dozen wicked inheritors who would hasten her to her grave. In Harmony she would subdivide her fortune [among a number] for whom a small legacy will not be a motive for desiring her death. . . . Artémise will have 1800 friends simply in souvenir of her loves of alternation and inconstancy. Those among them who, by monogynie, conserve no friendship for her will get small

sums by way of legacy.... Thus Harmony knows how to take advantage of inconstancy to create legions of friends for everyone.

Thus Harmony will be composed of a veritable "swarm of bonds," "bonds which replace the seeds of enmity in civilization."[30] What all this means, if we grant Fourier's assumptions, is that instead of the deeper but limited dyadic bonds of modern society, Harmony will be characterized by much more extensive but much more casual bonds of friendship. This is a novel point that Fourier makes and it is worth considering. The "civilized" family, as based upon a dyadic bond, was a disastrously selfish one. It was the worst sort of dyadic relationship possible since it formed the basis for the "familist" bond, one which further isolated individuals. Famly members were at best "indifferent" to the outside world; if they did not become secret enemies in regard to one another, they became secret enemies to other families. Fourier asks "[does harmony] exist in a bond that renders the family an enemy inclined to despoil all neighboring families?"[31] Family bonds were extremely difficult to break. Separated spouses were so bitter that they judged each other "worthy of nothing." Sons and daughters never really break the family bond.

Fourier mocked those "austere republicans" who promoted a regime based upon bonds of political fraternity. The liberation of the instincts implied that one or two ideas could not form a basis for political order. Republican virtue or its progeny, revolutionary asceticism, were also forms of restraint. "Virtue consists in forming the greatest possible number of bonds of all kinds."[32] Those "who desire that all men be brothers in Jesus Christ or in equality," those who wish to forge an "infinitely larger bond of friendship," fail "to consider that to thwart the development of one of the cardinal passions is to thwart them all."[33]

Fourierist friendship, extensive and patterned, is the alternative. But in selecting that alternative Fourier does not explore all its consequences. We tend to think of friendship, as well as sexual love, in dyadic terms. But friendships are certainly not as exclusive as sexual dyadic couples. It is much easier for us, even corrupted by civilization as we are, to imagine three or six or a dozen friends than to imagine the same numbers as lovers. But even if we take Fourier's example of the omnigene Artémise who had 1800 lovers, it would be difficult for us, nay impossible, to seriously regard all 1800 as friends. Even if it is true that Fourier has the Court of Love compiling records in its "amorous archives" of the intensity and duration of these affairs (we are assured that these records are "extremely accurate" for the purpose of inheritance), how many can we seriously give the description "friends"?

Fourier spoke of friendship as a "residue" or "trace" of sexual love, a sort of effervescence that attaches to past lovers. Thus sexual infidelity was virtue; there were saints of infidelity and even an "amorous nobility" in Harmony. To participate in the latter includes the requirement that an individual declare himself sentimentally attached to one woman or man at the same time that she or he has a physical relationship with another. After all, "anyone is capable" of having a simple "banal dyadic relationship."[34] Sexual promiscuity produces a halo effect of friendship. But how do brief lovers become friends? The relationship is anything but automatic. The one-night stand or the affair may produce absolutely no emotional ties. How can this residue produce time for shared experiences of friendship when individuals are moving with such religious dedication from affair to affair?

Fourier heaped scorn on the practice of "civilized" orgies in which participants hid their faces in darkness. But are relationships in Harmony much different? Fourier began his theory on the presumption that sexual love in civilization was a brutal and inhuman activity. Needs were so frustrated by marriage and morals that sexuality was solely a physical activity devoid of tenderness and concern. But sexual love is anything but transcended in Harmony. Friendship is in fact separated from physical love. It is on Fourier's own admission a residue or trace, a feeling that occurs after love has dissipated. As for friendship itself, one is reminded of the sort of friend that moves away and whom one has contact with once a year by a brief note at the bottom of a Christmas card. That sort of relationship may be pleasant enough but it is not the kind around which one would wish to build his life. These bonds are of the sort that are devoid of the agony and frustration of deep ties of affection; they are more like engaging remembrances, affectionate nothings on a greeting card. Instinct may be released in Fourier's utopia but it is an ironic note indeed that the character of human relationships that emerge from it should be so lacking in emotion.

As for that enormous intricate edifice of amorous institutions, a bureaucracy that is so devoted to human happiness that it is willing to search the world over to satisfy our most unusual need — well, one wonders how it really compares to that paltry, pathetic institution of the family, each composed of four or five members and arranged largely by chance and misguided devotion, in providing us with some measure of security and happiness.

KARL MARX AND FREDERICK ENGELS: DYADIC ROMANCE

The "successor" to utopian socialism pushed the family away from the center of social and political criticism. The family, no longer a focal point of analysis, was portrayed as a dependent institution. Like a lump of clay, the family changed throughout history. "One cannot in general speak of 'the' Family," announced Marx and Engels in *The German Ideology*.[1] As a consequence, there is surprisingly little in the writings of Marx (1818–1883) and Engels (1820–1895) about "smashing" the family in order to liberate universal sentiment. The family — now in its bourgeois form — was being smashed by the economic order itself. The *Manifesto* barely argued the proposal to abolish the family, though it was recognized that "the most radical flare up at this infamous proposal of the Communists":

> The bourgeois family will vanish as a matter of course when its complement vanishes, and both will vanish with the vanishing capital.[2]

The word "vanish" is instructive. For despite their ridicule of the family, its "dirty existence" in relation to "the holy concept of it in official phraseology," and their insistence that the key to the transformation of society lay elsewhere in greater historical forces, both Marx and Engels returned to the family at crucial points in their theories. The angelic couple, Fourier's nemesis, eventually becomes their center of attention. The relationship between man and woman was seen as the "most natural relation of human being to human being"; "it therefore reveals the extent to which the human essence in him has come to be nature to him."[3] Marx and Engels reduced the family to the dyad, the relation of man to woman, and made it not only an analogy for all relationships in communism but also the standard of what is natural. In an unusual sense, then, the family, in its truncated form as romantic dyad, is introduced as both the standard and the pinnacle of human development and becomes Marx's utopian solution to the family: "The direct, natural, and necessary relation of person to person is the relation of man to woman."[4] This celebration of the dyad, romantic and constrained as it appears from Fourier's perspective as well as from our own, is not without its logical inconsistencies. But let us follow the argument now and assess it after we have a complete picture.

THE ORIGIN OF THE FAMILY

The only work by Marx and Engels directly devoted to the family is *The Origin of the Family, Private Property and the State.* Based upon Lewis Henry Morgan's *Ancient Society* as well as Marx's own notes, Engels' *The Origin of the Family* is designed to extend the thesis of a materialistic conception of history back to prehistoric times. But on this central question, Engels, who is generally regarded as the more crude interpreter of the materialist doctrine, is not always clear. In the beginning of the first chapter, Engels approvingly quotes Morgan on the identification of "the great epochs of human progress" with "the enlargement of the sources of subsistence." In the preface to the first edition, however, the development of the family is described as taking a "parallel course" with the periods lacking "such striking marks of differentiation."[5] Here the family as a reproductive unit stands alongside the conventional notion of materialism in terms of the production of material objects. Presumably, the two coordinate bases interact with one another and with the more sophisticated version of materialism; both interact with nonmaterialist configurations. This schema is rather close to Fourier's, who often spoke of economic structure and family organization as the twin pillars of civilization. But Engels also seems to suggest that the reproductive base subsides as a determinant of change with the general development of wealth.[6] Thus the family is no longer a pivot in modern society.

The Origin of the Family is generally consistent on this point. The first forms of reproduction are natural in the sense that they reflect human needs independent of economic constraint. The very first form of the man-woman relationship was one of complete promiscuity, even devoid of any incest taboo. "Every woman" belonged "equally to every man and every man to every woman."[7] Next comes group marriage, which Engels defined as "mass marriage of an entire section of men scattered over the whole continent with an equally widely distributed section of women."[8] Gradually, group marriage incorporated incest taboos, first according to generations and then for sisters and brothers and cousins. Within the structure of group marriage a certain amount of pairing developed. These dyads were "unstable, floating relationships" and mistakenly perceived by missionaries as a "promiscuous community of wives."[9]

Engels might have traced this progressive narrowing of acceptable sexual relationships to the growth of the gens (clan) as an effective social unit. Instead he sees the gens as beneficiary of the reproductive base: "In this ever extending exclusion of blood relatives from the bond of marriage, natural selection continues its work."[10] Tribes with a gentile constitution were "thus bound to gain supremacy over more backward tribes."[11]

The pairing family is the basic unit of the lower stage of barbarism. For Engels it is the last form of family life to reflect natural conditions and represents something of a model for the family of the future. The pairing family is still a "loosely linked" dyad and as such is subordinated to the gens, which is still the basic social structure. "Individual sex love" plays a small part in the development of the pairing family. Marriages are arranged by relatives; they are easily dissolved. Two important consequences flow from the fragile nature of the pairing family. First, the independent household is still neither necessary nor desirable. Therefore the communistic household inherited from group marriage is maintained. The woman is master of the house and since the house represents the basis of the community itself it is "the material foundation of that supremacy of the women which was general in primitive times."[12] Second, descent was still reckoned only in the female line. Group marriage is matrilineal, the father of a child being unknown; inheritance went to the mother's gens. The pairing family still reflected this original framework. In conclusion Engels notes that the division of labor bewteen the sexes was determined by quite other causes than by the position of woman in society. The general position of women was "not only free, but honorable."[13]

This was as far as "natural selection" could proceed: "there was nothing more for it to do in this direction."[14] Heretofore history centered around the reproductive base. More specifically, women made history. Engels was uncomfortable with Bachofen's mother right, but he positively despised the dominant patriarchal school which he characterized as "still completely under the influence of the Five Books of Moses."[15]

The impetus for change came with the domestication of animals. It was followed by cattlebreeding, metalworking, weaving, and agriculture and finally, by the introduction of "human cattle" — slaves. Engels is not willing to pinpoint the moment that property came into the hands of the family rather than the gens. He notes, however, that from this point labor power is able to produce surplus over maintenance. Women have an exchange value and are bought along with slaves.

One more development was necessary to destroy the pairing family. As long as descent was determined only in the female line, property was inherited within the gens. The father's wealth returned to blood relations on his mother's side. Since the children of the dead father belonged to their mother's gens they were "disinherited." In the absence of a surplus this system met with no opposition. Separation or death in the context of the marriage pair simply involved the man's few instruments of labor returning to his gens, just as the woman retained the household goods. As the new wealth increased, however, it made man's position in the family more important than the woman's and "created an impulse to exploit this strengthened position in order to overthrow, in favor of his children, the traditional order of inheritance."[16] "Mother right, therefore, had to be overthrown, and overthrown it was."[17] Engels regarded this revolution as "one of the most decisive ever experienced by humanity." The result was the "world historical defeat of the female sex" and the birth of monogamy:

> The man took command of the home also; the woman was degraded and reduced to servitude; she became the slave of lust and a mere instrument for the production of children. This degraded position of the woman, especially conspicuous among the Greeks of the heroic and still more of the classical age, has gradually been palliated and glossed over, and sometimes clothed in milder form; in no sense has it been abolished.[18]

Engels concludes that monogamy was "the first form of the family to be based not on natural but economic conditions — on the victory of private property over primitive, natural communal property."[19]

Two Families: Bourgeois and Proletarian

The reproductive base had receded as a determining factor in history. It is important to note that Engels' discussion of the family concludes less than a third of the way through the book. The remainder of *The Origin of the Family, Private Property and the State* is taken up with the analysis of the gens and its eventual replacement by the state. For however "decisive" the "world historical defeat of the female sex" had been, it took place without disturbing the constitution of the gens itself. Since no historical institution receives more adulation than the "wonderful" system of the gens, we are left to conclude that the monogamous family lay silent for centuries, even after the rise of states, adapting only slightly to various economic frameworks.[20] Yet family structure anticipates modern class society. Engels quotes from Marx's notes:

> The modern family contains in germ not only slavery (servitus) but also serfdom, since from the beginning it is related to agricul-

tural services. It contains in miniature all the contradictions which later extend through society and its state.[21]

The treatment of the modern family by Marx and Engels is characterized by their insistence that it is nothing other than an economic institution. The rupture of man from his natural self that private property initiated was mirrored in man-woman relationships; the bourgeois family changed none of that. At this point, the perspective of Marx and Engels is less persuasive. Both writers emphasize the change in marriage under capitalism from parental arrangement to "free contract." Engels' description captures the transition:

> But a contract requires people who can dispose freely of their persons, actions, and possessions and meet each other on the footing of equal rights. To create these "free" and "equal" people was one of the main tasks of the capitalist production.... Marriage according to the bourgeois conception was a contract, a legal transaction, and the most important one of all because it disposed of two human beings, body and mind, for life.[22]

But Marx and Engels were unwilling to accept the bourgeois family's emphasis on love as a basis for marriage as well as its preoccupation with its children. Engels did acknowledge some impact of the former and reminds us that the bourgeoisie "had their romance and their raptures of love."[23] But all this was only "on a bourgeois footing, and, in the last analysis with bourgeois aims."[24] Most often Marx and Engels preferred to see the concept of bourgeois love in marriage as an ideological trick of the worst sort. The *Manifesto* harangues its readers for even thinking that modern marriage has *any* basis in love:

> Our bourgeois, not content with having the wives and daughters of their proletarians at their disposal, not to speak of common prostitutes, take the greatest pleasure in seducing each others' wives.[25]

"Bourgeois marriage is in reality a system of wives in common"; the real bond of the family was "boredom and money." Only "here and there" could "family affection be found."

The alleged child-centered character of the bourgeois home particularly angered Marx. *Capital* reports page after page on the brutality of child labor. The *Manifesto* sums up his feelings thus:

> The bourgeois claptrap about the family and education, about the

hallowed co-relation of parent and child, becomes all the more disgusting, the more, by the action of Modern Industry, all family ties among proletarians are torn asunder, and their children transformed into simple articles of commerce and instruments of labor.[26]

There is no question that Marx and Engels regarded the modern family as in a state of severe dissolution. Capitalist development made family relationships impossible. Thus their comments on the future of the family are related to their view that capitalism was headed for a cataclysmic conclusion. The future economic structure of society could be foreseen by the development of working class organization and class consciousness. Political organization would rest upon the economic achievements of capitalism.

If we take a moment to review Marx's scenario for the death of capitalism, we can see how he regarded the family's future as a parallel development. The unique feature of capitalism as opposed to all other modes of production was its revolutionary character. Changes, not only in the technical basis of production, but also in the functions of the laborer and in the social combinations of the labor process, incessantly wrench the social and economic order from any moorings and create "social calamity." Capitalism's processes of disintegration and consolidation were ultimately bound with each other.[27]

The constant movement of a capitalist economy produces, on the one hand, a new consolidation of the economic system as a whole; on the other, the same process breaks down these general functions to tiny technical operations within the factory, reproducing the "old division of labour with its ossified particularizations."[28] The whole process is reflected in human terms as well. The consolidation of the labor process in its capitalist form destroys human relationships by moving working people from one branch of production to another, constantly threatening their livelihood, and by suppressing their detail function making them superfluous. The industrial reserve army is the key to this system in that it represents both the devastation of capitalist production and the basis for a new consolidated economic order.[29]

The same process of disintegration and then consolidation at a "higher" level characterizes Marx's discussion of the family under capitalism. In *The German Ideology* Marx introduced a distinction between the "concept of family" and the "real body of the family." The concept of the family corresponds to the ideology of the bourgeois order. But the concept of the family is torn apart by the mode of production, the foundation of bourgeois ideology itself. Marx notes a conflict between the will of bourgeois society, which produces the concept of the family and emphasizes "obedience, piety, marital fidelity" and the basis of bourgeois society, which is actually dissolving the family (as concept). But he notes that even this notion of an internal family bond as a basis for the social order was abandoned by eighteenth-century philosophers.

This dissolution is already apparent among the proletarians. They no longer have families in the sense in which bourgeois ideology sets out the concept. The family still exists, however, as a "real body" and Marx gives the following examples as part of his description: "property relation, the excluding relation toward other families, forced living together — relations produced by the existence of capital, etc."[30]

The disintegrative impact on the family is discussed in detail in *Capital*. Marx contended that "parents think of nothing but getting as much as possible out of their children."[31] As children grow up they "do not care a farthing, and naturally so, for their parents and leave them."[32] The size of the working class family revealed a desperation which was well beyond an explanation that rested upon the luxury of parental love of children: "the absolute size of the families stands in inverse proportion to the height of wages ... [it] calls to mind the boundless reproduction of criminals individually weak and constantly hunted down."[33] Marx notes that the exploitation of children had been a feature of all societies. But the medieval apprenticeship system had some redeeming characteristics. Often it educated a child and provided him with a livelihood. But the new division of labor made children valuable only as commodities:

> ... the children employed in modern factories and manufacturers are from their earliest years riveted to the most simple manipulations, and exploited for years, without being taught a single sort of work that would afterwards make them of use, even in the same manufactory or factory.[34]

Nevertheless, the integrative forces of capitalism were already making themselves apparent. Marx noted that the begrudging establishment of technical schools for the sons of the workers showed the beginnings of necessary trends immanent in capitalist production. But these schools and the regulation of labor by the Factory Acts were only "mere interference" with the exploiting rights of capital compared to the regulation of "home labour." The new laws were viewed "as a direct attack on the *patria potestas*, on parental authority."[35] What follows is one of the most perceptive and revealing pages of *Capital*:

> The tender-hearted English Parliament long affected to shrink from taking this step. The force of the facts, however, compelled it at last to acknowledge the economical foundation on which was

based the traditional family, and family labour corresponding to it, and also had unloosened all traditional family ties. The rights of children had to be proclaimed.[36]

There is so much that can be said about this analysis. The concept of right, now applied within the family, looked like, and indeed at one level it was, a further individualization of the liberal order. Parents could no longer be trusted to exercise their authority. In the Lockean symbols of the Employment Commission, parents had been exercising "arbitrary and mischievious power over their young and tender offspring."[37] Such "absolute power" could not be tolerated; children could claim as their "natural right" their values as "intellectual and moral beings."[38] But, of course, this victory was not what it seemed. Marx reminds his readers that it was not the misuse of parental authority that created capitalist exploitation of children but precisely the opposite: "It was the capitalist mode of exploitation which, by sweeping away the economical basis of parental authority, made its exercise degenerate into a mischievious misuse of power."[39] The proclamation of children's rights was an advance toward collectivism, both in its realization of the final destruction of the family as an economic unit "outside" society (its affective base had already been destroyed) and in the intimation that there will be a "new economical foundation for a higher form of the family and of the relations between the sexes."[40]

The same sort of analysis is offered on the impact of capitalism on women and their relation to the family. The rise of the monogamous family had forced the withdrawal of women from society. The household and household work lost their public character and became a private service. The wife became "head servant, excluded from all participation in social production."[41] The antagonisms of capitalist production are again reflected in the new proletarian family:

> . . . if [a woman] carries out her duties in the private sphere of her family, she remains excluded from public production and unable to earn; and if she wants to take part in public production and earn independently, she cannot carry out her family duties.[42]

Thus the new position of woman in the working class in relation to her family was frought with contradictions. Her desperate search for work under the most degrading conditions nevertheless "at last breaks down the resistance which male operatives in the manufacturing period continued to oppose to the despotism of capital."[43] Prostitution also increases. It, after all, is a form of work and a public one at that. But prostitution and monogamy are "inseparable contradictions, poles of the same society":

For with the transformation of the means of production into social property there will disappear also wage labor, the proletariat, and therefore the necessity for a certain — statistically calculable — number of women to surrender themselves for money.[44]

THE COMMUNITY OF WOMEN

Up to the point of the overthrow of capitalism, the family is an adjunct of the economic order. All the transformations wrought by modern industry, disintegrative and integrative, are felt by the family. The family reels with each new development of capitalism — the creation of classes around the means of production, the use of the machine and division of labor within the factory, the progressive deterioration of the working class — and is itself transformed. If we are to give weight to Marx's account of "crude communism," the family is to be subjected to one final blow, the "communalization of women."

> Communism is in its first form only a generalization and consummation of this relationship. It shows itself as such in a twofold form: on the one hand, the dominion of material property bulks so large that it seeks to destroy everything which is not capable of being possessed by all as private property. It seeks to abstract by force from talent, etc. For it the sole purpose of life and existence is direct physical *possession*. The category of the laborer is not done away with, but extended to all men. The relationship of private property persists as the relationship of the community to the world of things. Finally, this movement of counterposing universal private property to private property finds expression in the bestial form of counterposing to marriage (certainly a form of private property) the community of women, in which a woman becomes a piece of communal and common property.[45]

In crude communism a woman is treated as "the spoil and handmaid of communal lust."[46] There is no joy in this form of revolutionary free love. Women are used in the same way that private property is despoiled. The envy that leads to the desire to destroy becomes a form of competition itself and ends with a "leveling down proceeding from the preconceived minimum."[47] The man-woman relationship, and the form that it took as marriage, is no longer used only as an analogy for the system of private property. The relationship between man and woman, with the woman as a form of property at once exclusive and general, is a real primary form. The destruction of both occurs under crude communism. In fact, Marx goes as far as to take the man-woman motif, particularly in its form as prostitution, and make it the generalized metaphor of crude communism. The sexual metaphor is the dominant basis for the description of society. The community of women actually "gives away the secret" of this form of communism:

> Prostitution is only a *specific* expression of the *general* prostitution of the laborer, and since it is a relationship in which falls not the prostitute alone, but also the one who prostitutes, — and the latter's abomination is still greater — the capitalist, etc., also comes under this head.[48]

It is most intriguing that sexual liberation should take the form of abasement of women by men. There is no question that man is the aggressor here. It is he who makes woman a "piece" of communal and common property. It is he who "negates personality ... in every sphere."[49] It is he who lets loose his own envy to make communalization of women a real social form in itself until *his* "avarice" finally "re-establishes itself and satisfies itself."[50]

But why should this abasement take place? Marx is careful to remind us that this is a "thoughtless" communism and not his model of its true or final stage.[51] Yet in some ways, that difference is not the point. Crude communism appears to be a necessary state of development. Why would men — especially the men of the working class whose families allegedly already bear the marks of real sexual equality — extend the desire to destroy and degrade to women? A more appropriate image would describe sexual relationships in no more pleasant but more equalitarian terms. Would not both men and women degrade themselves, taking from sex its personal and exclusive element? A casual but mutual degradation would certainly seem more appropriate. The "glass of water" approach seems more fitting with Marx's general model.[52] Or could not women treat men as the servant of communal lust?

Part of the answer to Marx's insistence that sexual relationships under crude communism should look more like a gang rape than a night at a singles bar might be related to the restrictions of the sociology of knowledge.[53] But a more complete response is possible. Marx preferred to see the overthrow of capitalism as a revolutionary event with physical force as the major element of transition. In his *Critique of the Gotha Program* and elsewhere, he emphasized the difficulties in building the proper economic base from this transformation. But force, in first overthrowing capitalism and then in effecting a complete alteration in attitudes, was central and this approach indeed characterized his entire mode of analysis. Next to the centrality of force as a basis of Marxist analysis is the commitment to destroy private property. So long as these two principles remain at the center of analysis, when Marx discusses the family or sexual relationships in general he would be inclined to provide an image very much like the one he did. If women are an extension of private property, then they will be forcefully destroyed as such. *"Everything"* will be "destroyed which is not capable of being possessed by all."[54] It is true that men are treated as commodities under capitalism but not in terms of their sexual relationships. If this point is pushed, it is the working-class man who is denied the community of women under capitalism. He is deprived of the favors of bourgeois women while the wives and daughters of the working class are at the disposal of the bourgeois. He is then, from Marx's viewpoint, taking back his own human property — the community of women has, after all, existed from time immemorial — along with material goods.

There is another reason for Marx's description of sex under crude communism. Nowhere is Marx more Hegelian in method than in his treatment of sex and the family.[55] In the *Manuscripts* this approach surrounds all his predictions, with the sexual model subsuming all others as typifying reality. Sex must represent a perfect "infinite degradation" for it to emerge pure and "direct and natural" in the final state. And what could be a more perfect negation of private property than the communalization of women? Mutual degradation misses the Hegelian point. Since Engels' "world historical defeat" of the female sex, men have regarded women as property. Only with the destruction of women as private property can the woman as an object of physical possession cease to exist. If, as Engels said, prostitution — as the essence of oppressive communality — "degrades the character of the whole male world," then male domination as *degradation* must be complete and total for the Hegelian zenith to be reached.

COMMUNISM AND THE FAMILY

The stage is now set for the final reunification of man and woman and the re-emergence of the reproductive base of which Engels spoke in the *Origin*. Sexual relations will now be direct and natural, the model of all human relationships. We are now in a position to see the historical culmination of the relationship between the sexes. Engels drew a picture of "natural" sex in prehistory. But a primitive sexuality was casual and impersonal. It lacked both jealousy and commitment. The rise of monogamy was the result of economic factors; "individual sex love" had a small part in it. Yet "individual sex love" emerged in the classical era through the concept of Eros. But Eros existed outside the institution of marriage and for the most part outside society. Moreover, it lacked the modern element of reciprocity. The Middle Ages carried the idea of love to a new level. Before that time one could not speak of individual sex love. But "chivalrous love" was still conceived as existing outside marriage in adulterous relationships. Marriage was still a "political act"; "the interest of the *house* must be decisive, not the wishes of the individual." Engels asks "What chance then is there for love to have the final word in the making of marriage?"[56]

We have already described the bourgeois contribution to the family. Its major innovation in terms of love is the ideology of the "free" contract and the individual freedom to select a partner that this allegedly provides. But what emerges out of the cauldron of crude communism? Strange as it might seem, Marx and Engels envision the bourgeois family as being replaced by the dyad. Love under communism will take the form of exclusive coupling: "Sexual love is by its nature exclusive."[57] The "desire for sexual intercourse" is awakened by "personal beauty, close intimacy, similarity of tastes."[58] It will be intense and demanding: "our sex love has a degree of intensity and duration which makes both lovers feel that non-possession and separation are a great, if not the greatest calamity. . . . "[59] Naturally, the relationship will be characterized by equality and reciprocity, the feature so lacking in Rousseau's concept of romantic love. Unless one takes seriously the steely Hegelian dialectic upon which it rests, one cannot help but see an irony in communism culminating in the concept of individual sex love. First, there is the question of how such an individualized love can emerge from the community of women. But on a broader level the general question has always troubled skeptics of Marxism. Understanding how the centralization of political and economic power will wither away rather than further consolidate runs far deeper than merely shedding bourgeois sensibilities or ridding oneself of a fixation upon the concept of the dictatorship of the proletariat. Marxism represents one side of a fundamental divide on the issue of whether the separation of society into relatively autonomous parts or the elimination of them is the road to freedom.

Yet on the movement from crude communism to the final stage, there is an even more glaring problem. By itself the dyad is the most "unsocial" of human relationships. The sort of dyad that Marx and Engels describe is particularly so. In the romantic dyad the desire for mutual self-possession is so intense that both Rousseau and Fourier were probably better observers of its impact on society. When Rousseau used the dyad as a basis for political philosophy he placed the couple in a setting outside society. Fourier's angelic couple, who before their transformation fit perfectly the Marxist model, are depicted as enemies of society who elicit envy wherever they go. The unsocial quality is further demonstrated by the way the romantic dyad sees itself in terms of society. Restraints on the couple's conduct are judged as stemming from irrational and jealous motivations. The couple sees itself in a state of war with society. Its terms of peace are isolation, a demand rarely met by the outside world.

Engels' focus on adultery as the historical form of romantic love should have provided him with the key to this problem. For the adulterers' status outside society rests only in part upon the institution of monogamous marriage. Their social crime, assuming the affair has a romantic basis, is that the coupling estranges them from the demand for routine in the social order. Commitments to children, friends, and co-workers as well as to wives and children are strained. But it is the excitement that comes from challenging these relationships in favor of a single new and intense one that provides adultery with its fascination.

At this point we must mention that feature most often employed to "stablize" the dyad and introduce it into the social order — the couple's responsibility to children. In the Marxist analysis, while the direct and natural relationship between man and woman finally emerges in the purest individual terms, children never return to the care of their parents. Engels explicitly makes the communalization of children a necessary corollary for the emancipation of the dyad:

> The care and education of the children becomes a public affair; society looks after all children alike, whether they are legitimate or not. This removes all the anxiety about the "consequences" which today is the most essential social as well as economic factor that prevents a girl from giving herself completely to the man she loves.[60]

Communist education is not simply a matter of continuing schooling with productive labor at an early age. We saw how much emphasis Marx placed upon the education provisions of the Factory Acts in terms of their impact on the family. He castigated the authors of the Gotha Program for calling for the prohibition of child labor. This was an "empty, pious wish," the realization of which would be reactionary since "an early combination of productive labor with education is one of the most potent means for the transformation of present-day society."[61] The work unit was to be the economic and socializing basis under communism. The housekeeping and childrearing duties of the mother were to be taken over by society. In prehistoric group marriage the large kinship unit was the economic base of the family. But the final reunification of humanity had no place for a kinship base. The form of the family in history was not absolute; now "it is obvious that the fact of the collective working group being composed of individuals of both sexes and all ages must necessarily . . . become a source of human development."[62] The state's takeover of parental authority in the working class and the technical schools was the first indication of this new form.

Would there be such an institution as parenthood under communism? In the sense that parents would individually or in part raise children and feel a special affective bond toward their own, the answer must be in the negative. The parental bond, like lesser social bonds, disappears into the whole. The only social unit that appears to continue to exist outside the whole is the dyad. Marx's and Engels' demarcation and support of this single bond is in this sense unique. It is the only relationship that stands at all apart from society. Even the model of bucolic hunter-fisherman critic of the final stage as described in *The German Ideology* is different from the model of the romantic dyad. The hunter-fisherman critic is a dilettante in a positive sense of the word. He freely moves from one activity to the next. The image that Marx portrays is one of contentment and fulfillment. Compare this with the language of "individual sex love." The latter is characterized by "intensity," "risk," "exclusivity," "desire," "need," "possession," "emotion."[63] In this sense, lovers are anything but free; romantic literature has always emphasized the traumatic and compulsive nature of love. A sweet insanity it may be, but nonetheless it is still described in part in socially pathological terms. Marx's "scientific socialism," in large part, continued to accept this portrayal.

FREUD: PARRICIDE AND PATRIARCHALISM

The birth of the psychoanalytic movement marked a revolutionary approach to the understanding of the modern family and its relationship to the political order. Yet the discoveries of Sigmund Freud (1856–1939) and his followers have left an extremely ambivalent legacy to the assessment of the modern family. On the one hand, there is the recent view that Freud attempted to provide a biological defense of the modern family replete with arguments for the inferiority of women.[1] On the other hand, there is the view that Freud's theories represent the discovery of universal cultural laws that are the key to our political transformation.[2] We shall have an opportunity to fully examine both these positions later. Our task now is to review and assess Freud's contribution to the knowledge of the family. We will proceed by dividing Freud's thought into three portions: his revision and transformation of the patriarchical thesis into a new theory of the family; his discovery of the unconscious and its significance for family life; his speculations concerning the relationship between instincts and family and civilization.

THE PRIMAL CRIME

At the center of Freud's analysis is the Oedipus complex. The drama of slaying one's father and sleeping with one's mother forms the "nuclear complex" of all neuroses and is the culminating point of infant sexuality whose aftereffects decisively influence the sexuality of the adult: "The task before each human being is to master the Oedipus complex; one who cannot do this falls into a neurosis."[3] Freud had insisted that "its recognition has become the shibboleth which distinguishes the followers of psychoanalysis from its opponents."⁴

The Oedipus complex was itself the result of the denial of sexual relationships with one's mother. The "natural" inclination of human beings is to select as the sexual object that person he has loved since childhood. Freud constantly emphasized the traumatic character of the incest taboo. It represented "the most drastic mutilation which man's erotic life has in all time experienced."

When and under what conditions was the incest barrier raised? The answer to this question, which, after all, represents the theoretical justification of psychoanalysis itself, was to occupy Freud's attention throughout his life. The "natural" condition of man, one which gave free rein to the sexual instinct, was left behind in "ape-like prehistory." In *Civilization and Its Discontents*, Freud suggested that the first beginnings of family life corresponded with the "adoption of an upright posture."⁵ This new gait reduced the factor of olfactory stimuli but consequent exposure of the genitals produced a visual stimulus that guaranteed a continuity of sexual excitation. In Freud's words "the moment came when the need for genital satisfaction no longer made its appearance like a guest who drops in suddenly, and after his departure, is heard of no more for a long time, but instead took up its quarters as a permanent lodger."⁶ The male now had a motive for keeping his sexual objects near him. The first family was created and the "threshold to civilization" was reached.

Freud's account of the movement from this primitive family to the system of exogenous kinship with the incest barrier is contained in *Totem and Taboo*. Curiously, it remains Freud's most controversial work, despite the fact that its thesis is central to his whole system. *Totem and Taboo* (with the exception of *Moses and Monotheism*) is likewise Freud's boldest work. Unlike *The Interpretation of Dreams* and the *Three Essays on Sexuality* it is based entirely on analogy, the comparison between the behaviors of neurotics and primitive people. Freud was not unaware of the purely speculative character of his efforts, but insisted that it was a hypothesis which "may seem fantastic but which has the advantage of establishing an unexpected unity among a series of hitherto separated phenomena."⁷

The link between the neurotic and the primitive which so fascinated Freud was the series of "compulsive prohibitions" to which both adhered. The "taboo" in each was characterized by an unconscious motivation. Neurotics are unable to tell the analyst the reason for their prohibition. They only believe that its violation will be followed by a certain and unbearable disaster. The tabooed person or object has enormous powers for good and evil. Contamination with the object shows no regard to motive. A primitive who accidentally eats the food of a chief is as "guilty" as one who purposely ate it. The tainted person or object can, however, sometimes be cleansed through rigid ceremonial procedures. Freud concluded that the sternness of taboo suggested that its violation was "a renunciation of something really wished for."[8] He then proceeded to discuss three prominent taboos — those regarding enemies, rulers, and the dead. In each he found the existence of extremely ambivalent attitudes. While primitives are noted for their savagery, the slain enemy is an object of remorse. The treatment of rulers is extremely complicated; Freud attempts to sum it up in terms of two principles — rulers must be both guarded and guarded against. On the one hand, the ruler is elevated to the position of a god; on the other, his life is subject to so many restrictions that one can find numerous examples of individuals in primitive societies who must be physically forced to accept a status of authority. A dead person, the object of love and affection in life, turns into a demon. There is a touching taboo as well as a taboo on speaking the name of the deceased. Freud notes the similarity to the neurotic's pattern of mourning. He concludes that there is a "hostility, hidden behind tender love, [that] exists in almost all cases of intense emotional allegiance to a particular person."[9] The neurotic suffers from the wish to see his beloved one harmed and thus creates a system of obsessive reproaches. The primitive projects his hostility outward by attributing malevolent behavior to the dead. Freud closes this portion of his discussion of taboos by concluding that emotional ambivalence was much stronger among primitive than modern people. Taboos themselves are the result of this ambivalence. In fact, the taboo represents "the oldest form in which we meet the phenomenon of conscience."[10]

The groundwork for what Freud called his "fantastic" hypothesis is now almost complete. He registers his dissatisfaction with current explanations of the incest taboo. Westermarck's theory of incest dread as an "innate aversion" against sex among those living together is rejected out of hand in the light of the experience of psychoanalysts. The principle of natural selection is rejected as well. It was "ridiculous to attribute hygienic and eugenic motives such as have hardly yet found consideration in our culture to these children of the race who lived without thought of the morrow."[11]

Freud notes Frazer's reluctance to explain the riddle of the incest taboo and the attendant difficulty of determining the relationship between totemism and exogamy under those conditions. (Psychoanalysis was able to shed a "single ray of light" on this problem.) It is at this point that Freud introduces his famous account of the circumstances of the "primal crime." This is the similarity of outlook toward animals shown by the child in civilization and primitive man. Both see animals on equal and intimate terms. Occasionally the child develops an animal phobia. Analysis has established that the problem was "in every case the same: the fear at bottom was of the father."[12] Anthropology tells us that the father is regarded as the tribe's ancestor. The animal totem is the father. Freud can scarcely hide his elation when he notes that the main commandments of totemism — not to kill the totem animal and not to use a woman belonging to the same totem for sexual purposes — agree in content both to the two crimes of Oedipus and to the child's primal wishes whose reawakening forms the nucleus of all neuroses.

One more elaboration of the totemistic religion is presented before Freud presents the primal crime itself. This involves the ritual of the totem feast. The clan takes the forbidden animal, kills it, and ceremoniously eats it. Mourning and lamentation of this death are followed by a festival. Here Freud's real speculation begins. Perhaps Darwin was correct in positing a primal state of society governed by a violent, jealous father who keeps all the females for himself and drives away the growing sons. Nowhere has this primal horde been observed. The most primitive form of human organization, still in force among some tribes today, is "associations of the totemic system, and founded on matriarchy, or descent through the mother."[13] If we could explain how one resulted from the other, we could also establish our "unexpected unity among a series of hitherto separated phenomena." Here is part of the result of Freud's detective efforts:

> One day the expelled brothers joined forces, slew and ate the father, and thus put an end to the father horde. Together they dared and accomplished what would have remained impossible for them singly. Perhaps some advance in culture, like the use of a new weapon, had given them the feeling of superiority. Of course, these cannibalistic savages ate their victim. This violent primal father had surely been the envied and feared model for each of the brothers. Now they accomplished their identification with him by devouring him and each acquired a part of his strength. The totem feast, which is perhaps mankind's first celebration, would be the repetition and commemoration of this memorable, criminal act with which so many things began, social organization, moral restrictions and religion.[14]

However, the brother clan proved to be an ineffective organization. Each member aspired to the role of murdered father and was the other's rival among the women. "Thus there was nothing left for the brothers, if they wanted to live together, but to erect the incest prohibition — perhaps after many difficult experiences — through which they all equally renounced the women whom they desired, and on account of whom they had removed the father in the first place."[15]

The hypothesis of the primal crime provided not only an explanation of the origin of exogamy and totemism but a theory of civilization itself. Freud never departed from the basic framework of this model. In *Group*

Psychology and the Analysis of the Ego he sandwiched a period of gynecocracy between the primal crime and the new patriarchical family. This allowed him to explain the existence of mother deities. As to the movement from matrilineal societies to the patriarchal family Freud had little to say. He notes that the new family was only a shadow of the old: there were many fathers, each limited by the rights of others. At one point he suggests that a projection might have occurred. The woman who was the prize and allurement to murder was "probably turned into the seducer and instigator to the crime."[16]

But the primal father was the real object of Freud's attention. The final development of the patriarchal unit, so prominent in Engels' formulation, did not seem to him to be a crucial historical moment. What did trouble Freud was the question of how the trauma of the primal crime was transmitted from generation to generation. Ironically, when Freud approached this problem he intended to deprecate the historical reality of the primal crime. The change might have been accomplished in a less violent manner and still have conditioned the appearance of the moral reaction. The continued ambivalence toward the father was the result in part of the "inheritance of psychic dispositions" and in part, the transmission of psychic processes from one generation to the next:

> For psychoanalysis has taught us that in his unconscious psychic activity every person possesses an apparatus which enables him to interpret the reactions of others, that is to say, to straighten out the distortions which the other person has affected in the expression of his feelings. By this method of unconscious understanding of all customs, ceremonies and laws which the original relation to the primal father had left behind, later generations may also have succeeded in taking over this legacy of feelings.[17]

AMBIVALENT PATRIARCHY

If we just look at Freud's contribution to anthropology we can begin to sketch the outlines of his transformation of the patriarchical idea. We have already used Freud's hypothesis of the primal crime in our discussion of Hobbes. There we noted that Freud's approach challenged Hobbes' radicalism by bringing murder — or murderous wishes — into the household itself. Hobbes in his own revision of his patriarchical thesis had been unwilling to admit that the son stood in a state of nature in relation to the father. Freud's willingness to incorporate this element represented the radical side of treatment of patriarchy. He certainly drew a picture of the family that was patriarchal. But the family drama consisted of rebellion against the father. Each son challenged in each generation. The incest taboo represented the defeat of the sons but at the same time it recalled their victory. The son could not sleep with his mother, but neither could his brothers. Moreover, he was no longer deprived of all women.

The conservative side of Freud's theory can be further delineated by briefly comparing it to Engels', a project we will also return to later. Engels too contended that civilization was patriarchal, but he reserved that characterization at least to the period of introduction of domesticated animals. Various family forms predated the "world historical defeat of the female sex." Freud, however, traces the dawn of civilization to the murder of the father. He thus reaches the paradoxical conclusion that because of the primal crime civilization is coterminous with both the monogamous family and patriarchy. If one wishes to remove patriarchy as a basis for the social order, it is necessary to return much further back in history than Engels' celebrated gens. Humans might even have to resume walking on all fours.

All of this represents only half of Freud's transformation of the patriarchal thesis. The patriarchal idea is composed of two motifs. One asserts that patriarchy is the most natural form of social organization and that the family is coterminous with patriarchal rule. In a sense, Freud even outdid this portion of the patriarchal motif by bestowing upon the primal father not only unlimited authority but also exclusive sexual rights over the entire social unit. In Freud's words, he was the "superman whom Nietzsche expected only from the future"; a leader who "need love no one else," a man of "a masterly nature, absolutely narcissistic, but self-confident and independent."[81] The second portion carries patriarchal symbols to politics, usually as the foundation for a theory of authority and obligation. Here too Freud seems to follow the patriarchal model. *Group Psychology and the Analysis of the Ego* raises the question of how groups are formed and maintained. Freud openly departs from a liberal conception of politics. Group formation is a much deeper phenomenon than mere interest aggregation. The common direction of thoughts, the deterioration of the individual psyche, and the high emotional level of group members suggest a "state of regression to a primitive mental activity."[19] The group — be it random crowd, church or army — is "a revival of the primal horde."[20] Freud's emphasis in *Group Psychology* was on leadership. If the group could be understood in terms of the primal horde, its leader then represented the dreaded and loved primal father. The primal father was the first to create group psychology by forcing his sons into sexual abstinence and consequently into emotional ties with him. The modern group's leader functions through the power of some aim-inhibited libido. The only difference is that the followers' belief that the leader loves them all equally and justly is an "idealistic" modeling of the sons' knowledge of being equally persecuted by the primal father.

The movement in the opposite direction — from group to individual psychology — is also explained on the basis of the organization of the primal family. The social contract founded exogamy. After an unspecified period of matriarchy, some individual may have been moved to free himself from the group and take over his father's part. Freud describes this individual as the first epic poet, for he invented the heroic myth that one son, acting alone, slew the primal father. Thus the creation of the heroic myth is "the stop by which the individual emerges from group psychology."[21]

In his last work Freud reapplied the same theme to the Judeo-Christian heritage with a double effect. He hypothesized the existence of two Moses, one an Egyptian noble who introduced monotheism to the Jews and another, a Jew, who succeeded him. The first Moses was killed by rebellious tribes and collective remorse brought forth the belief in a Messiah who would undo the great murder. The death of Christ, the son, added both an overlayer and a progression to the original sin of parricide. The polytheistic tendencies of early Christianity served as an aggressive outlet to the earlier crime, while expiation devices such as communion, which Freud saw as a refurbished totem feast, stood alongside them. Christianity incorporated a complicated version of the hero myth; the judicial murder of Jesus and his resurrection was a repeat of the parricide in heroic terms. Christ was "the resurrected Moses and the returned primeval father of the primitive horde as well — only transfigured, and as a Son in the place of his Father."[22]

Thus we see that the dualism of Freud's work characterizes the second portion of the patriarchical mode. The twin wishes of rebellion and worship, irrevocably rooted in prehistory, form the dynamic of all civilization. The extraordinary tenacity of these wishes is the basis for social order. In *Totem and Taboo* Freud traced religion and ethics to the psychic complicity in the common crime. Twenty-five years later in *Moses and Monotheism*, his position remained virtually unchanged. The drama of the primal crime is repressed but emerges again and again from the memory traces of the human race. The cycle of early trauma, defense, latency, outbreak of neurosis, partial return of the repressed material is repeated in different degrees of severity in each family, in each group and religion in civilization. The story of "Little Hans," the boy afflicted with animal phobias, re-enacts the same neurotic fear of the primitive before his totem, as does the Catholic worshiping a fearsome and angry God and the soldier placating the whims of his general. Patriarchy does indeed define our obligations to authority at large — it does so through the strongest of connections, our libidinal desires — at the same time it provides the framework for our renunciation of them, again through the same avenue.

The father-son relationship was itself an ambivalent one. Freud's theory of patriarchy reflects that tension.

THE DEMYSTIFICATION OF FAMILY LIFE

Thus far we have confined our analysis to a general or, in Freud's terms, a phylogenetic history of the family. But as we suggested, the struggle with the father occurs within each of us individually. This struggle is the premise of psychoanalysis as a therapeutic discipline. We can now see Freud's contribution by giving his presentation of the little dramas of human life. Space forbids us from offering a complete picture of Freud's discovery of the unconscious and its relation to childhood development. What interests us here is the general orientation of Freud's analysis of individual human growth in the context of the family.

One of the most prominent features of Freud's treatment of the family seems to escape our attention today. This is the assumption — it is never argued — that the family is exclusively an institution revolving around instinct. Nowhere in all of his writings is the family portrayed as an economic institution or even an institution with a major economic function. In *Civilization and Its Discontents* the first family arises from the male's desire to have his sexual objects near him. The movement from the primal to the exogamous family was occasioned by sexual jealousy directed at the father. The motive of general security is loosely linked to family organization but only as a by-product of the sexual instinct. Nor does Freud see the family as solely an agency of civilization in general. The family does indeed perform the crucial function of channeling sexual instincts which is necessary for the maintenance of civilized life. But the reasons for this function also run counter to the interests of civilization. In an important sense, the family is an enemy of civilization:

> The more closely the members of a family are attached to one another, the more often do they tend to cut themselves off from others, and the more difficult is it for them to enter into the wider circle of life. The mode of life in common which is phylogenetically the older, and which is the only one that exists in childhood, will not let itself be superseded by the cultural mode of life which has been acquired later. [23]

We shall take up this point in a moment. For the present it will be sufficient to note that for Freud the family could be defined entirely as an institution that grew out of the psychic needs of its members.

The sexual instinct makes its appearance in infancy. At its earliest stages it is autoerotic and anaclitic. In terms of the latter, it originates in the self-preservative function (hunger) through breastfeeding. The sexual instinct "leans" on the self-preservative function and only later makes itself independent of it. Infant sexuality knows no sexual object. It is not directed toward another person; the child "gratifies himself on his own body." Moreover, the sexual instinct appears in its earliest stage in a "pregenital" form, first as oral (or "cannibalistic") organization and then as "anal-sadistic". From this point on the child must go through a series of difficult transitions in order to reach normal adult sexuality. First there is a narcissistic stage (introduced somewhat later by Freud) and then the initial selection of a sexual object. The object selected is the mother. This desire can never be fulfilled and the child experiences intense hostility toward the father. But the father is also a source of affection, so that hostile wishes directed toward the father are mixed with fear for his life. Mercifully, this phase ends abruptly and does not emerge again until the child reaches puberty. During the latency period the tender stream of sexual life is predominant. The child learns to accept the help and affection of his parents. The whole process of object selection appears again in puberty and the child must somehow complete three tasks: (1) detach his incestuous libidinal wishes from his mother; (2) come to terms with his father; (3) find a sexual object with some similarity to his mother.

Several points need to be made about this presentation. The most obvious point, although its direct impact has receded somewhat, is the demystification of family life that results from Freud's theories. It is all very well to say that Freud merely put in theoretical perspective what every nursemaid knew firsthand, but the relationships between parent and child were laid bare in a manner that had to have a profound impact on understanding of the family. The demystification goes far beyond the imagery of the suckling infant as a bundle of sexual desires. For what so shocked the European medical profession is not the major point. What Freud exposed was the tremendous frustration and agony that characterizes all family life: there are the difficulties a child has in coping with phantasies of mother love and consequent fear of castration and the murderous wishes he harbors against his father and his brothers and sisters. There is the phenomenon of infantile amnesia, which dams up these feelings and causes the individual to look upon his childhood as if it were a "prehistoric time," concealing — often forever — the beginning of his sexual life and the source of his complaints. There is the series of repressions and sublimations that often break through from their libidinal home to hound the adult.

Freud himself never underestimated the enormous burdens of psychological development: "These tasks are set to everyone; and it is remarkable how seldom they are dealt with in an ideal manner."[24] Later writers would openly raise the issue in terms of something like this: "If the family is the tangle of fears and frustration that indeed it is, by all means let us rid ourselves of this horrible institution." Freud rarely thought of the family in quite these terms. We shall see why in a moment. But let us pursue the subject of demystification a bit further. Freud's exposure of the nature of sentiment in family life occurred at a moment in history when the family was coming to be regarded as an institution that was primarily designed in terms of sentiment. Husband and wife were to be portrayed as lovers and children as one of the fruits of that love. There is also further irony that as the family was to turn inward as a unit, casting off the authority of the broader kinship unit, Freud would make the discovery of the tremendous burdens laid upon us by the father figure. The family was an institution of instinctual repression. It fights against the interests of civilization which attempts to carry that repression beyond it. But it laid the groundwork, albeit a tenuous one, for further instinctual renunciation. "Over and above the struggle for existence, it is chiefly family feeling, with its erotic roots, which has induced the individuals to make their renunciation."[25] Thus the sentiment that Freud saw as fairly exploding family life was the outward manifestation of instinctual repression. This was a novel way of portraying life in the family, especially if we look at the view of the family as refuge from society, as an institution that allowed its members to express tender sentiments openly. The family as a haven for love and lovers is challenged by Freud. The challenge is not complete, as we shall soon discuss, but this image is radically different from, say, the Lockean view. In the language of psychoanalysis, the latter represents an idealized image of family life.

In the previous section we noted the many resemblances in Freud's theory to the traditional formulation of the patriarchal thesis. Freud's diagnosis of civilization as a patriarchal affair has angered contemporary radicals. It is true that Freud's transformation of patriarchalism had its conservative undertones. The rebellion against the father is openly presented but the challenge is never successful. The normal male might "smash" the Oedipal complex in that he is able to come to terms with a sexual object outside the family. But civilization requires such instinctual renunciation that the Great Father will turn up elsewhere, in religion or political formations. The remorse from murderous wishes is so great that the longing for the return of patriarchal authority explains far more of our individual or group life than the rejection does. But if we add the impact of the demystification proposed by psychoanalysis we receive a more complicated picture.

All political and social theories have their demystifying elements. This is the general method by which they make room for their own world view. Other images of the world must be exposed and pushed aside. Ideologies do not gain hold through establishing a patina over other world views. There is much truth then in Freud's own description of the primal crime as a "scientific myth." If respect for the father as aim-inhibited love can be translated into a partial resolution of the Oedipal complex and its fear of castration, and if a woman's gift of a child to her husband can be translated into a resolution of penis envy, two of the major devotional symbols of family life — paternal affection and mother love — are now seen as outcomes of the tangle of sexuality within the family. And these are "normal" resolutions.

But the "abnormal" case histories of Freud's can illustrate the demystification impulse just as well. Take the case of the manic woman who would lead her doctor to her excrement and claim it as the baby she had produced that day. This certainly is a bizarre and pitiful story. Our hearts reach out, and rightly so, to this unfortunate human being. Here is part of Freud's analysis:

> If he is not aware of these profound connections, it is impossible to find one's way about in the phantasies of human beings, in their associations, influenced as they are by the unconscious, and in their symptomatic language. Feces — money — gift — baby — penis are treated as though they meant the same thing, and they are represented too by the same symbols.[26]

This woman's behavior was a reaction to the demands of her Oedipal neurosis. They are not appreciably different from any young female's struggles. The general equation "gift — feces — penis — baby" was in this case arrested in its infantile anal stage, but any young mother undergoes these transitions.[27]

Let's take another case, Freud's famous treatment of the "Rat Man." Early in the analysis, a young man related to Freud his horror and obsession with an alleged Oriental torture. A bucket of rats is placed under a man's buttocks and they burrow their way into the victim's anus. Freud was able to unravel the symbolism of the rat punishment by determining how other incidents were incorporated into the obsession. The patient associated money with rats (his father's legacy and gambling debts), children with rats (his own infantile desire for punishment for aggression), the penis with rats (his fixation with anal eroticism), prostitutes with rats (his correlation of sex with disease). But the neurotic afflictions of the Rat Man are again not so very different from all our tribulations. Freud recounts a behavior pattern of the Rat Man that is especially instructive in this regard. The patient would arrange his day so that he would be working until midnight, the time in which he phantasized that his father would appear. He would then stop his studies, which had been pursued with great diligence, get up to open the door as if to allow his father to enter. He would then return to his room, turn on all the lights and examine his penis before a mirror. Freud noticed how this sequence illustrated the Rat Man's intense desire to both impress and appease his father and at the same time, in the thinly disguised masturbatory act, show his defiance. "Thus," Freud concludes, "in a single unintelligible obsessional act, he gave expression to the two sides of his relation with his father."[28] The source of the Rat Man's neurosis was a traumatic incident in which his father punished him for masturbating. But the cautionary tale in this case history reaches back to the unconscious memory of our common complicity in the primal crime, the central thesis that Freud at this point had not fully formulated.

There is an additional point that deserves to be highlighted aside from the obvious one that behind the Rat Man's neurosis, bizarre as it was, stood all the signposts that characterize normal human development. This is the contention, which is the central therapeutic claim of psychoanalysis, that once the patient is able to translate his obsessional symbols back to their source he is on the road to recovery. That is, the patient must undergo his own process of demystification, translate his own general symbols back to his infantile experiences in his family. In this case, the rat obsession must be reduced to ordinary symbols of familial experience (children, devotion, and love) and then to the instinctual renunciation that lay behind them (masturbation, guilt, and fear of castration).

All of this is not to say that Freud incorrectly diagnosed the Rat Man's neurosis. The point it raises is that in Freud's dualism, in this instance instinct and family, the two never are permitted a synthesis. The sexual instincts are channeled and directed by the institution of the family. But the sexual instincts are too strong and the demands of the family too high for the conflict between the two ever to really cease. Accommodations are made, of course, but even in normal adults they are imperfect. The instinctual side of conflict is largely hidden. Freud's analogy of the sexual instinct as a river bed is helpful here, for aside from the suggestion that it is channeled and often dammed, the image conveys the concealed nature of sex drives. Being both hidden and separate, the sexual instincts, as they are housed in the libido, require demystification techniques for their discovery. In this respect, Freud's approach shows similarities to Marx's doctrine of materialism. The latter has its own demystification process as well. The symbols that move people both to action and restraint are exposed as manifestations of economic forces. Marx's method, for all the problems of the dialectic, is never as dualist as Freud's; but since the socialist drama has an ending, it is less uncompromising. Presumably, at some point the demystification process as a critical tool will no longer be necessary. We saw that on Marxian terms such an ending holds out little hope for the family as an institution. But on Freud's terms, too, the future of the family is not bright. To the extent that the family is held up for exposure as an institution of instinctual renunciation, how is it to survive the demands of instinct? Long before the advent of radical therapists, Freud himself would ask, "For why should it be such a specially hideous crime to commit incest with a daughter or sister, so much more than any other sexual relations?"[29] His response was that however "mysterious, grandiose, and mystically self-evident" our answer is, it is nothing more than the "perpetual will of the primeval father."[30] This is a puzzling formulation for a writer with a reputation as the "one conservative genius of modern culture."[31]

INSTINCT, FAMILY, AND CIVILIZATION

Let us continue with our discussion by examining the final part of Freud's work as it relates to the family. Here we confront directly Freud's famous formulation of the antagonism between instinct and civilization. This portion of Freud's thought represents his conservatism at its deepest and most profound point. But there is an ambivalence in Freud's conservatism that has important implications for the treatment of the family.

A helpful way to begin is to make a general distinction between two kinds of conservative thought. Both variations emphasize the innate aggressive impulses of human beings and the limited capacity of reason as well as love to restrain these instincts. However, one version (which includes theorists such as Aristotle, Burke, and Hume) takes as its major premise the belief that the historical accumulation of experience as reflected in certain symbolic representations and as incorporated in certain institutions is the best guide for restraining those impulses. The other version (which includes theorists such as Carlyle, Lawrence, Dostoevski, and Nietzsche), places its bets upon the power of a single figure to mold and restrain the aggressive appetites of the mass of human beings. Thus both kinds of conservatism openly grant the necessity for repression and its source in human nature. The latter, however, which is certainly the boldest, finds a certain delight in casting its lot with an individual who himself rises above the demands of repression. Of course, this is an extremely general view and hopefully it is not a deceptive one in that it is not designed primarily to place Freud in some corner.

It hardly needs to be said that Freud's major structural premises agree with the general disposition of conservatism. This appears to be especially so after the reformulation of the pleasure principle that made it the servant of the death instinct. The basic conflict between instinct and civilization was fixed. Freud's not totally unsympathetic treatment of socialism concludes as follows:

> Aggressiveness was not created by property. It reigned almost without limit in primitive times, when property was still very scanty, and it already shows itself in the nursery almost before property has given up its primal, anal form; it forms the very basis of every relation of affection and love among people....[32]

Civilization can accomplish only so much. The precept "love thy neighbor" cannot significantly restrain the instincts:

> ...men are not gentle creatures who want to be loved, and who at the most can defend themselves if they are attacked; they are, on the contrary, creatures among whose instinctual endowments is to be reckoned a powerful share of aggressiveness. As a result, their neighbor is to them not only a potential helper or second object, but someone who tempts them to satisfy their aggressiveness on him, to exploit his capacity for work without compensation, to use him sexually without his consent, to seize his possessions, to humiliate him, to cause him pain, to torture and to kill him.[33]

Nor can common goals work to restrain instincts: "instinctual passions are stronger than reasonable interests."[34] Thus civilization is "perpetually threatened with disintegration."[35] It attempts to restrain men's aggressive instincts by psychical reaction formulations. Aim-inhibited libido is summoned up on the largest scale so as to strengthen the common bond. Thus the sexual dyad must be restricted for libidinal energy to flow toward larger units. One gets the impression that the whole attempt is a hopeless endeavor. No better analogy conveys Freud's view than his description of the superego watching over the ego "like a garrison in a conquered city."[36]

What of the two conservative strategies? If we look at Freud closely we find that he openly accepts neither of them. He does, however, seem to be attracted to the newer version. The great man is assuredly the primal father:

> We know that the great majority of people have a strong need for authority which they can admire, to which they can submit and which dominates and sometimes even ill-treats them. We have learned from the psychology of the individual whence comes this need of the masses. It is the longing for the father that lives in each of us from his childhood days, for the same father whom the hero of legends boasts of having overcome. And now it begins to dawn on us that all the features with which we furnish the great man are traits of the father, that in this similarity lies the essence, which so far has eluded us, of the great man. The decisiveness of thought, the strength of will, the forcefulness of his deeds, belong to the picture of the father; above all other things, however, the self-reliance and independence of the great man, his divine conviction of doing the right thing, which may pass into ruthlessness. He must be admired, he may be trusted, but one cannot help also of being afraid of him. We should have taken a cue from the word

itself; who else but the father should in childhood have been the great man?[37]

In *Moses and Monotheism*, Freud, after rejecting the modern inclination to trace social change to impersonal factors, asks himself as much as the reader whether the emphasis on the great man is not a "retrogression to the manner of thinking that produced creation myths and hero-worship, to times in which historical writing exhausted itself in narrating the dates and life-histories of certain individuals — sovereigns or conquerors?"[38] Freud's answer, however, is contained in the last quotation. If we accept the transformation of the patriarchal thesis, our new-found self-knowledge would seem to keep the great man in perspective. He is merely a father idealized and projected from our libidinal longings.

The reason for Freud's tentative embrace with the great-man theory, with all its patriarchal overtones, is that he has no other suggestions for the continued maintenance of civilization. How else can civilization procure the necessary libidinal attachments to large groups? In what amounts to a magnificent parody of Locke, Freud worries that without the requisite leadership role all the world would become like America:

> This danger is not threatening where the bonds of a society are chiefly constituted by the identification of its members with one another, while individuals of the leader type do not acquire the importance that should fall to them in the formation of a group. The present cultural state of America would give us a good opportunity for studying the damage to civilization which is thus to be feared.[39]

Thus the patriarch is necessary after all. He is not the primal father, whom Freud compared to the Nietzschean Superman, but the longing for him is still crucial to civilization. The trade-off which civilization proposes, little fathers in families and ideological substitutes in groups, is an exchange of a portion of psychic happiness for a portion of security.

If Freud's embrace with great-man conservatism is muted, he never entertains the alternative proposed by traditional conservatism. Habit and tradition are only (outward) manifestations of instinctual renunciation. In fact, Freud never even bothers to argue against them. If habit and tradition represent the superego of a particular epoch of civilization, they are based upon the "impression left behind by the personalities of great leaders — men of overwhelming force of mind or men in whom human impulsion has found its strongest and purest, and therefore its most one-sided, expression."[40]

But all this is a strange brand of conservatism. It leads to an awkward defense of civilization and a peculiar defense of the family. For what Freud is saying is this: Your most deeply held attachments are simply idealized formulations of instinctual frustrations. As sublimations, they may produce great works of art and some measure of individual security. But civilization, despite the efforts of centuries, has not managed to restrain aggressive instincts very successfully. Thus you are unhappy and with good reason. You are called upon to make enormous sacrifices in your instincts. You must reject the original source of love and seek out "strange and unloved" partners. They must be of the opposite sex, of limited time duration, and directed toward only the satisfaction of genital sexuality. Despite these accommodations our society will still not let you live in peace with even this restricted attachment. It needs your libidinal energy to sustain itself. Moreover, the bargain you made with civilization does not always protect you against murderous neighbors despite the renunciation of your own aggressive instincts. Nevertheless, in order to perpetuate this contract you are called upon to emotionally connect with certain figures and symbols that you now know are nothing more than infantile projections of psychic longing. These great men are too unbalanced individuals. Under different circumstances they might have become neurotics or "ordinary" criminals.

PART II

Rousseau's children are now forgotten,
And he might be forgotten, too,
If he had not sent them to an orphan asylum
To free himself for the writing of books.
But oh! to be remembered
For deserting your children,
For the sake of learning the violin,
And not to learn it!

–*Edgar Lee Masters, "Perry Rouston," from* The New Spoon River

8

ABOLISHING CHILDHOOD

If we look at the effects of these first six theorists as a whole, it is relatively easy to outline common features. First there is the attack on the patriarchal model leading to its complete rejection or to an attempt to base it on new foundations. Hobbes stripped patriarchy of its moral symbolism. The major thrust of Locke's work is to construct a model of the family on a different basis. Fourier and Marx tied patriarchy conceptually to a dying economic order. Rousseau and Freud, the two writers who were intent upon transforming the old model of the family, used opposite methods but managed to achieve similar results. Rousseau offered a version so romanticized that it seemed to lead him to propose an alternate model, one which denied the family altogether, and that could better approximate his idealized views of social bonds. Freud, whose approach bears resemblance to Hobbes', so demystifies patriarchy that the universal validity that he attributes to it lessens its moral impact.

The attack on patriarchy gave rise to an analysis of the concept of the dyad as the fundamental unit of the family. The dyad was a new and useful way of looking at male-female relationships. It not only leads to viewing bonds in reciprocal and relatively equal terms, but it tends to foster a theoretical separation, along with the family structures that surround it, from their previous immersion in the social order. The discovery and treatment of the dyad in this regard is most interesting in analyzing the theorists we have presented. That the dyad is much more difficult to fit in the broader social order is brilliantly revealed by Rousseau. His couple — admittedly conceived in patriarchal terms — stands outside the political and social order. All the basic units of modern politics and their ideational forms are the enemies of the dyad. Dyadic families, like defeated guerillas, must retreat to the countryside. But when Rousseau sets out to transform the modern state, he too casts away the dyad. In these respects, Freud's image of the dyad as an antisocial relationship in "demonstration against the herd instincts" parallels Rousseau's position.

Locke's concept of the dyad is probably the most free from the old patriarchal base. While he was not at all anxious to scrutinize the basis of the family once he removed the previous base, one receives important indications of its subsequent deterioration in the society of the "free and rational." Thus the dyad is seen as less immediately threatening because of the very looseness of the attachment.

The dyad comes under direct attack in "utopian" socialism. Thus, as we suggested, Marx's embrace of the dyad as a pure form of love in the future seems less consistent with socialist principles than the allegedly obsolete utopian formulation. In any case, it was the Marxist version of socialism that offered a momentous revision in the service of the dyad by recommending the removal of children from the family.

Part II continues our examination of the family. We will focus here on the "child" in a dual sense. First, and most broadly, we will examine a variety of writers who are, in a figurative sense, the children of Locke, Hobbes, Rousseau, Freud, Marx, and Fourier. Like the sons and daughters of the modern family, these writers sometimes question and rebel against their ideological parents. But like all children coming of age, these writers are the heirs of their parents' hopes and fears. Their rebellion often involves a disguised appeal to the standards of the parents. But there is also a more literal focus to the following chapters. The child has now become a social and political problem. The uniqueness of childhood and the uniqueness of the parent-child relationship, like the uniqueness of the dyad, are now an unbearable social fact. The abolition of the child stands alongside the abolition of the family as part of the agenda of political thought. Rawls is troubled by the special treatment the child receives. Is the parents' affection for the child a partly unconscious act of treason, a subtle but stubborn refusal to fully accept the dictates of distributive justice? But liberation from childhood itself is the strongest motif. For R. D. Laing the relationship between parent and child is a knot formed from the strings of guilt and frustration. Reich seeks to free the child from sexual repression; for Marcuse, youth became the new proletariat. Beneath this ideology of liberation lies an attempt to free individuals from the burden of parenting. Ostensibly, this measure is justified in the service of the dyad. But the liberation of the child is really a step in the liberation of the self. In this sense, then, the uniqueness of childhood, despite its relative historical novelty as a concept, is a challenge to both individualism and collectivism in the forms in which we have seen them. As long as childhood remains special or unique, the collective world of the free and rational or the liberated self remains incomplete. Uniqueness must be reinterpreted in terms of radical dependence as Hobbes suggested (and as the group of philosophers we shall examine have shown) or in terms of some sort of deception. In the latter case, childhood is an invention of the powerful to enslave others. In this chapter we shall begin to examine both these efforts and begin to show that with the abolition of the child goes the abolition of the dyad itself. For childhood involves a process of human regeneration. Break that link and other social institutions will attempt to fill the void.

PARENTHOOD AS TUTELAGE

Let us begin by briefly reviewing Locke and Rousseau once more, but this time with an eye toward their concept of parents and childhood.

There are differences between Locke's and Rousseau's conception of the child and these of course parallel their treatment of authority in general. Yet in these important respects the two writers held common premises. Both envisioned the child as a separate entity who progresses to adulthood in stages, both recommended a period of tutelage by adults, and both by and large accepted the family as the tutelary agency. Locke refused to accept the Hobbesian fiction of infant consent and declared that we all "are born Rational; not that we have actually the Exercise of either; Age that brings one, brings with it the other too."[1] Rousseau's *Emile* is a primer of developmental child psychology. "Mankind has its place in the sequence of things," and Rousseau outlines the development of childhood from infancy through adolescence, alerting the reader to the crisis which can accompany each stage. Locke's *Thoughts Concerning Education* is a much less systematic work than *Emile* but no less attentive to the details of child development, from diet to education.

Parental tutelage is a crucial element in the theories of both Locke and Rousseau. The model of parent as tutor is quite different from that of a conventional patriarchal parent. The inequality between parent and child is profound, but the parental role is essentially one of the teacher rather than a ruler. Locke was adamant on this point. Parental authority "puts no scepter into the Father's hand, no sovereign power of commanding."[2] "Honor" and "respect" are the only duties owed to the parent when the child comes of age. The parent as tutor owes the child "nourishment and education." These tutelary "bonds of subjection" drop off "like swaddling clothes" at nonage.[3] Rousseau's tutelage model is much more demanding. *Emile* begins with the plan to "raise a wall round your child's soul." A sense of urgency and peril surround Rousseau's description of Emile's childhood: "The child must come first, and you must devote yourself entirely to him." The exposure of the child to the world is delayed as long as possible.

Rousseau recommends a late weaning. Emile is taught "no history, no metaphysics, no morals" until adolescence. Rousseau demands complete silence on the question of sex education in order to "prolong innocence."[4]

There are differences between the tutelage models of Locke and Rousseau. The affective basis of the family, so central to Rousseau's analysis, is cautiously approached in Locke's. It is true that in seeking to tear down the barriers of patriarchy Locke argued for a much freer relationship between father and son and that he hoped to create his own concept of a nidal climate. But the word "free" is the important description. The father's task is one of providing the groundwork for independence:

> Though I have mentioned the Severity of the Father's Brow, and the Awe settled thereby in the mind of Children when young, as one major Instrument, whereby Education is to be managed; Yet I am far from being of an Opinion, that it should be continued all along to them. . . . I think it should be relaxed, as fast as their Age, Discretion and Good Behavior could allow.[5]

Fathers are destined to become friends to their sons, sharing the "knowledge of their Estates and Concerns." Thus Locke would be able to make his case for the uniqueness of childhood as well by outlining the necessary tasks set for the parent. Locke's judiciousness in politics is mirrored in his image of the "careful" father. He is one who uses punishment sparingly, teaches the child respect for servants and steers him away from pursuits like music which "waste so much of a young man's time, to gain but a moderate skill in it."[6] This sense of economy in family matters must temper the "ways of Tenderness and Affection, which parents never want [lack] for their children."[7]

Of course a sense of economy is urged by Rousseau as well. But it is designed largely as a guide to focus emotion. The romantic individualist seeks perfection through personal awareness and for Rousseau this awareness required the tutor to gradually introduce the child to a threatening environment.

The interrelationships between Locke and Rousseau's models of childhood and parental authority are extremely subtle. Moreover, there is the question of complications and refinements introduced by modern psychology. But this much can be safely said. Both theories contain within them explosive elements that prepare the way for an ideology of children's rights. The Lockean approach is especially well suited as a model of parental authority for an advanced industrial society. Childhood is a training period for acceptance into the world of the free and rational. Locke's family, held together by contract, is the "specialized institution" designed to function not as an economic or political unit or even as an island of sentiment but as an agency of socialization. However, Locke's model has no impelling logic which demands that it be the family who introduce the child to the world of the free and rational. Once the family exits from Locke's system, we are left with a set of protorational beings who have the right to expect "nourishment" and "education." With just another slight push, one might ask why children indeed are exempted from the status of the free and rational. Why, if parental authority drops like "swaddling clothes," is any special effort necessary to introduce the child into the liberal adult world of freedom and rationality?

At one level Rousseau's model suggests an alternate position in regard to parental and political authority. The preparation of the child for independence from the social order and the isolation of the family itself from the demands of society leads one to view Rousseau's model in terms of producing the alienated citizen. The draconian, indeed totalitarian, techniques of Emile's tutor are designed to inculcate a sense of self-awareness and self-control so that the child can resist the temptations of society. Of course, Rousseau himself was not content to limit himself to the alternative offered in *Emile.* When he offers the more inclusive model in the *Social Contract,* parental authority and its role in preparing a stable state of alienation is abandoned.

But even if we limit ourselves to Rousseau's *Emile,* we find that it too contains elements which threaten the parental-tutelage model. Rousseau provides no link between the liberated self and the tutelage of Emile. We are reminded that the father "owes men to humanity," but what if the adult search for liberation is so demanding, so exhausting, that parenthood itself becomes a burden which threatens the development of the self? Closely related is the issue of the authority of the parent himself. Can a theory that places such a premium upon individual self-development continue to justify such complete subjection from the child? Ought the tutor's "little rebel" be liberated from the tutor as well?

THE PROBLEM OF PUNISHMENT
Within the tutelage model itself, however, there emerged an almost intractable problem: the question of the use of force as a punishment. Force and violence formed an integral part of the old patriarchal unit. *Patria potestas* provided the general theoretical basis for the use of force but severe physical punishment was deemed necessary to maintain discipline, transmit educational ideas, please the gods, even expel evil spirits.[8] Examples are legion. Erasmus, John Wesley, Frederick the Great, Lady Jane Grey, and Henry VI complained bitterly of their childhood treatment. In ancient Greece, boys were flogged by their parents before the altars of Diana. Child sacrifice remained a problem throughout most of ancient history (a point which was not left unreported by Locke). In what must

prove to be one of the major ironies of cultural history, Christian parents whipped their children on Innocents Day to make them remember the massacre of the innocents by Herod. Force was deemed indispensable as a way to break a child's will. For a time Reformation ideas even added support to this belief. Children were "imps of darkness." Signs of "willfulness" could indicate demonic forces. They must be "broken" and "beaten down."[9]

There is no strict logic that forbids the use of force in the tutelage model. Several factors, however, moved away from corporal punishment. The notion of childhood itself as a developmental process provided for a reinterpretation of a child's apparent signs of "willfulness." Locke constantly reminds his readers that when "parents so heap Rules on their children" it is "impossible for the poor little ones to remember a tenth part of them, much less to observe them."[10] The new affective basis of the family itself and the creation of a nidal climate increasingly made the use of force seem a bizarre rather than a natural and necessary practice. But what is most striking about child education in Locke and Rousseau is the view of authority they seek to present. Locke wishes to produce a free and rational man, one who never submits to "arbitrary authority." He insists that children can "learn to Dance and Fence without whipping; nay Arithmetic, Drawing, and co. they apply themselves well enough to without beating."[11] There is a hint of suspicion over the motives of parents and teachers who use force: ". . . there is something strange, unnatural, and disagreeable . . . in the Things required in the grammar-schools, or in the Methods used there, that children cannot be brought to, without the severity of the Lash, and hardly with that too; or else, that it is a mistake, that these Tongues could not be taught them without Beating."[12] Physical force produces only an external obedience, and an external submission to authority is never "good on the Mind." It lessens the "Authority of the Parents, the Respect of the Child."[13] Children can distinguish early "betwixt Passion and Reason": "And as they cannot but have a Reverence for what comes from the latter, so they quickly grow into a contempt for the former; or if it causes a present Terrour, yet it soon wears off; and natural inclination will easily learn to slight such scare-crows, which make a noise, but are not animated by Reason."[14]

Rousseau chides Locke for his emphasis upon reason ("these children who have been constantly reasoned with, strike me as exceedingly silly")[15] but in many ways his approach is similar. For Rousseau wishes to inculcate a kind of self-sufficiency, which, while it is not dependent upon a fine logical sense in the child, nevertheless requires a sense of limit that the child will accept internally. Take this example. Rousseau is given charge of a "capricious" child for a few weeks. The first night the child awoke at midnight and demanded that Rousseau light a candle. This he did. The next night the child made the same request. Rousseau acceded but told the child not to do it again. The next night the request was refused and Rousseau chuckled as the child unsuccessfully attempted to light the candle himself. When the child shouted and knocked over chairs, Rousseau tells his readers that he almost lost his temper. But he recovered, lit the candle, and took it to another room: "What a noise there was! This was what I expected, and took no notice. At last the noise ceased; I listened, heard him settling down, and I was quite easy about him. Next morning I entered the room at daybreak, and my little rebel was lying on a sofa enjoying a sound and much needed sleep after his exertions."[16] The child had learned his own limitations. "Willfulness" had been defeated — and without one strike from the parent.

It should be mentioned how delicate and difficult parenting is according to the tutelage model. Authority must be freely accepted but the child as its object is in some ways a figure beyond the comprehension of the parent. "Childhood has its own ways of seeing, thinking, and feeling," said Rousseau. But childhood is not a static category. Each age has its temptations and modes of thinking. Thus even in the context of intimacy the parent is charged with something like reaching for a moving target at dusk. If one thinks about this task for a moment, one can see how gloriously utopian is the model of authority in the tutelage model. Authority freely accepted by an adult without physical threat, without bureaucratic rules, without anticipation of immediate benefit is a rare occurrence. Imagine the difficulty of achieving such authority in the context of childhood!

Nevertheless, it is precisely this general model that the modern family accepted as a guide. Bernard Wishy has reported a number of examples offered in childrearing manuals for parents who struggled with this new form of authority. Here is a case from Catherine Sedgwick's best seller of 1835, *Home*. The book is designed to illustrate how parents could "completely" spare the rod and yet save the child. A family pet had torn a boy's kite. The child was so angry at his sister's kitten that he threw the animal into a pot of water boiling in the hearth. The family was horrified. They sent the child to his room for two weeks allowing him to leave only for school. "Social ostracism, the sorrow of those who love him, his offense to peace and love in the family . . . are the burdens on his conscience."[17] At the end of this period, the boy asked his father for forgiveness. He was asked if he had gained "strength to resist the sin of temper." The boy "knew" his father wanted proof of his conversion. "I had to wait till something happened to try me." Twice at school a friend had tried to provoke him to fight. The second temptation made him raise his fist to hit his friend:

"Oh, Wallace!"

"But I did not, father, I did not, I had to bite my lips though so the blood ran!"

"God bless you, my son."[18]

At this point the father decides that now is the moment to effectively offer a moral maxim. These trials are important. Virtue and good were only possible with free will; it was better to be virtuous through temptation than to be incapable of sin. At this point the boy confesses that he worries about failure in the future. The father embraces his son and reassures him of his confidence. The mind of teacher and student are one.

Modern childrearing manuals are less concerned with virtue and sin, but the question of physical punishment still takes up a large portion of the instruction. Parent Effectiveness Training (P.E.T.) portrays itself as a way to raise "happier, more responsible and more cooperative children . . . without being *either* strict (authoritarian) *or* lenient (permissive)."[19] It promises to avoid the temptation not only to use force but also many reward techniques in general. Here is an approved example of an incident between a mother and her two-year-old that rivals Rousseau's techniques:

> I was cooking dinner one night and my daughter was gurgling happily on her rocking horse. Then she took the straps used to buckle the child on and began to try to buckle the straps herself. Her face reddened and she began to scream in a high-pitched voice as her frustration mounted. I found myself getting angry at her screaming, so in my usual fashion I knelt down to do it for her. But she fought me and kept screaming. Now I was ready to pick up her and the rocking horse and deposit them both in her room, slamming the door to shut out the noise. Then something clicked in me. So I knelt down, placed my hands on top of hers and said, "You're really mad because you can't do that yourself?" She shook her head, "Yes," stopped the screaming, and a few belated sobs later was again happily rocking away. . . .[20]

There are also the books of Haim Ginott that recommend "therapeutic conversations" between parent and child. Joan Beck's *Effective Parenting* contains a delightful discussion of a child who tells lies and what a parent should do about it. Lying may be the result of an active imagination, fear, embarrassment, or lack of trust. She emphasizes the Lockean notion of parental example ("Never tell a child you are not home") and concludes with a Rousseauan percept: "A small child almost always tells the truth, as he sees it, until he is taught otherwise."[21]

We are now in a good position to assess two recent developments in the general area of childhood: research on family violence, including child abuse, and the children's-rights movement. No expert would allege that parental violence directed against children was unknown before the recent series of studies documented its existence. As we have seen, the image of murder in the household was vividly painted by both Hobbes and Freud. What is novel in this reasearch is a sensitivity to violence and force particularly, between parent and child, which leads to a search for new explanations for its causes. David G. Gil has argued that since various forms of physical punishment (spanking, slapping) are culturally sanctioned, they must be regarded as constituting the "basic causal dimension of all violence against children in American society."[22] Richard J. Gelles has attacked the so-called psychopathological model of child abuse. Child abusers do not, according to Gelles, exhibit any definable set of personality characteristics. Violence against children must be related to the general social environment: "Child abuse can be seen as a form of deviant behavior instead of being seen only as a result of individual pathology."[23] On the related question of the relationship between physical punishment and child behavior, studies emphasize the counterproductive nature of *any* corporal punishment.

Research which attempts to focus the circumstances of violence against children reveals factors that can be directly traced to the tutelage model. Violence against children is more likely to be perpetrated among the working class and the unemployed and poverty stricken. The sex of the child abuser is more likely to be female. The "most dangerous period" for the child is from three months to three years of age. Unwanted children are candidates for physical abuse, as are children from "mixed" religious backgrounds and children in families with spouse conflict. If indeed there is an empirical relationship between physical punishment and child abuse, it appears that these specific factors exacerbate or trigger the linkage. On the whole, researchers seem to relate these factors to the standard of the tutelage model.

Gil suggests that loss of employment can so damage the caretaker function that the relationship between parent and child is stripped down to one of anger and frustration. Others emphasize the less verbal environment of the "lower"-class family and the higher level of violence such a family regularly endures. Gelles argues the normally close relationship between a mother's self-esteem and child behavior explains the high incidence of female child abuse. The very high incidence of infant abuse suggests that when "reason" is limited as a basis for social interaction, physical punishment (and the chance that it will get out of hand) is increased.

What research in child abuse seems to indicate, then, is that the tutelage model fails under certain economic conditions. It may well be that corporal punishment itself so contaminates the objectives of the tutelage model that it needs to be eliminated entirely. But parental tutelage without physical force represents an extension of the model rather than a rejection of it. Indeed, one can make the argument that familial violence is a consequence of the breakdown of the family. This argument is rejected by the following set of advocates.

THE CHILDREN'S-RIGHTS THEORISTS

The new theorists of childhood accept either the Lockean view of the rational individual or the Rousseauan one of the liberated self. Some even seem to hold to an uneasy combination of both. Thus John Holt writes: "I propose ... that the rights, privileges, duties, responsibilities of adult citizens be made available to any young person, of whatever age, who wants to make use of them."[24] Richard Farson gives his prologue a more Rousseauan cast: "The issue of self-determination is not the heart of children's liberation. It is, in fact, the only issue, a definition of the entire concept. The acceptance of the child's right to self-determination is fundamental to all the rights to which children are entitled."[25] Thus the Lockean period of tutelage is rejected as unnecessary. The Rousseauan model of self-awareness is short-circuited. The child is not to be prepared for a sense of self-awareness as a means to remain independent from society. On the contrary, for Farson there is no image of society at all, only a swarm of liberated individuals.

Behind this basic premise of the child as a fully rational self capable of self-determination stand three basic themes: the insistence that childhood itself is an exclusively cultural institution; the use of a vocabulary of oppression to explain the existence of childhood; the exploration of the strategies of political action to overcome that oppression.

The claim that childhood is an artificial or even unnatural category rests upon two assertions of the children's-rights theorists. Many point to the historical relativity of childhood. Childhood is a local and recent invention, "not some universal part of the human condition." The basic source of authority on this point is Phillipe Ariès' *Centuries of Childhood*. Ariès has claimed childhood was unknown throughout the Middle Ages and that children freely moved within the adult world as apprentices and holders of class lineages. We shall note in later chapters that the position of Ariès offers only limited support for the movement. But for now it will suffice to mention that Ariès' contention that childhood was in part the self-serving creation of the bourgeois family fits neatly into the view of children's-rights theorists. For if children had been captured, subdued, and segregated from adult life as a consequence of the structure of the modern family, childhood can be seen as not only a cultural invention but an exploitive one at that. Rousseau's famous dictum is subjected to expansion. If children were born free, and remained so in medieval society, then why are they in chains?

The use of Ariès offers a double support. Children were regarded with "gay indifference" by the medieval aristocrat. Only when patriarchy was enclosed in sentiment was the child to be imprisoned by the institution of childhood. For the children's-rights theorists, affection of parent for child is a tool of domination, an attempt by the bourgeois to introduce "uniformity" throughout the population. Holt goes as far as to suggest children do not "need" love. By the time infants are six months old, "or even younger," they have their own "well-developed purposes, needs, and preferences."[26] Our affection for our children is part of a well-developed ideology of the child as a love object. We "use" children and devise a theory to justify our actions, much as do men who "use" women as sex objects. Farson's book begins with a list of terms of "affection" used to describe children, making it clear that "babe," "little one," "bairn," "bambino," "tat," "tad," "cherub," "urchin," "tyke" are employed as marks of inferiority.[27]

Historical relativity may suggest alternative ways to organize society. Biological necessity may indicate limits to social change. Children's-rights theorists have begun to challenge the massive body of writings that sees childhood, social construct though it be, as somehow corresponding to physical and emotional development. In her critique of developmental psychology, Arlene Skolnick suggests that the view of stage development from infancy to adolescence be replaced by a two-step model: ". . . there is essentially one step up from childhood to the adult level and that transition takes place at around five to seven."[28] John Holt is unwilling to accept even this bifurcation. "If children do not learn the ropes faster in our society . . . it is in part because they do not have to. . . ."[29] The earliest age he mentions for the right to vote is six, although he insists that "ultimately, I want the right to vote for people of any age. No one should be left out."[30]

Why then does "childhood" exist? The conventional Marxist answer has always emphasized the economic base of childhood for the bourgeoisie. Children were hostages to the future. Now childhood is seen in terms of emotional rather than property interests. Parents have a psychic "vested interest" in the child's dependency. Children who act competently and intelligently "threaten us." Reform must somehow "free" us from almost pathological emotional ties to our children. If we wish to be free, we must free our children. "There is no way to have a liberated society until we have liberated children."[31]

Thus for children's-rights theorists childhood represents an oppressed stratum: Segregated and impotent, children are "excluded from almost every area of life."[32] Corporal punishment is only one aspect of their "slavery." John Holt lists the following rights that children require: the right to vote, the right to work, the right to own property, the right to travel, the right to choose one's guardian, the right to guaranteed income, the right to legal and financial responsibility, the right to control one's learning, the right to use drugs, the right to drive. Richard Farson's list is very similar. He adds the right to sexual freedom.

In fact, it is the alleged peculiar relationship between parent and child that requires such measures. One of the major descriptions of the relationships between oppressed and oppressor in the Marxist model of class in a capitalist society involved the absence of emotional ties between worker and capitalist. Oppression that took as its base the cash nexus made capitalism a unique, and so it was argued, a transitory system. Thus children's-rights advocates most frequently resort to earlier models of oppression as their model. Holt argues that children are sensitive to faces because "like all slaves ... they learn to look at and read the faces of their rulers in order to sense what will happen next."[33] Children are the last group of slaves and "having [our] own home-grown slaves is very satisfying."[34] This, says Holt, is the "one use" of childhood. Thus the rights listed above can help break the pathology of attachment between parent and child. If only parents could be made to realize the "extraordinary emotional and financial burden" that children entail. If only they could "admit without shame or guilt that they don't much like these young people who live in their houses, worry them half to death, and soak up most of their money...."[35] Unfortunately, children too may insist on being "Uncle Toms and Aunt Toms": "We can predict that children will be their own worst enemies in the movement of their liberation."[36]

Children, now so excluded from adult life, ought to take their place immediately in society as independent human beings. But, of course, children are "so oppressed and incapacitated that it is not at all likely that they will be able to act on their own behalf." Until children can develop strength and vision as a group, "we will need more, not less, adult advocacy."[37] Lawyers and judges, psychiatrists and educators, social workers and political reformers appear to be the approved vanguard for these efforts. The new-class basis of suggestions offered in this proposal is clearly reflected in the lists of rights.

Farson considers the implications of the child's "right to economic power." We need to rid ourselves of the Dickensian view of child exploitation. Children are not "weak, innocent and incompetent." As long as the government can insure safe conditions and working hours, all "protective" legislation ought to be eliminated. Very young children should be provided with government allotments, perhaps placed in trust by panels of children's advocates: "The incapacity of the child in infancy should only mean that extra steps must be taken to guarantee the protection of his rights."[38] Holt, departing somewhat from this belief about the uniqueness of childhood, contends that children love the kind of work in which they "get their hands on, or better yet in, materials."[39] Cooking, painting, cleaning are ideal occupations for children. Of course, "greedy" parents may attempt to compel their children to work. Then steps would have to be taken to insure the child the right to dispose of his money as he sees fit.

The "right to choose one's guardian" (Holt) and the "right to alternative home environments" (Farson) also reveals the political direction of the new theorists of childhood. Holt would have three choices available to children: first, to live as dependents "under the care and control" of their parents ("primary guardians" in his words); second, to live as dependents "under the care and control" of people other than their parents ("secondary guardians"); third, to live as fully independent citizens, financially and legally responsible. It is the second alternative that so excites Holt's reformist sensibilities. The relationship of secondary guardian and child would be voluntary and provisional. They might make the agreement last *sine die* or choose a month and year of termination. Holt explains that the terms would be much like the pact that a student makes with the university. Although it reappears in different forms, liberalism's contract is ubiquitous. Infant consent now takes this form: Secondary guardians could say to the child, "If you are going to do things like this, we don't want you living with us anymore; find someone else...."

Groups can function as secondary guardians as well. One of the largest, says Holt, is already in existence — the armed forces. Many young people might prefer a "less personal relationship with a different kind of community — the sort of thing children get when they go to camp or boarding school."[40] Holt admits that such concentration communities of children would develop rules for their inhabitants — a time for coming in at night, work details, rules about guilt, and the like — and that this development may appear to present a contradiction. After all, families were characterized as virtual prisons. But in a voluntary organization "there is no contradiction at all between freedom and rules."[41] Love it (or at least tolerate it) or leave it. Young people will, after all, have some guaranteed minimum income. They can take their money somewhere else.

Farson offers some more variations on the problem of enforcing the right to alternative home environments. Communes are one possibility, but he is skeptical. The counter-culture commune is a bit too unreliable. Contractual arrangements for property relationships are never carefully worked out. Communes often develop a narrow ideological discipline. If some network could set the terms for such ventures, Farson would be more sympathetic. Two other alternatives are more strongly recommended; child-exchange programs and children's residences. The model for the former is the foreign-student exchange program. Familes could "swap children, children who have created a problem for their parents, or simply children who would like to have the chance to experience new situations."[42] Child swapping is now in existence, but it is "informal and haphazard." Counseling and contracts would rationalize the system. Children's residences would be permanent camps organized by a "network staff" and financed along the lines of the Social Security system.

THE CHILD AS DISPLACED PERSON

The claims of children's-rights theorists illustrate a curious ideological direction. On the one hand, these theorists do offer truly radical proposals in the sense that they are attempting to apply to children the standards of individualism, rational and romantic. In fact, in some respects there is more ideological consistency in the writings of the children's-rights theorists than in Locke and Rousseau themselves. Since children are both free and rational, society need not require any special institutions of entry, however narrowly functional. This ideological "advance" shows itself most strikingly in the characteristic presentation of these thinkers. For the children's-rights theorists insist on a level of abstraction that surpasses both Locke's world of the free and rational and Rousseau's *promeneur solitaire*. All cultural and historical features of childhood are arbitrary. Parental emotion is illusory or self-serving. Every dimension of society, every network of human interaction, is treated as anomaly, except, of course, the rights of individuals. Thus educational systems, families, economic structures must be treated as needless encrustations. What is real is what is a right. Since rights, in either the Lockean or Rousseauan sense, form only a part of our social existence, social theory must consistently operate at a high level of transcendence.

It is the abstract quality of the children's-rights theorists that permits a curious sensitivity in viewing family relationships. Practices that do not fit a rights model are scrupulously examined. For example, Farson can recount in detail the oppressive nature of a society without children's furniture catalogues that feature both left- and right-handed desks. He can repeat in the most vivid terms the tortures inflicted by the child abuser. But he can also so freely explore the question of pedophilia that he is able to conclude that "in many instances, the child is a willing participant."[43] Consent, of course, can be engineered. The child may have been threatened, seduced, or cajoled. But, after all, "engineered consent is not only a problem for children ... adults have an identical problem in understanding the issue of consent."[44] Incest, too, may show hidden consensual arrangements. The failure of a child to report incest behavior "apparently comes from some understanding of such confidences and not as a result of threats or retaliation."[45]

There is a reason for such imbalance in assessing the role of force in the life of the child. Once it is decided that a relationship can be conceived in terms of a right, the abstraction pushes away any insights that might be reached through a contextual analysis. Autonomous beings, in either their sexual or economic activities, need to be protected against restrictions on their actions. Sexual or economic relationships between adult and child are now seen as relationships between consenting parties. Any examination of an underlying dependence suggests ulterior motives on the part of the critic. Resistance to children's rights is "understandable" because it "threatens our entire system, our way of life." All this is, of course, a curious circular argument. We are reminded that children are not weak and dependent, except to the extent that historical and cultural patterns have made them so. Any signs of different kinds of dependence in the new world of children's rights are in the mind of those with little faith in the capacities of human beings to live in a truly free society. Thus in some ways, the role of force and violence in family life is even more deeply submerged in this new view than in the most idealized model of conventional family forms. In the latter, violence could be recognized at least as an aberration from the norm. We have even suggested that the perception of parental violence as a pathology was in part the result of the acceptance of the new tutelage model. Even most of the researchers on familial violence, while they emphasize its frequency, measure it against inconsistent patterns of childrearing within the tutelage model. The new theorists of childhood bury the problem of violence behind an iron veil of rights. If the right is protected, the question of force is rejected. In some ways, this is a return to Hobbesian doctrine.

But the rejection of the tutelage model, however radical in its implications, also suggests a retreat. For the relationship between parent and child as presented by Locke and Rousseau offered a utopian view of authority. Paternal but not patriarchal, developmental and ultimately temporary, the tutelage model combined rational and emotional elements of authority in a unique fashion. The abandonment of this model represents not an abandonment of authority as such but a resort to what is seen as a surer, more consistent form of authority.

Despite what the children's-rights theorists say, they offer us a form of authority over children that is as paternal as any found in the tutelage model. The immediate elevation of the child to the status of adult places him directly in the world of the free and rational. Armed from birth with a state-financed income allowance and carrying his Social Security and voter registration card, the child progresses through day-care centers to child-exchange programs and youth camps. His expenditures or credits are supervised by a benevolent and efficient bureaucracy. His entrances and egresses are protected as well. In fact, the rite of passage, universal in form if not in content across all societies, is erased by bureaucratic administration. If this scenario looks too severe, let us contrast it for a moment with middle-class adulthood in current advanced industrial society. For the most part this lifestyle is smooth and uneventful. We do progress through a series of career paths and we spend our time relatively freely. We are subject, of course, to taxes and to a certain mismanagement of administered services. In the new children's-rights model, however, we would be freed from the idiosyncrasies of being parent-educators, freed from that peculiar form of authority that is so different from the kind to which we adults are now subject, freed from the emotions involved in transmitting one's failures and successes to a human being of the next generation. In short, we would be individuals finally and completely free and rational. At last we would be freed of the memories of the past. We would also, of course, be freed of the concept of a future. For the future would now be reflected in a new person (child) whose life would be identical to but independent from our adult life. There has always been a jerky sort of reformism encased within the general tutelage model. Perhaps this explains why parenting is subject to so many fads in modern society. The question can always be newly asked: "Isn't there a better way to raise children?" But without parents or children, an irremediable stolidity takes its place. To assure that a proper transmission would be secure, the professional would supervise rights of self-determination.

Certainly a kind of utopianism does appear in this aspect of the new world of children's rights. The burden of parenthood is eliminated as is the burden of childhood. But primary importance of the new world lies elsewhere. For the child of this new world takes on all the characteristics of a displaced person. He has many homes but as a consequence is homeless. He has in his possession a whole panoply of human rights but has no power to enforce any of them. He is subject to no authority, except, of course, the authority of those institutions that guarantee him his freedom. He can foresee no future generation, for the capacity to form a generation is not available to him; generation is defined in political, or more properly, in bureaucratic terms. What broader and more stable system of authority can be imagined? Only one in which we are all displaced persons.

9

LOCKE'S CHILDREN: THE END OF THE FAMILY IN LIBERAL THOUGHT

John Locke's political thought left the family in a quiet purgatory. Locke did much to outline the features of the modern family that might fit into the new liberal order of the "free and rational." He provided a picture of the family as an institution with relatively equal spouses who presided over the creation of a new kind of individual. Marriage was a contract and there are contractual overtones to his depiction of the parent-child relationship. What Locke left unexamined, however, was the basis of the modern family itself. The family was a natural institution despite the fact that it was modeled after the contrivance of the constitutional order. Men were certainly not born free and rational, but the family, the institution of the free and rational, would make them so. Thus the naturalness of the family lay not in the aspirations and temperaments of the individuals who composed it — these were the same as those of the citizen — but in its universal functional performance. Families existed in the state of nature exactly as they do in society. Whereas the just political order may require the most judicious attention, the family was a much more simple affair; its basic principles could set it in motion and natural inclinations could, by supplementing them, do the rest.

We have just seen how subsequent theorists attempted to further rationalize Locke's concept of the family. Children not only do not "need love," they need no authority either, save that derived from consent. Liberal ambivalence to the family does not derive solely from its insistence upon the axiomatic status of free and rational citizens. If it did so derive, liberal revisionists might have been able to find a place for the modern family.

In a world which has seen liberalism challenged by other world views, we tend to forget that the great power of liberal ideology, a source of radicalism that can transcend historical period, is its ability to submit every social practice to rational analysis. As the objects of liberal analysis change, we can find its adherents more openly asking: Is the family really rationally necessary? Liberalism, at first in moments of self-doubt and then as a simple matter of social policy, came to the conclusion that men and women need to be *made* free and rational. When the question of social engineering reopened not only the liberal imagination but created a whole new professional liberal stratum in society, the universal functional necessity of the family was then questioned. Liberals would begin to ask with some suspicion in their voices if the family is the proper agency for the nurturing of the free and rational.[1] Remember that questions regarding the desirability of the modern family came rather late in liberalism. Liberalism had reached a de facto accommodation with the family partly by restricting the principles of rational individualism to family life and partly by supporting the new family form itself.[2]

One must be reminded that the dominant model of man in liberalism, rational individualism, leaves room for a range of alternatives with respect to the family. One is the route offered by Locke. But liberalism contains collectivist pulls from other directions and can take the form of two polar types. We saw the way Hobbes relentlessly pursued rational individualist premises until they justified a collectivist order and the denial of the basis for the modern family. The Hobbesian alternative is very much alive in contemporary liberal thought. We shall take a look at it in a moment. The other alternative is more recent and reflects liberalism's accommodation with collectivism.[3] Thus we have reserved our analysis of it for now.

THE FAMILY AND THE CONCEPT OF ENGINEERED INDIVIDUAL DEVELOPMENT
The easiest way to begin is to note briefly the major departures from Locke's rational individualism. Locke's basic premise was that men are by nature free and rational. Except for children and madmen, the social and political order had no need to promote the liberal individual; he came to the arena of citizenship in full bloom as a free and rational man, out of the bosom of the family. But Locke's premise was an analytic one and would undergo a good deal of scrutiny. It came first with John Stuart Mill, who brought liberalism to its initial internal crisis of self-confidence by challenging the epistemological status of rational individualism. All of us may *potentially* be free and rational, but not with "present wretched education and social arrangements."[4] For the moment we must rely upon competent judges and pay close attention to the hindrances against the creation of the rational individual.[5]

Mill compared human beings to plants. Some sprout luxuriantly and reach "a great development in this heated atmosphere and under this active nurture and watering" while others, even from the same root, "which are left outside in the wintery air, with ice purposely heaped all around them, have a stunted growth...."[6] Thus was born the concept of "individual development" as a sort of yardstick that would measure the attainment of the status of the free and rational. Mill had imbued a tradition of liberalism with a sense of self-consciousness about its own premises that is rare in internal ideological change. The liberal, once he had broken down the barriers of custom and authority, could not assume the world of the free and rational. The liberal individual must be nurtured, "developed" in the new image.

Several factors prevented a direct and swift conclusion to this change. One was Mill's own deep-seated skepticism which often warred with his commitment to progress. Another factor, closely related, was Mill's belief that the proper route to self-development must be in large part individually attained. There could be no revolutionary transformation along the lines of the creation of a new Soviet man. "The spirit of improvement is not always a spirit of liberty, for it may aim at forcing improvements on an unwilling people ... the only unfailing and permanent source of improvement is liberty, since by it there are as many possible centers of improvement as there are individuals."[7] But Mill's commitment to the individual search for development would have profound implications for his own idea of individuality, especially as it relates to the family.

The principle of individual development as a replacement for Locke's axiomatic free and rational man and Bentham's utilitarian calculator eventually produced its own ossification. For instance, T. H. Green made the goal of morality individual development and did so in a clearly analytic fashion.[8] With Hegelian certainty the state is assigned the task of aiding this development:

> institutions of civil life ... render it possible for a man to be freely determined by the idea of a possible satisfaction of himself, instead of being driven this way and that by external forces.[9]

Thus Green's philosophy eliminates both Mill's doubts and his caution. Liberalism had lost an insight that came to it after much struggle. Locke's free and rational men were not axiomatic but the path to their creation was. This form of liberalism had closed up again and as yet it has still not broken out of this new mold. One can see this tendency even in Mill. It will be helpful for us to review it by looking at his celebrated "The Subjection of Women." Mill's general purposes in this courageous essay are at once carefully drawn and direct. The Victorian family virtually enslaves women. No liberal society can live with this anachronism. The present legal

barriers to the emancipation of women in property ownership and entrance to the professions must be eliminated. But Mill's general ideological
predilections outstrip his central purpose. I cannot resist laying the
statement of principle of *On Liberty* beside that of "The Subjection of
Women." Here is the central premise of the former:

> The object of this essay is to assert one very simple principle, as
> entitled to govern absolutely the dealings of society with the
> individual in the way of compulsion and control, whether means
> used be physical force in the form of legal penalties or the moral
> coercion of public opinion. That principle is that the sole end for
> which mankind are warranted, individually or collectively, in
> interfering with the liberty of action of any of their number is
> self-protection.[10]

And here are the opening lines of the latter:

> The object of this Essay is to explain as clearly as I am able, the
> grounds of an opinion which I have held from the very earliest
> period when I had formed opinions at all on social or political
> matters ... That the principle which regulates the existing social
> relations between the two sexes — the legal subordination of one
> sex to the other — is wrong in itself, and now one of the chief
> hinderances to human improvement; and that it ought to be
> replaced by a principle of perfect equality....[11]

Now Mill would certainly respond that there is no contradiction between the self-protection principle and the principle of perfect equality.
Women are certainly entitled to benefit from the principle of self-
protection. The key here, however, is the principle of perfect equality.
Mill's entire policy framework is equality before the law but his ideological
impulses are barely able to contain this formulation. Three premises in the
essay are used to support the argument for legal equality. They are suited
for a much broader appraisal of the family than that for which Mill ostensibly uses them. It is here that we do see the conflict between the two
principles.

Let us briefly present them:

First: Women can be seen as an oppressed people but the source and
nature of their repression is unique. "Men do not want solely the obedience of women, they want their sentiments."[12] Of course, all forms of
oppression have an affective tie. Without some sort of psychological
bonding, tyrannies could not exist. But Mill presents us with the idea of
oppression whose major source is affection: "All the moralities feel then

that it is the duty of women, and all the current sentimentalities that it is their nature, to live for others, to make complete abnegation of themselves, and to have no life but in their affections."[13]

Mill never tells us what so many theorists now tell us, that the affective tie must be broken in order to achieve female emancipation. His policy argument is only a legal one. But Mill takes the next requisite step for such a proposal. The affective basis of the Victorian family is self-serving. An "instinct of selfishness" has made men hold women in a state of affective subjection "by representing to them meekness, submissiveness, and resignation of all individual will into the hands of a man, as an essential part of sexual attractiveness."[14]

Second: If the family is to be tolerated, it must be an equalitarian institution. The following selection illustrates how Mill saw equality before the law, one basis of the self-protection principle, as a means for a broader and deeper conception of equality:

> The equality of married persons before the law is not only the sole mode in which that particular relation can be made consistent with justice to both sides, and conducive to the happiness of both, but it is the only means of rendering the daily life of mankind, in any high sense, a school of moral cultivation. Though the truth may not be felt or generally acknowledged for generations to come, the only school of genuine moral sentiment is society between equals ... society in equality is its normal state.[15]

Family relationships must be identical to those of citizens: "The true virtue of human beings is fitness to live together as equals; claiming nothing for themselves but what they as freely concede to every one else...."[16] Mill looks closely at the free and rational family and takes Lockean thought an important step further. The family needs no ultimate sovereign. It is not true that in all voluntary associations one must be master. Mill uses the model of the business partnership and grafts it onto liberal constitutionalism. The contract can provide the basis for a preappointed division of powers between the two parties: "each being absolute in the executive branch of their own department, and any change of system and principle requiring the consent of both."[17]

It would be unfair to say that Mill took a step toward conceiving the family as an institution that was phenomenologically bureaucratic. But he did feel that the portrayal of internal family functions in bureaucratic terms was a necessary measure to restrain the "exaggerated self-abnegation" of women. Mill contended that such self-sacrifice was an "artificial" ideal of the sex. Women must learn to be no more self-sacrificing than the best men. The transformation of the women to the world of the free and rational can take place within the family but only if the family is part of a society of equals.

Third: Once a particular kind of family is posited as the only desirable one and it is accepted that its existence is not axiomatic, one is confronted with the task of promoting it. Mill concluded that the Victorian family was "a school of despotism."[18] Unfortunately, and there is indeed a wistful tone to Mill's argument on this point, the practice of citizenship is not sufficient as "a school of society in equality." Citizenship "fills only a small place in modern life, and does not come near the daily habits or inmost sentiments."[19] The state has a direct interest in family forms. "The family, *justly constituted,* would be the real school of the virtues of freedom."[20] There will be no moral progress until people "practice in the family the same moral rule which is adopted to the normal constitution of human society."[21]

PARSONS AND RAWLS: TWO FINAL EFFORTS

Mill never took further steps in presenting a theoretical critique of the family. His larger theory was too avowedly pluralist to allow an easy push in this direction. Moreover, Mill apparently accepted the notion that the woman's social role would still be primarily a familial one.

Let us briefly look at two attempts to deal with the family from the perspective of rational individualism. It may be that the works of Talcott Parsons and John Rawls represent the last liberal efforts to find a place for the modern family in the context of rational individualism. Both writers offer us systematic theoretical structures designed to capture the stable elements of liberal society. Both theories, for all their apparent internal logic, provide little more than a holding action in maintaining the family in liberal thought.

Parsons' well-known penchant for abstract theorizing and endless categorization only partially conceals his initial concern for the modern family. High divorce rates and low birth rates, a more permissive sexual morality, the decline of the broader kinship unit, and the "loss of family functions" would seem to indicate that the family was disintegrating as a social institution. But Parsons insists that while some of this disorganization is of a "serious character," most of it represents the strain that accompanies all structural change. Divorces usually occur in the early stages of marriage and in any case, "divorce certainly has not led to a general disillusionment with marriage."[22] The birth rate represents a process of readjustment rather than some continuous trend of disorganization.

Parsons concludes that the family is now being reduced to its "root functions." While there is a decline in certain features traditionally associated with families, this does not represent a "decline of the family" in a more general sense:

> We think the trend of the evidence points to the legitimacy of the
> relative stabilization of a new type of family structure in a new
> relation to a general social structure, one in which the family is
> more specialized than before, but not in any general sense less
> important, because the society is dependent *more* exclusively on it
> for the performance of certain of its vital functions.[23]

This is an ingenious argument. Parsons sees evidence of decline all around
him, yet he concludes that this disorganization will go no further. He sees
the "loss of function" everywhere. The family does not engage in much
economic production; it is not a significant unit in the political power
system; it is not a direct agency of integration in the larger society. Why
then is it likely for the family to stabilize in the performance of its two
remaning "basic and irreducible" functions, the socialization of children
and the stabilization of adult personalities? Here is Parsons' answer:

> If, as some psychologists seem to assume, the essentials of human
> personality were determined biologically, independently of in-
> volvement in social systems, there would be no need for families,
> since reproduction as such does not require family organization. It
> is because the *human* personality is not "born" but must be
> "made" through the socialization process that in the first instance
> families are necessary. They are "factories" which produce human
> personalities.[24]

In other words, Parsons cannot imagine a society that does not have some
agency to perform these functions. Therefore the family's disintegration
can proceed only so far. Then it must stop and restabilize around these two
"basic and irreducible functions." Locke's free and rational men must be
created and Parsons assumes that the family is the natural institution for
this function. He never considers that there is no necessary reason why
social institutions must continue to perform their designated functions.
He never considers that, despite the fact that personalities must be made to
continue a stable order, a stable order is a human contrivance that can fail
and fail miserably. Complete social disintegration is a reality that is
beyond the scope of Parsons' vision.

But even apart from this point, Parsons' actual reconstruction of the new
stable family reveals serious flaws. The modern family is the result of the
modernization process in general. Parsons gives special attention to the
disjunction between the family as an organization and the larger society.

It is above all the pressure of the modern occupational system and its mode of articulation with the family which accounts for the difference between the modern, especially American, kinship system and *any* found in non-literate or even peasant societies. The family household is a solitary unit, where, once formed, membership and status are ascribed, and the communalistic principle of "to each according to his needs" prevails. In the occupational world, status is achieved by the individual and is contingent on his continuing performance.... Occupational organization in the modern sense is the sociological antithesis (of the family).[25]

Yet Parsons insists that the occupational organization of society *"must* be at the expense of the relative predominance of the kinship unit" but not of the modern family itself. The fact that the family is exempted in Parsons' mind from complete absorption into the occupational system is related to his belief in basic and irreducible functions. But he also believes that there is a link between both systems and that this is enough to satisfy the demands of an occupational organization of the larger society. Income may not be derived from the cooperative effort of the entire family, but it is the result of the father's occupational role. This is an example of "interpenetration"; the husband-father holds a "boundary role" between the two systems.

The role of the father as instrumental leader has import within the family as well. The father brings rationality into family dynamics as representative of the instrumental character of the outside world. He is both leader and technical expert. But the mother's expressive role, while firmly anchored within the family, is not devoid of instrumental content. In a technological society, childrearing tends to be regarded as an applied science. Thus while the mother tends to specialize in the expressive direction, "she is heavily involved in the attempt to rationalize these areas of human relations themselves":

> The mother not only "loves" her children, but she attempts to understand rationally the nature, conditions and limitations of that love, and the ways in which its deviant forms can injure rather than benefit her child. In this, as in other respects, the development we have been outlining is an integral part of the more general development of American society.[26]

Thus we begin to see that despite Parsons' initial reconstruction of the family as being precipitated by the boundary problem created by the occupational organization of the larger society and his open presentation of function in the family based upon sex differentiation, he has gone rather far toward picturing the modern family as a rational organization. And if the family is indeed largely organized on this basis, why then is it so indispensable?

Parsons' use of Freud appears to preclude an affirmative response to this question. Freud is used exclusively as Parsons' model of child development. But Parsons' Freudianism is extremely diluted and rationalized, despite the use of Freud's terminology and categories. A few examples can make our point. The smashing of the Oedipus complex and the resultant struggle to find love with strange women, so graphically and poignantly described by Freud, is a much easier process for Parsons because it is almost virtually guaranteed by the "geometry" of family structure. The child is *naturally* drawn away from the family in seeking his erotic attachments.

Parsons never adopts the primal father thesis as an explanation for group behavior and even challenges Freud's account of the sex drive. Freud was on the right track, we are told, but he lacked "a systematic analysis of the structure of social relationships as systems in which the process of socialization takes place."[27]

The functional analysis of Parsons has all the elements of a conservative theory of the family. The family is an intricate and indispensable functional unit, perfectly balanced to produce "normal" adults and to keep "normal" adults stable:

> To sum up, the family is part of the larger society and must be integrated in it. The basic point of reference for analyzing the structure of society is this institutionalized societal value system. In social terms this means that, within limits, the family type will vary as a fraction of the kind of wider social structure, and hence value-systems, in which it is integrated. This is reflected in the balance of the four fundamental need-disposition components of the Oedipal personality, which in turn forms the basis on which the societal value-system can be internalized and the differentiations of role-participation within it worked out.[28]

Instrumental and expressive roles are carefully balanced in society, although Parsons himself denies rigid sex typing. In this broad sense it is difficult to see the modern family as in any great degree "isolated," given its perfect mesh with the common values of the larger society. But this, of course, is the problem with Parsons' analysis. If the family was so balanced and supportive of the general social structure, why in recent years has it changed so radically from Parsons' own description? The answer is either that Parsons' image was originally a highly idealized model of the family or, if it was not, that Parsons seriously underestimated the fragility of the modern family in its role as a specialized agency that performs "basic and irreducible" functions.

But Parsons at least is able to tuck the family away into an important corner of social and political life. John Rawls does not appear to have that luxury. Let us offer a general word or two on *A Theory of Justice.* Rawls' mammoth effort will, I think be historically credited with two achievements. First, he carried the concept of the social contract, a major though not exclusive tool of liberalism, to its highest form of theoretical abstraction. The men who are poised to make the social contract stand in an "original position" behind a veil of ignorance. They are deprived of knowledge about their individual talent, wealth, even their own personalities. Nothing, save the pressing need for a social and political order acceptable to all, is to be part of their calculations. Second, and it is to this purpose that the device of the original position is designed, he brought the idea of distributive justice to the center of liberal ideology. The two principles of justice, equality of opportunity and the difference principle, are the principles that *"free and rational* persons concerned to further their own interests would accept in an initial position of equality as defining the fundamental terms of their association."[29] In short, Rawls shows us how Kantian — and socialist — liberalism can become.

If the free and rational chose the principles of justice that Rawls tells us they would, would they select the modern family to help carry them out? Every impulse of Rawls' theory moves him to answer negatively. Doubts about the utility of the family in promoting the principles of justice dot Rawls' masterpiece:

> ...the principle of fair opportunity can be only imperfectly carried out, at least as long as the institution of the family exists....[30]

> Even in a well-ordered society that satisfies the two principles of justice, the family may be a barrier to equal chances between individuals.[31]

> The consistent application of the principle of fair opportunity requires us to view persons independently from the influences of their social position. But how far should this tendency be carried? It seems that even when fair opportunity (as it has been defined) is satisfied, the family will lead to unequal chances between individuals. Is the family to be abolished then? Taken by itself and given a certain primacy, the idea of equal opportunity inclines in this direction.[32]

In each case Rawls draws back from his own comments. Perhaps "there is less urgency to take this course"; perhaps the difference principle and the priority rules it suggests "reduces the urgency to achieve perfect equality of opportunity"; perhaps "it is impossible in practice to secure equal chances of achievement and culture for those similarly endowed...."[33]

One critic has noted that on this point, and on others, Rawls "flinches" from accepting his own conclusions.[34] But Rawls does not let matters rest here. He returns to the family. On the question of stability of the just society, the family has been brought to the forefront. But even here it is not presented without a certain foreboding:

> Now I shall assume that the basic structure of a well-ordered society includes the family in some form, and therefore that the children are at first subject to the legitimate authority of their parents.[35]

Here Rawls flinches from the opposite direction:

> Of course, in a broader inquiry the institution of the family might be questioned, and other arrangements might indeed prove to be preferable.[36]

Despite this evidence of doubt, Rawls draws us a picture of the family at the center of the social and political system. Look at this description of the same family that so challenged the principles of justice:

> The parents' love of the child is expressed in their evident intention to care for him, to do for him as his rational self-love would incline, and in the fulfillment of these intentions. Their love is displayed by their taking pleasure in his presence and supporting his sense of competence and self esteem.... In general to love another means not only to be concerned for his wants and needs, but to affirm his sense of the worth of his own person. Eventually, then, the love of the parents for the child gives rise to his love in return.... A new affection is in time called into being by the evident love of the parents.[37]

Within the family the child learns of love and authority. The sentiments of justice are firmly fixed in his heart so that he naturally comes to learn of "morality of association" and finally of public principles of justice in the "morality of principles."

Irony abounds here. After declaring his doubts about the family's ability to support justice, Rawls gives us a picture of the most doting parents.

These are the same kind of parents who would willingly and brazenly slant the fair-opportunity principle in favor of their child. Rawls behaves as if he were a Christian who publicly expresses his doubts about his faith and then registers his child into a parochial school.

The family stills appears necessary for the production of the free and rational even when the free and rational have decided to "further their interests" by adopting the principle of "equality as defining the fundamental terms of their association."

But how long can we count on liberals to flinch?

10

HOBBES' CHILDREN: ABORTION, INFANTICIDE, AND RIGHTS

The attempt to pursue the implications of rational individualism until they reach collectivist foundations, what we have called the Hobbesian alternative in liberal thought, is clearly evident in contemporary political thought. But today's neo-Hobbesian philosopher is not a system builder. Nor is his method used so boldly to support his own ideological premises.[1] Thus one has to dig a bit to find these Hobbesians. We are forced then to approach the new attitudes toward the family on a policy-issue basis. Their treatment of abortion is especially suitable for our purposes. It brings out in stark relief the Hobbesian alternative as it related to the family. Four essays provide the basis for our analysis: Judith Thomson's discussion of the fetus' right to life, Roger Wertheimer's analysis of the "liberal" and "conservative" attitude toward the fetus, and Michael Tooley's and Mary Ann Warren's attempt to define the concept of personhood in relation to the fetus.[2] The editors of *Philosophy and Public Affairs* have commended the pieces appearing in their issues for "introducing greater rigor and opening up entirely new questions." They have "permanently altered the character of the debate," and "constitute an indispensable source for anyone wishing to think further about the problem of abortion."[3]

PHILOSOPHY AND THE BIZARRE SITUATION

What precisely is the nature of this "greater rigor" and what "new questions" have been opened up? The factual background of abortion is changing but in its essentials it remains the same as Soranus described it in the second century. Medical technology allows limited fetal surgery as well as safer abortions. It holds out the possibility of cloning and *in vitro* pregnancy. Yet at the date of this writing, women have babies and they do so as a result of sexual intercourse with men. But contemporary philosophical discussions center around the same questions: What constitutes human life (or "personhood")? Professor Warren notes that "the fundamental question in the long history of abortion is, 'How do you determine the humanity of a being?'" Thomson is, for the sake of argument, prepared to pretend that the fetus is a person. The traditional standards by which human life is defined are still accepted in varying degrees by the philosophers in question: the mother's sensation of life or "quickening," the "human resemblance" that the fetus bears, the potentiality of the fetus for personhood, the principle of consciousness as a basis for human life, the ability of the fetus to feel pain.

Yet one can only begin to appreciate the novelty in these articles by considering the conclusions. Thomson argues that to grant a fetus the right to life is not necessarily to place the prospective mother under a moral obligation to complete her pregnancy. Her defense of abortion includes not only cases of rape, malformed fetuses, and extreme economic conditions, but unplanned pregnancy as well.

She admits that it would be "indecent in the woman to request an abortion, and indecent in a doctor to perform it, if she is in her seventh month, and wants the abortion just to avoid the nuisance of postpoining a trip abroad."[4] But "greedy, stingy and callous" actions need not be unjust ones. While there may be cases in which abortion is unjust killing, Thomson suggests "there is room for much discussion and argument as to precisely which, *if any*" fit that category. Roger Wertheimer laments the nature of the whole abortion argument. "When seen in its totality the conservative's argument *is* the liberal's argument turned completely inside out." The arguments of pro- and anti-abortionists "are equally strong and equally weak, for they are the same argument, an argument that can be pointed in either direction." We must point the argument in either direction, not by logic but by our response to the facts. He asks for the creation of a moderate position. Since the nature of the abortion argument seems to preclude a compromise, Wertheimer contends that the moderate "would have to *invent* a new set of moral categories and principles."[5]

The fears of anti-abortionists are realized in the positions taken by Tooley and Warren. Both amputate the concept of personhood from the description of the fetus. In Warren's words, "Some human beings are not people and there may be people who are not human beings."[6] Comatose patients and "defective" human beings fall in the former category as well as fetuses. Robots, computers, and extraterrestrial beings compose the latter. She concludes that to ascribe full moral rights to human nonpersons is "absurd." Tooley employs self-consciousness as a criterion for person-hood. Fetuses certainly do not meet such a standard; nor do infants. Thus "infanticide during a time interval shortly after birth must be morally acceptable." Tooley solves what he calls a "practical moral problem" of infanticide by suggesting that it can be satisfactorily handled by choosing some period of time, such as a week after birth, "as the interval during which infanticide will be permitted." Yet even this seven-day grace period is subject to modification: "This interval could be modified once psychol-ogists have established the point at which a human organism comes to believe that it is a continuing subject of experience and other mental states."[7]

In philosophical analysis the reader is cautioned against any revulsion that might result from reading these essays. Peter Singer has recently suggested that appealing to our feeling is a "superficial way of doing ethics," since "our ethical 'feelings' very often turn out to be inconsistent when their implications are unravelled." Philosophers must "demand reasons instead of feelings of horror."[8] As we shall see, this pride of philosophers under discussion shares his position as well.

To what reasons do these philosophers appeal? While the standards of analysis are traditional ones, the philosopher submits them to a process of reasoning that can best be described as bizarre. Although the range of examples offered in support of abortion is full, there is a uniformity in the reasoning underlying them.

Thomson utilizes the following examples:

> 1. You wake up in the morning and find yourself back to back in bed with an unconscious violinist. A famous, unconscious vio-linist. He has been found to have a fatal kidney ailment, and the Society of Music Lovers has canvassed all the available medical records and found that you alone have the right blood type to help. They have therefore kidnapped you, and last night the violinist's circulatory system was plugged into yours, so that your kidneys can be used to extract poisons from his blood as well as your own. The director of the hospital now tells you, "Look, we're sorry the Society of Music Lovers did this to you — would never have permitted it if we had known. But still they did it, and the violinist now is plugged into you. To unplug you would kill him. But never mind, it's only for nine months. By then he will have recovered from his ailment, and can safely be unplugged from you." [pp. 4–5] Is it morally incumbent on you to accede to this situation?
> 2. Suppose you find yourself trapped in a tiny house with a growing child. I mean a very tiny house, and a rapidly growing child — you are already up against the wall of the house and in a

minute you'll be crushed. The child on the other hand won't be crushed to death; if nothing is done to stop him from growing he'll be hurt, but in the end he'll simply burst open the house and walk out a free man. [p. 8]

3. If Jones has found and fastened on a certain coat, which he needs to keep him from freezing, but which Smith also needs to keep him from freezing, then it is not impartiality that says "I cannot choose between you" when Smith owns the coat. [p. 9]

4. If I am sick unto death, and the only thing that will save my life is the touch of Henry Fonda's cool hand on my fevered brow, then all the same, I have no right to be given the touch of Henry Fonda's cool hand on my fevered brow. [p. 11]

5. If the room is stuffy and I therefore open a window to air it, and a burglar climbs in, it would be absurd to say, "Ah, now he can stay, she's given him a right to the use of her house — for she is partially responsible for his presence there, having voluntarily done what enabled him to get in, in full knowledge, that there are such things as burglars, and that burglars do burgle." [p. 14]

6. Suppose it were like this: people seeds drift about in the air like pollen, and if you open your windows, one may drift in and take root in your carpet or upholstery. You don't want children, so you fix up your windows with fine-mesh screens, the very best you can buy. As can happen, however, and on very, very rare occasions does happen, one of the screens is defective; and a seed drifts in and takes root. Does the person-plant who now develops have a right to use your house? Surely not.... [p. 15]

7. [Suppose that a box of chocolates is given to one of two brothers.] There he sits stolidly eating his way through the box, his small brother watching enviously. Here we are likely to say, "You ought not to be so mean. You ought to give your brother some of those chocolates." My own view is that it just does not follow from the truth of this that the brother has any right to any of the chocolates. [p. 16]

8. A violent aggressor nation has threatened us with death unless we allow ourselves to be enslaved by it. It has ... a monster missile launcher [with interior tunnels that can only be triggered by a trained team of] very young children, two-year olds in fact. The children will be killed if the system is disabled by bombing them or the launcher. Of course, some very high-minded people may say we must not bomb in either case: after all, the children are innocent! Lower-minded people, like me, will say we can bomb in either case.... [p. 120]

Wertheimer's examples are these:

> 9. . . . respect for a fetus cannot be wrung from us as respect for a Negro can be. . . . After all, there is not much we can do with a fetus; either we let it out or we do it in. I have little hope of seeing a justification for doing one thing or the other unless this situation changes. [p. 49]
>
> 10. Close your eyes for a moment and imagine that . . . the relevant cutaneous and membranous shields become transparent from conception to parturition, so that when a mother puts aside her modesty and her clothing, the developing fetus would be in full public view? [p. 47]
>
> 11. Or suppose instead, or in addition, that anyone could at any time pluck a fetus from its womb, air it, observe it, fondle it, and then stick it back in after a few minutes. [p. 47]
>
> 12. Suppose that dogs or things could and did talk. . . . [p. 49]
>
> 13. If we build robots with a psychology isomorphic with ours and a physical structure comparable to ours, should we award them civil rights? [p. 48]

Tooley's:

> 14. . . . it is obvious that if we encountered other "rational minds," such as Martians, the fact that their physiological make-up was very different from our own would not be grounds for denying them a right to life. Similarly, it is clear that the development of human form is not in itself a morally relevant event. . . . The appeal is, I think, purely emotional. [p. 68]
>
> 15. Suppose at some future time a chemical were to be discovered which when injected into the brain of a kitten could cause the kitten to develop into a cat possessing a brain of the sort possessed by humans. . . . [Suppose some "neutralizing chemical" could be injected to stop the development. Since it is not wrong to kill or arrest the development of chemically induced rational animals,] neither can it be seriously wrong to destroy a member of homo sapiens which lacks such properties, but will naturally come to have them. [pp. 75–76]

Warren's:

> 16. Suppose that our space explorer falls into the hands of an alien culture, whose scientists decide to create a few hundred thousand or more human beings by breaking his body into com-

ponent cells, and using these to create fully developed human beings, with, of course, his genetic code. We may imagine that each of these newly created men will have all of the original man's abilities, skills, knowledge, and so on, and also have an individual self-concept, in short, that each of them will be a bona fide (though hardly unique) person. . . . I maintain that in such a situation he would have every right to escape if he could, and thus deprive all of these potential people of their potential lives; for his right to life outweighs all of theirs together, in spite of the fact that they are all genetically human, all innocent, and all have a very high probability of becoming people very soon, if only he refrains from action. [p. 134]

Sixteen examples (and there are variations) are used to analyze the morality of abortion. But what examples! The world of the philosopher is filled with people seeds, child missile launchers, Martians, talking robots, dogs, kittens, chimps, jigsaw cells that form human beings, transparent wombs, and cool hands — everything in fact but fetuses growing in wombs and infants cradled in parents' arms. The sixteen examples force one to ask why the philosopher's imagination is set loose to explore every possible moral dilemma *except* those which people confront in their everyday lives. The philosopher's response is that we cannot confront the human condition directly. One might pass off as philosophy a "taboo rather than a rational prohibition." The revulsion to infanticide "is like the reaction of previous generations to masturbation or oral sex."[9] For these writers visceral philosophizing must surely be avoided. If the cost involves discussing injections into kittens rather than saline solutions into fetuses or Martian physiognomy rather than fetal development or Henry Fonda's cool hand rather than parental care, so be it.

Philosophers have moved into the world of fantasy in the same way and with the same verve that social scientists moved into the world of quantifiable facts. We are admonished to liberate ourselves, both from what are viewed as merely personal feelings and from the superficiality of unordered reality, in order to steel ourselves for the consequences of the real objectivity of a method. But the attainment of objectivity through fantasy exacts a cost that is quite high and not readily discernible. Nearly all of the sixteen examples are models of extreme moral situations. Either our own life is threatened or we are placed in the position of threatening others, or we find ourselves confronted with a set of facts that throw our moral habits into chaos. It is very questionable whether the moral dimensions of our lives can be clarified in circumstances in which the very basis for morality is no longer present. Most moral principles are based upon certain social conditions; among them are regularities in human relations. On these terms moral systems are able to encompass relatively complex rules involving individual calculations, assessments of the motivations of self and others. There are also sets of excuses for failure, under relatively fixed circumstances, to do one's duty. Moreover, moral systems are based upon the good faith of others. In extreme situations none of these conditions exist. People do not know whom to trust, and they cannot take for granted existing social roles; they no longer know which actions are excusable and which ones are not. The extreme condition forces us to contract whatever morality we have left. A quiet dispassionate egoism, consistent only with the demands of the situation, appears as a sensible, even laudable, mode of behavior. In situations of extreme suffering, say Thomson's tiny dwelling which houses you and the growing child, a calm and dispassionate murder, to save one's own life of course, can be seen as a necessary and even vaguely heroic action. What was one supposed to do? If one kept one's inner feelings intact, the victim would surely have understood. All of us can now thankfully turn our heads away and, if not forget the incident, push it into our unconscious. How can one speak of murder under such unbearable stress? This is why Thomson's eighth example is so helpful to her case. After partially laying her example before us, she whispers, "So far, so good. Nothing bizarre yet."[10] There is her warning. If the reader believes he still has hold of conventional moral sense, he is now forewarned. Not only does a violent aggressor nation threaten to destroy us, but it uses children to trigger its missiles. Any anticipated just-war doctrine must now cope with murder of innocents. Only now she can make her case with ease and almost make it appear noble: "Of course, some very high-minded people may say we must not bomb in either case: after all, the children are innocent! Lower-minded people, like me, will say we can bomb in either case: after all, it is the violent aggressor nation which itself imposed that risk on the children."[11] It takes an extremely confident thinker to ascribe low-mindedness to her own views. But the confidence is justified. A bizarre fantasy is placed before us. Our own survival is threatened and ironically we are forced to accept a "realistic" alternative. Anything other than a flat, calculating egoism is folly, an escape from "facts." Never mind that the facts are fantasy or, at most, distillations of those bizarre real-life situations that are so rare as to cause people that do live through them to refer to them as unreal. Think carefully and you will commend me, we are exhorted — place your high-minded morals aside. Thomson knows the argument is now won. Two pages were spent on constructing the analogy. Only a sentence needs to be devoted to abortion itself. The aborted fetus is not innocent, even in the technical sense. The belief in innocence is only "a play on the word" which made it seem that the fetus "did fall under it."[12]

The use of the bizarre confrontation with a new reality serves the same purpose for the philosophers as the extreme situation based upon some lifeboat analogy. Seven of the sixteen examples deal with talking robots or chimps, "human" cats, Martians, or cloning. The desired effect here is to show us that our moral convictions are based upon limited experience. We are instructed to expand our conception of humanity in order to later collapse it when confronted with the issue of abortion. In dealing with the human physiognomy of the fetus, Tooley reminds us that Martians might not look like human beings at all, yet their different physiological make-up "would not be grounds for denying them a right to life." From this he draws the conclusion that "the development of the human form is not in itself a morally relevant event."[13] Extraordinary conclusions follow from extraordinary examples. An argument that has served as the basis for refuting all manner of racial and ethnic prejudices for centuries, an argument that was given a timeless eloquence in the speech of Shakespeare's Shylock, is now, on the basis of the rumination that there may be Martians who think like humans but look like tables or chairs, to be disregarded as not a "morally relevant event." Our feelings of empathy and even compassion rest on an appeal that is "purely emotional."

Let me quote from a recent account of abortion and let the reader judge whether the "purely emotional" reaction to the human form is an unimportant one without sociological and even philosophical import:[14]

> One day driven by my own need to arrive at a measure of clarity, I go into the room, place my stuff on the floor next to the garbage cans and pull on a pair of gloves. Planting myself in front of the table, balanced, legs slightly apart, I remove with one hand the lid of a bucket. . . . I look inside the bucket in front of me. There is a small naked person in there floating in bloody liquid — plainly the tragic victim of a drowning accident. Then, perhaps this was no accident because the body is purple with bruises and the face has the agonized tautness of one forced to die too soon. I have seen this face before, on a Russian soldier lying on a frozen snow-covered hill stiff with death and cold.

Does this emotional reaction — one which triggered an association with another human death — become not morally relevant because we can imagine Martians who do not look like us? There are many differences — speech, mannerisms, customs, and, of course, variations in physical characteristics — which have led people to regard one another as nonhuman. Yet what greater bond is available to allow human beings to reach across walls of hatred than the perception of the simple connection between their own image and that of others? We even may leave aside the mythical significance of the desire to have a god who also looks like us. The universal human reactions to a smile or to a grimace from pain allow us to forge a social bond. No doubt it is a meager enough basis for such a bond, often left fallow and corrupted by other social pressures. Wertheimer's argument 9 that respect for the fetus cannot be wrung from us in the way respect for the Negro can because "there is not much we can do with a fetus" is an inadequate one.[15] Whatever strength it has is based upon the assertion that the fetus is some isolated "thing," biologically quite independent of "personhood." Yet one wonders what these philosophers have in mind as a substitute.

GREEDY INDIVIDUALS

The question of abortion, as important as it is, is only a part of larger questions about human life and the conditions under which we ought to live. In this respect, the examples of these philosophers are even more instructive. Let us take these examples quite seriously: not just as clarificatory metaphors for arguments about abortion but as parables which can reveal their view of the world.

A number of years ago, Lewis Coser wrote a very provocative article in which he outlined the concept of a "greedy organization."[16] The greedy organization sought to reproduce individuals without a private self, sucking up the individual's substance, leaving only a shell. Coser suggested that part of the failure of utopian communities to survive for very long could be traced to the nature of their own organizational structure. Individuals were so socialized into community norms that they had no values to transmit *as parents* in the next generation. But our philosophers of abortion have carried liberalism into the opposite direction. For they have conjured individuals that are able to reject the emotion of communal solidarity in a way that makes them "greedy individuals." They are not greedy in the traditional sense of being driven by desire for money. Their greed is of a subtler and far more deadening sort.

The image of the greedy individual pervades the discussion of each of our philosophers and it is a pity that it should take the form of the traditional liberal's doctrine of rights. This becomes quite clear in Thomson's treatment of abortion. Each of her examples is designed to make the case of a *right* to abortion on the part of the mother even if the fetus has the *right* to live. In example 4 the sick person has no *right* to receive Henry Fonda's cool hand; in example 5 the burglar has no *right* to burgle even if I leave my house unattended; in example 7 the unfairly treated brother has no *right* to my candy. The claimant in each case here, the sick person, the burglar, the brother, the child crusher, is a surrogate to the fetus. (What an irony that while common sexual language has been condemned as dehumanizing, unborn children can by analogy be described as burglars and people seeds!)

The person of diminished capacity, once a troublesome point for the traditional natural-rights theorists, now becomes a cornerstone for our philosophers. A fetus cannot reason, cannot claim his or her rights, and may have a limited capacity for pain. How easy it is to make the case for its demise on a rights basis. We saw how Hobbes found the issue of diminished rights a mixed blessing in forming his account of obligation. Children were creatures who stood outside the covenant but at the same time were subject to parental authority.

With Hobbes, parent-child relationships stand in an awkward juxtaposition. On the one hand, the cold rationalism of Hobbes prevents any real examination of the relationship; on the other hand, the force of the historical reality of the state of nature depends upon the proliferation of the family. If it didn't, the state of nature would have been even shorter than Hobbes himself had feared. But the world of the twentieth-century philosopher is not at all so harsh. The most compelling motive for family organization, protection against invaders, is absent. Life is much more comfortable, so much so that couples can contemplate esthetic abortions, balancing the gender and regulating the order of appearance of their children. Tooley introduces a further wrinkle in an attempt to reproduce Hobbesian calculation: that perhaps one ought to provide compensation to a mother who does not abort a fetus.

The main point, however, is that a rights model takes as its basis self-sufficient rational human beings. A good portion of humanity at any given moment does not fit that criterion and children and those who are about to become children make up the bulk of the segment of that population. Since a rights model is designed to make us aware of our self-sufficiency as moral agents, it says little about solidarity among human beings. Let me illustrate by examining briefly how these philosophers approach issues which place a burden upon a rights view of reality. Two tendencies are predominant: (1) an unwillingness to examine relationships that cannot fit into a rights mode; (2) a definite willingness, even a positive desire, to constrict the import of the description "human." Thomson is very much concerned that some people are inclined to use the term "right" too broadly: "This use of the term is perhaps so common that it cannot be called wrong; nevertheless it seems to me to be an unfortunate loosening of what we would do better to keep a tight rein on."[17] By keeping a tight rein on rights, Thomson is able to argue that "nobody is morally required to make large sacrifices, of health, of all other interests and concerns, of all other duties and commitments, for nine years, or even for nine months, in order to keep another person alive."[18] She asks: "In some views having a right to life includes having a right to be given at least the bare minimum one needs for continued life. But suppose that what in fact is the bare minimum a man needs for continued life is something he has no right at all to be given?"[19] Let's leave Henry Fonda and the violinist aside for a moment. Children require great sacrifices of health, time, money, even emotional stability. Women submit to discomfort, pain, and reduced sexual capacity during pregnancy. They bear stretch marks. Parents loose sleep, give up hobbies, lose mobility, money, privacy. Even with comfortable incomes and pregnancy leaves, these are large sacrifices. So large, in fact, that portions of a whole generation inbred with a rights model have decided to remain childless. On Thomson's standards, *no* pregnancy ought to be brought to term on the basis of rights.

Now Thomson is not an insensitive person; she recognizes frivolous reasons for abortions. She mentions a woman who contemplates abortion in her seventh month just to avoid the nuisance of postponing a trip abroad. We will be merciful and not continue to explore the difference between a trip abroad and maintenance of a "life style" or general career advancement. If our interpretation of Thomson is correct and no abortion is a violation of right, she does, nevertheless, seem willing to mark off some as "positively indecent." In fact in examples 1 (if the hookup is only nine days), 4, and 7, she argues that help on sharing is required out of decency. But what is the difference between an indecent act and a violation of rights? Thomson argues that the law can help, that there is a distinction between a minimally decent Samaritan and a good one. But we know that even if we refrain from everything the law forbids, and do not cheat, murder, and steal, but do *nothing* to *help* others, the resultant society could still be a very unpleasant one. The fact that there was no law broken when 38 persons stood by and let Kitty Genovese be killed indicates the importance of fostering relationships of aid when the law is silent. It appears that decency for Thomson is not equivalent to a supererogatory act, for the woman who aborts to go on her trip is subject to moral condemnation and the woman who unhooks the violinist is not. If this is the case, decency as a concept stands behind respect for rights and supererogation in terms of moral rectitude. And if that is the case, Thomson has presented a more extreme case then we have been giving her credit for. But as with her discussion of rights, she is anxious here to keep a tight rein on the concept of decency. For decent actions often require sacrifice. The brother must give up his chocolates; Henry Fonda must fly in from California.

What Thomson fails to see is that in a good society decent actions are probably as important as respect for rights. A rights model does little to explain those personal relationships that lie beneath the contractual view of life, and which set the tone for relationships among friends, lovers, parents and children. Our anger at the refusal of one to share a bounty (even a box of chocolates) with another is as severe as if it were a violation of rights. To say that an action is "positively indecent" is a strong moral condemnation that admits an important violation of human interaction, one which if violated regularly would make respect for rights meaningless. Who would want to live in a society in which everyone was positively indecent to another and at the same time positively scrupulous in respecting another's rights? And would such a society be possible?

Warren and Tooley present the concept of the greedy individual in even clearer relief. Warren sniggers at Thomson's notion of indecency. "Whether or not it would be *indecent* (whatever that means) for a woman in her seventh month to obtain an abortion just to avoid having to postpone a trip to Europe, it would not, in itself, be *immoral,* and therefore it ought to be permitted."[20] She goes on to develop an extremely narrow definition of personhood. For Warren there are two senses of what we mean when we say an entity is human: the mere genetic sense, "the sense in which *any* member of the species is a human being, and no member of any other species could be,"[21] and the moral sense. Warren insists that the latter sense is the only acceptable one. A genetic humanity is neither necessary nor sufficient for establishing that an entity is a person. We would naturally be puzzled about her unwillingness to accept genetic humanity as a necessary condition for personhood, but Warren reminds us of "highly advanced, self-aware" robots and extraterrestrial beings.

What makes one a person (or human in the moral sense)? Warren suggests five "traits" and we list them below:[22]

1. Consciousness (of objects and events external and/or internal to the being), and in particular the capacity to feel pain.
2. Reasoning (the *developed* capacity to solve new and relatively complex problems).
3. Self-motivated activity (activity which is relatively independent of either genetic or direct external control).
4. The capacity to communicate, by whatever means, messages of indefinite variety of types, that is, not just an indefinite number of possible contents, but on indefinitely many possible topics.
5. The presence of self-concepts, and self-awareness, either individual or racial, or both.

She toys with the idea that 1 and 2 alone may be sufficient for personhood. Criteria 1–3 are "quite probably sufficient." In any case we are told that her claim is "so obvious" that "anyone who denied it, and claimed that a being which satisfied none of 1–5 was a person all the same, would thereby demonstrate that he had no notion at all of what a person is — perhaps because he had confused the concept of a person with that of genetic humanity."[23] Note how deftly Warren plies her trade. A fetus *might* be able to feel pain, but surely he or she is unable to reason, especially with *developed* capacity. What is shocking about this criterion 2 is that a two-year-old may fail to meet it. What this means, my readers, and let us be direct about this, is that we must restrain our emotions and come to regard an infant as not a person at all but a mere clump of genetic humanity. Are not then the comatose patient, the schizophrenic, the catatonic, the unaided mute, the paraplegic also in danger of slipping into that awful category "genetic human." I do not mean to push Warren down a slippery slope: the terrain appears to be of her own making. See how swiftly she disposes of the potentiality argument: "Thus, in the *relevant* respects, a fetus, even a fully developed one, is considerably less personlike than is an average mature mammal, indeed the average fish."[24] The fetus, a being who in a few months will have a consciousness and the capacity to feel pain, is *less personlike* than a "newborn guppy."

We must ask what the consequences are of this collapsing humanity, this clarification of the "confusion" over the genetic and moral senses of humanity. As with the other philosophers of abortion, Warren insists we cannot, must not, be guided by moral repulsion, "since mere emotional responses cannot take the place of moral reasoning in determining what ought to be permitted."[25] Let us leave emotion aside for a moment. Warren insists that "educating people to the kinds of moral distinctions we have been making here will enhance rather than erode the level of respect for human life." There are very few general laws of social science but we can offer one that has a deserved claim: *The restriction of the concept of humanity in any sphere never enhances a respect for human life.* It did not enhance the rights of slaves, prisoners of war, criminals, traitors, women, children, Jews, blacks, heretics, workers, capitalists, Slavs, Gypsies. The restriction of the concept of personhood in regard to the fetus will not do so either. Reminders that we are cruel to mammals and that we would need to extend humanity to Martians do not alter the picture. Nor does it change the result if the restriction is achieved in the context of philosophical analysis and through the concept of human rights.

It is interesting that Hobbes' dilemma should reappear in Warren's analysis. In responding to criticisms that her position justified infanticide, Warren reluctantly introduces emotion into her account. She is careful not to object personally to infanticide: "Inasmuch as most people, regardless of how they feel about the morality of abortion, consider infanticide a form of murder, this might appear to represent a serious flaw in my argument."[26] We must assume that if most people accepted the morality of infanticide, Warren would regard her argument as without the flaw. A casual empiricism is entered into this discussion. Since people "in this country and in this period of history" would be "deprived of a great deal of pleasure by an infant's destruction," infanticide is wrong for reasons analogous to those which make it wrong to destroy great works of art. Moreover, most of us would rather be taxed to support orphanages to preserve infants. But what if some resented these tax dollars and regarded them as a violation of the right to dispose of their income as they see fit? Warren has an answer for that as well:[27]

> On the other hand, it follows from my argument that when an unwanted or defective infant is born into a society which cannot afford and/or is not willing to care for it, then its destruction is permissible. This conclusion will, no doubt, strike many people as heartless and immoral; but remember that the very existence of people who feel this way, and who are willing and able to provide care for unwanted infants, is reason enough to conclude that they should be preserved.

What she never answers or even considers is how likely support for children is going to be in the sort of society she describes. She rests her case on "the very existence of people who feel this way." But earlier we were told that such "mere emotional responses" were an illegitimate basis for moral reasoning. The protection against infanticide rests upon feelings which she has spent pages attempting to dispel.

None of the philosophers we have reviewed have asked how individuals even within a single generation might be helped to establish relations of caring among one another. To pursue the latter direction involves seeking out patterns of affection and searching for conditions under which they can be sustained. These relationships of caring may provide the link between current generations and those of the future and the past. It does not require a romantic mind to see in the man-woman relationship, complicated as it is and distorted as it can become, the basis for a vital link between generations. Precisely how parenthood does serve to make and keep life human is a question beyond the scope of this chapter.[28] But certainly the maintenance of an affective tie that unites generations is an important part of what it is to be human, as important as the five traits of moral humanity we have been offered. There is something seriously wrong with theories that insist upon viewing fetal development through analogies which emphasize their growth as alien and threatening. If abortion can be justified only on those terms, with the images of the unborn as intruders upon our rights, then abortion does indeed lessen our own humanity.

11

ROUSSEAU'S CHILDREN: ROMANTIC ALTERNATIVES

Many critics have sarcastically noted the paradox of Rousseau's emotional ode to the family and his alleged dismissal of his own children to an orphanage. This behavior, which was so characteristic of Rousseau, does illustrate for us the nature of his writings. We outlined three alternatives that he offered: the familial bond in an apolitical setting, the citizen bond, with all the restrictions on family life that Rousseau thought it entailed, and the solitary life. We only mentioned the last alternative. While Rousseau lived the role of the *promeneur solitaire* most of his life, he seems to have felt quite guilty about it and only in his last work offers it to us as the best life.[1] The key to Rousseau in each case lies in his insistence that his utopias be self-willed. Even Fourier, the romantic gone resolutely collectivist, retains a voluntarist veneer to his sexual empire.

These alternatives tell us much about the nature of romantic individualism and its ambivalence in regard to the family. The fascination with self is much more rich, tormented, and intense than the liberal analogue of individual development. Accordingly romantic individualism rapidly slides back and forth from apparently contradictory alternatives in life. The romantic individualist is basically a personalist in politics but he will recommend strong institutional structures if he feels they can aid his search for the authentic self. He will swing, as Rousseau did, from libertinism to celibacy; from exploring the duties of dyadic love to the existential qualities of the sex act depersonalized.[2]

Rousseau's children, those contemporary political theorists who follow in the tradition of romantic individualism, reveal the same ambiguity.

However, there is a new element that characterizes current romantic individualism. While Rousseau in part created the emotional base of the modern family as part of his search for the proper setting for the authentic self, these writers are searching for new family forms. Thus Fourier looms close in the background; further behind is an even different image.

R. D. LAING AND THE PATHOLOGY OF FAMILY LIFE

A brief excursion into R. D. Laing's famous analysis of the family is the best starting point for our review. Laing portrays the family as a political institution grounded on a kinship-based affective tie. Family dynamics are generically totalitarian. They are compared to the "Nazi mystique of the Country and the Party." Two concepts designed to expose the tenacity of family ties are used to make the point. One is the "series," the structural creation of the family that permits it to distinguish itself from other groups. The series represents the passive aspect of group structure. It derives its unity not from the mutual affection of its members but from the sheer delineation by the family of itself as apart from other groups. Thus families survive by creating a world distinct from themselves and lay the perceptual groundwork for all sorts of nefarious distinctions: good/bad, male/female, white/black, Jews/Gentiles. These collections of serial objects, which from Laing's viewpoint are uniquely created by the family, result in a "conformity to a *presence* that is everywhere *elsewhere*." Any attempt to break down this dualism is met with an extraordinary reaction from the family:

> A crisis will occur if any member of the family wishes to leave by getting the "family" out of his system, or dissolving the "family" in himself. Within the family, the "family" may be felt as the whole world. To destroy the "family" may be experienced as worse than murder or more selfish than suicide.[3]

The other boundary defining concept of the family is the "nexus." Here group unification is obtained by an internal mechanism such as reciprocity and mutual affection. In a sense, Laing's two concepts of series and nexus parallel Parsons' instrumental and expressive roles. The series has an instrumental cast; its manifest function is the delineation of the family as a group. On the other hand, the nexus is a dynamic that arises from the presence of family members themselves; its function is instrumental. But Laing's analysis is designed to demystify the family. Beneath the "highest ethic of reciprocal concern" is the generation of terror, phantasy, and domination.

Laing's juxtaposition of the following "mappings" can make our point:

M (to fourteen-year-old daughter): You are evil.
D: No, I'm not.
M: Yes, you are.
D: Uncle Jack doesn't think so.
M: He doesn't love you as I do. Only a mother really knows the truth about her daughter, and only one who loves you as I do will ever tell you the truth about yourself no matter what it is. If you don't believe me, just look at yourself in the mirror carefully and you will see that I'm telling the truth.

M: You are pretty.
D: No, I'm not.
M: Yes, you are.
D: Uncle Jack doesn't think so.
M: He doesn't love you as I do. Only a mother really knows the truth about her daughter, and only one who loves you as I do will ever tell you the truth about yourself no matter what it is. If you don't believe me, just look at yourself in the mirror carefully, and you will see that I'm telling you the truth.[4]

For Laing this structural identity which permits the mapping of "evil" and "pretty" into our psyches shows us that he has not "recklessly generalized from particular instances of 'pathology' to the 'normal.'" He continues: "... the gap between what seems to be the abnormal or deviant or pathological, and what does not, may be more superficial than it appears at first encounter."[5] Never mind that another conclusion might be warranted, that the family like any social institution has the capacity for destroying as well as building human personality. The family has already been diagnosed as a pathological institution, an organic knot that is "tied, *very, very* tight — around the throat, as it were, of the whole human species."[6]

THE SEARCH FOR AUTHENTIC FAMILY FORMS

Laing's description of the family led him to advocate a life of Rousseauean revery. Only a solitary existence can produce a world without an inside/outside dimension. One must "disentangle himself from his body" to achieve a state of "discarnate spirituality." Romantic individualism took the form of mysticism:

This journey is experienced as "going further in," as going back through one's personal life, in and back and through and beyond it into the experience of all mankind, of the primal man, of Adam and perhaps even further into the beings of animals, vegetables and minerals.[7]

Other writers, however, have not been quite so anxious to take leave of this world. They are attempting to find a "self-actualizing" alternative to the modern family. The search for new family forms tells us much about the character of romantic individualism. Listed below are the most frequently cited alternatives:

(a) swinging
(b) single parenthood
(c) three-parent families
(d) group marriage
(e) communes
(f) open marriages
(g) gay marriages and families
(h) "childfree" marriages
(i) celibacy
(j) singlehood

Some of them (i and j) involve a denial of the family altogether, some represent truncated family forms (b, h), some are recommended in the name of pluralism (d, e, g) and some are offered as variations in the conventional family (a, f). All of them, however, are justified in terms of their "self-actualizing" potential in relation to the modern family. Each of those forms includes "self-actualization, autonomy, gender equality, intimacy in a variety of interpersonal relations, openness in communication, and sexual variety."[8] Variant family forms have become more visible, partly as a result of the "self-revelation" and the emphasis upon "'open' relationships."[9] "We are reminded that people have a variety of affective and sexual needs, and they increasingly come to realize that they may need a variety of intimate relationships within which they can be satisfied."[10]

If we look more closely at these new recommended family forms we receive a very clear picture of their basic unity. The most common critique of the modern family is its stability and permanence. The modern family is a "greedy organization," a totalitarian society in microcosm. If self-actualization is to be attained in a world that we all share, the postmodern family must be dissolved. Thus for a family form to be judged acceptable it must be voluntary, self-willed, and temporary; the family must reflect the wishes of the liberated soul.

The first step beyond treating the modern family as a pathological institution involves a relabeling of "deviant" family forms. If the modern family is dysfunctional in terms of self-actualization standards, then its failures must be seen as new modal types. The switch is much like determining the disease as a misdiagnosed normal state. This is not an easy turnabout to achieve. One recent analysis relies upon a distinction between "deviant" and "variant" to produce the desired effect:

> In terms of the larger social structure, they are similar in that both are non-modal forms in a presumed modality which is nuclear, though the nuclear form may undergo re-formation with divorce and remarriage. Both "deviant" and "variant" forms do, however, tend to affront the values embodied in the prevailing mores. "Deviant" forms, consensual unions, female-headed households, resulting from illegitimacy and desertion, child abuses, alcoholic parents, have "variant" counterparts, such as cohabitation, serial monogamy, and voluntary single parenthood. There are also communes in which children are allowed access to the sexual and drug-taking practices of their parents and which might be viewed as "abuse" in other contacts.[11]

How does one distinguish between child abuse and "sexual freedom" within the family, between alcoholism and "drug-taking practices"? The ingenuity of social scientists can be astonishing. Variant family practices are "voluntary or intentional formulations created with relatively high degrees of consciousness of their unusual character."[12] Deviant forms are "involuntary, unintentional results of inability to conform to model expectations."[13] In other words, if incest is committed with forethought and a social theory behind it, it is a form of political experimentation; if it is done on impulse it is the result of the brutalization produced by the modern family. The class bias here is too clear. Pathology cannot be equated solely with intentional action whether caused by structural strains on the conventional family or not. Therefore, changes in family organization must be seen as part of a larger process of change. Perhaps *all* practices that challenge the modern family must be labeled variant.[14] The category of deviant is to be eliminated; pathology now can be reserved solely for the modern family. Human misery can be blamed on the structural strains of transitions, necessary pain on the road to recovery.

THE FAMILY AS VOLUNTARY ORGANIZATION

The new model for the postmodern family is the voluntary organization. The family must be constituted so that one can move in and out of its structure with a minimum of effort. Each alternative on our list is especially able to cope with this new requirement. The "childfree" marriage allows for greater movement in and out of the dyadic tie and the home than does the conventional family. Childlessness, for example, may be one type of structural change that may be adopted by some couples who desire equal status linkages with the occupational system.[15] But childlessness only alleviates the problem. Only serial polygamy and "non-marital, semi-permanent living arrangements" can provide enough "flexibility."[16] Communes are always an attractive alternative because they fit the model of the "voluntary family."[17] They represent a family that is self-willed, without kinship, and in the words of one sociologist, without "all the weight a two-person bond must bear."[18] But in this model even the commune should provide easy egress. This is an option not readily available to such organizations in the past. The contemporary commune is "temporary and subject to much change and turnover of members, it is this kind of temporary system that some communes themselves seek . . . nothing should be forever . . . change is part of life."[19] One writer values the commune, the new alternative to the family, because it is such a "temporary option":

> . . . communes may constitute places of renewal, self-integration, and alternative experience. As extended kin networks and joint households offer reduced attractions for or contradict such experiences, intentional families tend to serve as way stations to self-knowledge. . . . Communal families moreover easily fit the modular conception of industrialized societies; ongoing communes, like the monasteries or Twin Oaks, can absorb and send forth members without internal disruption.[20]

One can see how this sketch of one Rousseauean alternative can slip into a Fourierist pluralism. It is true that in this version libidinal desires do not ooze throughout the social structure. But there is much concern over the unhealthiness and undesirability of sexual exclusivity in the dyad. Monogamy is a severe restraint upon self-actualization in sexual life: "It is the maintenance by one man or woman of the effective right to exclude indefinitely all others from erotic access to the conjugal partner."[21] In other words, monogamy involves restraining oneself to the "absurdity" of one single event. Falling in love and fidelity may mean no more than a lack of courage:

> There is a formal contradiction between the voluntary contractual character of "marriage" and the spontaneous uncontrollable character of "love" — the passion that is celebrated precisely for its involuntary force. The notion that it occurs only once in every life and can therefore be integrated into a voluntary contract becomes decreasingly plausible in the light of everyday experience — once sexual expression as a psycho-ideological system becomes at all relaxed.[22]

The latest euphemism, "recreational sex," is designed for more than two to play. But more importantly it requires political and bureaucratic institutions for the proper setting.

The real irony in the new romantic individualist approach to the family is that this new pluralism of family forms is hardly pluralistic at all. The various alternatives are presented as a veritable smorgasbord but are justified by a single monistic standard. And that standard must somehow be enforced. Not surprisingly the enforcement strategies are presented in the guise of pluralism. Variant family forms must develop "positive" and "supportive" ideologies, engender "social movements" in their behalf which finance long-term lobbying groups.[23] Spontaneity and experimentation must be politicized and rationalized.

THE BUREAUCRATIZATION OF NEW FAMILY FORMS

Earlier in this chapter, and in our discussion of Rousseau and Fourier as well, we noted that the romantic approach is not at all averse to supporting large bureaucratic structures in pursuit of its aims. The connection between self-actualization and professionalization, routinization and rationalization — the major characteristics of bureaucratic organization — is, despite their apparent irreconcilability, firmly made in the proposals of current romantics that go beyond endorsing the list of family alternatives.

Genetic technology is warmly embraced by many of these writers. The fascination with *in vitro* pregnancy is the result of its promise to free women from the "tyranny of their reproductive biology" and free men of the "implicit equation now made between husbands and fathers."[24] Cloning would "reduce the prime motive for marriage" and "dethrone the heterosexual couple."[25] The rationalization of reproduction entrained by genetic technology is hardly noticed in the rush to free us to pursue *individual* liberation. Childbearing could be a profession; professional breeders could be paid salaries, like today's athletes, for 15 to 20 years of their prime breeding time.[26] Mothers could live in "well-run dormitories, with excellent physical care, food and entertainment." Children conceived by professional breeders could be reared by "well-trained professional parent-teachers in age graded groups." Parenting is written off as an inappropriate self-actualizing act. Or perhaps we should let childrearing remain in the hands of "volunteers," using monetary rewards to elevate parenthood to "the status of a religious vocation." But the volunteers of children still must be separated from the nonparentally minded to receive training in special schools for their main future roles as producers and socializers of children. But they would have to vow to live with their spouses and children for life. They would naturally be paid for their parenting work but would be permitted to work at farming, handicrafts, or cottage industries. However, these primitives in our midst are likely to be troublesome:

> The disadvantage of such a system of socialization is that, if all family life were relegated to a select group, a deep social division between the family-oriented and the individually-oriented would soon emerge because of the different social values of each group. The family-oriented, even today, value monogamy, kinship, geographical stability, and their supportive religious beliefs, and disapprove of free sexuality, divorce, contraception, and abortion on demand. In contrast, the individually-oriented value flexible mating rules, efficient contraception, and abortion on demand in order to pursue their individual goals, be they travels, job hopping, creative work, or polymorphous sexuality. Encouraging production and rearing of children only by those with a family-oriented calling, while non-family-oriented are left free to follow their individual pursuits, is *probably not compatible* with a unified society.[27]

So much for pluralism.

A more rational proposal is offered in its place. Divide the world into child-oriented and non-child-oriented economies. "The world's population needs could adequately be met in the near future by just the currently overpopulated, underdeveloped countries."[28] Develop a "world system of child exchange" and have parents "ship their children to the low-fertility countries to supply their needs for labor."[29] Of course there is the problem of irrational "affectionate ties" to one's own biological children. One must devise an arrangement by which the underpopulated industrialized nations would buy "surplus children" at an early age. This would also insure that "qualified imported children" would have an opportunity to be educated for "administrative and professional positions."

Children are now depicted as commodities in a global economic market. One wonders what would happen if there were a sustained glut. In any case, children are so far beyond the scope of the self-actualizing adult's interests, that they are seen only as administrative replacements.

Less grandiose proposals reveal the same desire to free adults to search for appropriate life styles by bureaucraticizing the remains of the family. Carl Levett has suggested that a third parent be slipped into the modern family in order to reduce the "side-effects that accelerated individualization has had on parent-child relationships." But the selection and background of the third parent cannot be left to chance:

> The credentials and qualifications of a third parent should be

viewed in the framework of a professional careeer. The background of education, training, and experience would need to be heavily weighted in the areas of education, psychology and social work. Graduate work leading to a master's or doctorate degree would be a logical necessity.[30]

Then there is the question of day-care planning, an issue we will take up later. Suffice it to say that the professional is again the savior. He or she is judged "better trained, more patient, and objective in dealing with children than the mothers."[31] He or she may be more intellectually stimulating.[32] Studies that show the negative aspects of bureaucratic child-caring are passed over as biased. Such studies are inclined to favor individual as opposed to group development and achievement, or they confuse maternal separation with deprivation, or they are in general too much colored by cultural norms.[33]

We saw how demanding was Rousseau's search for the authentic self. In terms of the family, Rousseau attempted to find respite in his construction of romantic patriarchy. Today's writers are much more bold. Their search is more intense. Like Rousseau, however, they find they need help — but not in the quiet of isolated village life or even in the ego dissolution of the city-state. Fourier's collectivism provides some solace. It lets them out of the travails of dyadic relationships and removes libidinal frustrations. But Fourier, too, needed help in organizing his sexual utopia. The new romantics' abandonment of the family and selection of a bureaucratic world represents a natural and understandable conclusion to their quest. It is a more reasonable choice than Rousseau's alternative of the city-state. Rousseauan politics, after all, calls an end to self-actualization. It is designed more to prevent *amour propre* than to promote *amour de soi.* Fourier's model is more utopian. His sexual bureaucracy has a life of its own; it is neutral in respect to need, accommodating everyone, and it is self-perpetuating. The new romantics see the bureaucratization of everyday life in the same light. It will free them of the inflexible structure of the modern family and allow them to pursue their search for the authentic self. They do not appear to have even the slightest notion at all that they are constructing an iron cage, much more confining than the family, around their sweetest sentiments.

12

THE CHILD AS PROLETARIAN: MARXISM AND PSYCHOANALYSIS

In our chapter on Marx and Engels we have shown that the family was never regarded as an obstacle to revolution. Family forms always mirrored economic structure. Morgan's terminology did not perfectly correspond to Engels' purpose but the fit was close enough; savagery had group marriage, barbarism the "pairing family" and civilization monogamy. The watershed, of course, was the transition from pairing to monogamy and this was occasioned by the transition from primitive communism to slavery. When further productivity was halted by the pairing family, the latter was abolished. We even suggested that this relative unconcern about the family was one of the distinguishing features of Marxist socialism. The family need not be wrenched from its mooring in communal experiments; it would die a natural death, swept away by the economic transformations produced by capitalism.

That belief is still widely held by Marxists. Once the productive base was socialized, the family would disappear. Jobs and day care were Lenin's solution to the "family problem," if we could call it that. A recent orthodox Marxist account of the family shows some uneasiness over this formula. "The redefinition of the problem of the family from a moral to an economic problem marks a great advance."[1] But the experiences of Russia and China showed that classic Marxism provided less than a complete model. In the Soviet Union, women have benefited economically from proletarianization but the "psychohistorical heritage of male supremacy was scarcely challenged by the entry of women into industry."[2] In China, sexual life is governed by a severe puritanism. What can Marxists learn from these noble failures? The answer lies in providing women with "child care, public restaurants, laundries, canteens, recreation, etc."[3] Women with jobs again. Of course, socialists must pay more attention to personal life, yet they must recognize that "the prerequisite to realizing the promise of personal life is to abolish its forced separation and isolation."[4]

Those Marxists who have been preoccupied with the durability of capitalism have taken a look at the family close-up and attempted to re-evaluate its role as mere object of social transformation. We will look at two writers who have undertaken this task, Wilhelm Reich and Herbert Marcuse. The paths that their revisions have taken them will tell us more about the modern family and Marxism's struggle against it.

Reich and Marcuse have much in common. Both have written in circumstances that saw Marxist initiatives collapse in the face of what they saw as opportunities. Both have criticized the Soviet experience. Both have sought to refurbish Marx with Freud and rejected Freud in the process. Both have emphasized the role of sexuality in the continuing development of capitalism and searched for a new proletariat in youth. Nevertheless, they reached different assessments on the role of the modern family; they devised different theories of sexuality in support of Marx.

REICH: SEX AND CIVILIZATION

Reich began his career as a Freudian. He left Freud for Marx and eventually rejected both. His work is always more bold and unorthodox than Marcuse's. The latter's critique of Freud is more conventional than Reich's efforts during his Freudian period. Marcuse's Freud is made to fit his Marx, and Marx made to fit Freud. Reich never attempts a synthesis. Freud never fits his ambitions, nor does Marx. Both were makeshift structures that housed his current theories.

On what then do Reich and Marcuse agree? There is one simple point of convergence, the belief that the sexual drive can be safely released and connected to work. Marcuse calls his formula "libidinal work relations" and Reich, always searching for the plain speech of the working class, refers to "natural work democracy." The idea (as an outgrowth of Freud and Marx) is a simple one. We have already shown how Fourier anticipated it. Marx, of course, never had a theory of the libido, although the shape of pure communism was modeled after a sexual metaphor. Work was part of man's being but it was not play. To the extent to which he discussed sexual relationships, he empahsized the new mutuality between men and women. But the sexual sphere stood outside the world of work, so much so that the young Soviet communists were able to categorize sex as a "private matter," "outside the area of regulations."[5] Sexuality was seen in dyadic terms and Marx and Engels saw no conflict between dyadic sex and the economic collective.

Freud split this arrangement down the middle. The dyad was an open threat to the group. He could imagine a cultural community consisting of dyads who were libidinally satisifed with each other and connected with one another through work, but "this desirable state of things does not and never did exist."[6] Civilization simply would not have it and probably rightly so. Human aggressiveness was too strong to remain unrestrained, the satisfaction from work too weak to naturally carry itself. Moreover, the achievements of civilization rest upon sublimated instinctual drives.

Both Reich and Marcuse, having discovered sex in a Freudian sense, set out to attach it to Marxism. At its most basic level, indeed, this was the level with which Reich became most absorbed; this meant uniting sex to work. In the *Function of the Orgasm* Reich relates his discovery:

> The universal fear of the "evil" instinct has had a severely detri- mental effect on the work of psychoanalytic therapy. *Psycho- analysts had unquestioningly accepted the absolute antithesis between nature (instinct and sexuality) and culture (morality, work and duty) and had come to the conclusion that "living out of the impulses" was at variance with cure.* It took me a long time to overcome my fear of these impulses. It was clear that the *asocial impulses which fill the unconscious are vicious and dangerous only as long as the discharge of biological energy by means of natural sexuality is blocked.*[7]

It may have taken Reich a long time to overcome his fear of genital libera- tion. But this was not so with his patients. Their recovery was so thorough and rapid that he was baffled by it: "I did not understand how the tena- cious neurotic process could give way so rapidly."[8] Their new character seemed to function according to "different and hitherto unknown laws."[9] Reich was to conclude that Freud's description of the libido represented only a second layer of personality, an intermediate character layer which does indeed consist "exclusively of cruel, sadistic, lascivious, rapacious, and envious impulses."[10] Beneath this unconscious was buried a third layer, the biological core, which under favorable conditions showed man as "an essentially honest, industrious, cooperative, loving" animal.[11] Psychoanalysis had only exposed the second layer and had not been aware that "every natural, social, or libidinous impulse that wants to spring into action from the biologic core has to pass through the layer of secondary perverse drives and is thereby distorted."[12]

Reich's investigation of the first layer, the conscious self, remains the most respectable portion of his theory. Even after the *Ego and the Id* Freud had regarded the ego as an embattled force, usually under the sway of a demanding and reckless id and a zealous superego, and he openly ex- pressed his sympathy for it. Not so Wilhelm Reich. His first break with the

Freudians involved his insistence that neurotic symptoms were the result of an inadequate sex life. Sexual dysfunction was not merely one symptom of neurosis but was indeed the actual cause.[13] Thus Reich's therapy was ever so much more simple than Freud's: "Those who are psychically ill need but one thing — complete and repeated genital gratification."[14]

The outward manifestations of the neurotic thus became defenses against anxiety created by sexual repression. Reich developed his own therapy on the basis of his own view of neurotic behavior. In the light of today's methods of radical therapy, Reich's efforts have lost their shock value. He would bully patients and make fun of their physical symptoms. In Reich's own words "character analysis gives rise to violent emotional outbursts."[15]

The repressed individual formed a definite personality type. Reich contrasted a "genital character" with a "neurotic character." The neurotic character had sets of armor that protected him. He was polite, overpolite, highly moralistic, and ascetic. Barely hidden beneath the surface was a hatred for authority, sadistic impulses and fantasies, fear of rejection and pain. Thus Reich questioned the orthodox analytic technique of smashing the superego; doing this only left the antisocial layer exposed. It was the genital character which needed to be created, or more properly, to be found. In Reich's description we see a dualism as explicit as Freud's but now an eschatological theory is attached to overcome it. The genital character is everything the neurotic is not — open, kind, decent, and above all, sexually secure. Why was the neurotic character so common? This question and related ones troubled Reich:

> ...if the attributes of the genital character are so self-evident and desirable, why is the intimate relation between sociality and orgastic potency overlooked? — Why has the conception of a sharp antithesis between nature and culture, instinct and morality, body and spirit, devil and god, love and work, become one of the most salient characteristics of our culture and philosophy of life?[16]

Freud had been partially correct. Present-day culture was dependent upon the repression of instincts, but was "culture as such dependent upon sexual repression?"[17] Reich originally thought opposition to his new individual was "scientific cowardice." Later he became openly abusive of Freud's view: "One becomes a bit skeptical and asks how is it possible for the masturbation of small children and the sexual intercourse of adolescents to disrupt the building of gas stations and the manufacturing of airplanes."[18] Sexual repression was in fact a tool of a "minority's interest in material profit."[19] The patriarchal marriage and family was the organization form of repression, "the factory in which the state's structure and ideology are molded."[20]

The family as the sexual structure of society "interlaced" with the economic structure to reproduce the neurotic character. The family's repression of the natural genital sexuality of the child produced the authoritarian personality. He was fearful of authority, obedient, and crippled sexually. In the moral language of the reactionary, he was "good" and "docile." The family produced a morality perfectly adjusted to the authoritarian order. In fact, the family was the "authoritarian state in miniature," the order to which the child must learn to adapt as a preparation for the general social adjustment required of him later.

Thus did Reich's Freudo-Marxism return the family to a central role in socialism: the class order maintained economic domination; the family, sexual repression. Workers were so "infested" with the authoritarian ideology of family life that they were unable to rebel even under favorable economic conditions.

PRIMAL HISTORY REFASHIONED

Having established the family as an institution of domination, Reich searched for its origins. He found both Engels' and Freud's accounts unsatisfactory. What upset Reich most about Freud's primal horde was the supposition that patriarchy preceded matriarchy. In fact, Reich is probably correct on this point. Freud's discussion of matriarchy seems to be mostly an afterthought, an attempt to account for the existence of ancient female deities. For Reich, matriarchy was the first social organization and it formed the basis for another of his moral dualisms. Mother right represented primitive communism and the "farthest-reaching sexual freedom"; father right represented "private property, the enslavement of women, and sexual repression similar to one's own."[21]

But Reich was not entirely satisfied with Engels' formulation either. Natural selection was an inadequate explanation of exogamy. The harmfulness of incest is marginal and the concept of paternity itself must have been unknown to the primitive mind. Reich searches for a sociological explanation that in broad outlines shows similarity to Freud's: exogamy was the result of a violent act the traces of which we still feel. Reich replaces the primal father with the primal mother. The real unit of the maternal primal horde is the brother-sister dyad. And as Engels had his Morgan and Freud had Darwin and Atkinson, Reich has Malinowski as his anthropological mouthpiece. He cites Malinowski's account of a Trobriand legend of a primal mother who came from a hole, bore two children, a brother and a sister who lived in an incestuous relationship. The explanation of the incest taboo must rest then with the renouncing of sexual relations with the sister and the paying of tribute to her spouse. Reich's answer assumes that exogamy arose not from some kind of partition but from "primal catastrophe" between hordes. Here is the revision of Freud's hypothesis:

> There were two peaceful primal hordes, living at some distance from one another, and organized according to principles of nature-right, primitive communism, and incest. Economic or natural motives (change of hunting area) brought them into conflict with one another. The men of one primal horde, of necessity abstinent during the period of wandering, attacked the other horde; prohibition of sexual intercourse was introduced in the vanquished clan and tribute obligation thrust upon the previous brother-spouse. Thus endemic violence emerged from a previously peaceful society. Finally there developed a peaceful restitution through coalition formations. The permanent results were the institution of a system of marriage exchange with retention of economic advantages resulting from lasting sexual relationships (the future institution of marriage as well as the division of rank and a common chief as a symbol of the victorious clan).[22]

Reich's account has a great deal of structural similarity to Freud's. The incest taboo arose from acts of violence; there is a period of extreme instability caused by sexual insecurity; and finally there is social contract establishing restricted but stable sexual relationships. Sexual restraint is even seen as a result of power relationships. The defeated clan is the structural equivalent of the brother clan. What is missing, of course, is the primal father. The patriarch emerges as a *result* of the social contract and unlike the primal father his power is increased, not diminished, by the new social structure. The new "chief" represented the side victorious in the war.

In this manner Reich could explain both class division *and* "negative sexual morality" without abandoning the existence of an earlier stage of sexual and economic communism. There is no question that he puts Engels' theory on a firmer footing; the natural-selection hypothesis represented the weakest portion of Engels' account. Moreover, it greatly strengthened Reich's general efforts to unite sex and work. His venture into anthropology had established that "sexual suppression becomes a tool of economic enslavement" and that "sexual repression is of a socioeconomic and not of a biological origin."[23] In place of sexual morality there was the principle of "sex-economy." Sexuality would be self-regulated, "steadily alternating between tension and relaxation, ... consistent with all natural functions."[24] Morality functions as an obligation and creates both antisocial sex and work. The language of an ego-estranged "should" creates a sick "artificial, stiff self-confidence."[25] A sex-economically regulated structure "performs work in harmony with sexual interests, drawing from a great reserve of life energy."[26] For the genital character, sexuality and work are both sheer pleasure. "For the moralistically structured individual, work is an irksome duty or solely a material necessity."[27]

But like all social-contract theories, Reich's effort exhibits a serious internal inconsistency. If sex-economy governed the primal horde, why were relations with other groups so bloody? The hunters, you will recall, were looking not for women but for food. In several of his books, Reich deplores the way traders and soldiers "used" the natural sexuality of South Sea women. These "girls . . . do not know that you take their love as you would in a Denver brothel."[28] But Reich's primitive hunters treat women from other hordes in precisely the same brutal manner. It is true that they were "goaded on by sexual abstinence," but do several weeks of celibacy turn a noble savage into the "sexual swine" of civilization? And why in such a sexually free climate would the victors deny sexual relations to their defeated brothers? Reich, in attempting to refute the view that sex is a socially divisive force and one biologically unrelated to aggression, draws us a picture which seems to confirm these very contentions.

THE EROTICIZATION OF CHILDREN

The concept of sex-economy did not find a permanent home in Marxism. In *The Mass Psychology of Fascism*, Reich castigated Marxists for their neglect of psychic factors and their lapse into vulgar "economism." Marxists had failed to take into account the character structure of the masses, which was overwhelmingly neurotic. Every political party, even the church, played up to material needs and hunger. This left the fascists with an unchallenged opportunity to capture the sexual frustrations of the working and middle classes in the form of "organized mysticism." As one would expect, Reich focused upon the sexual symbolism of fascism and fitted it into his theory. Fascism was not simply the result of imperialistic interest or capitalist opportunism but the "expression of the character structure of the orgastically impotent man."[29] The mystical elements of fascism — race, blood, and nation — are religious in character and they represent a transformation of the "old patriarchal religion of suffering into a sadistic religion."[30]

Reich was not the first writer to discover the strong sexual element in fascist ideology. Fascist paraphernalia still adorn the shelves of pornographic shops. Freud has spoken of fascism in terms of cultural frustrations. But Reich turned this observation to an indictment of civilization itself: fascism was a reaction to a sexually "deadly sick society." The instincts "which the National Socialists so openly flaunted were pathological symptoms of secondary drives." And here is where Reich departed from the Marxists:

> The vulgar Marxist who thinks in mechanistic terms assumed that discernment of the social situation would have to be especially keen when sexual distress is added to economic distress. . . . Reality reveals an entirely different picture, and the economist is at a loss to know how to deal with it. . . . The explanation is: The suppression of one's primitive material needs compasses a different result than the suppression of one's sexual needs. The former incites to rebellion, whereas the latter . . . withdraws them from consciousness and anchors itself as a moral defense — prevents rebellion against *both* forms of suppression.[31]

But sexual repression does not produce complete docility. It creates a "secondary force in men's structure — an artificial interest, which actively supports the authoritarian order."[32] Substitute gratifications appear — sadism, homosexuality, and exhibitionism.

All of this meant that reliance upon the working class as a revolutionary force was misplaced. Reich's campaign for the liberation of children and adolescents became the *idée fixe* of all his later works. He denied Freud's belief in sexual latency in childhood. The "godlike" character of the child, his natural eroticism, must be permitted to emerge. The "household child" was neurotically tied to the sexually authoritarian family. Fathers demand "good" sons, mothers make "house pets" of their children to be loved and tortured at will. In language that was to be used by Laing, Reich blamed the Oedipal complex on the "triangular structure" of the modern family. Remove the child from the family at his third year and he would develop very differently.

Freud had made the Oedipal complex the central force of civilization. Reich removes it in one stroke by tearing the child from the family. Children should be confined to their own age group, encouraged to masturbate and "play genital games with others." Age-graded sex must be promoted through adolescence. Then adolescent sex would cease to involve a reactivation of incestuous desire (which was the result of sexual stasis anyway): "One can give up infantile pathogenic desires in adulthood only if the road to normal genital gratification is open and if such gratification can be experienced."[33]

Comparison of Reich's campaign to free the children with the classic Marxian formulation can be instructive. Not only are youth the new proletariat but their communalization is not enough. The eroticization of childhood would first destroy the family, the greatest bulwark against socialism since it perpetuated sexual repression, and then almost automatically and incidentally transform the capitalist order.

It is also worth noting that Reich kept the dyadic romance of Marxism completely intact. He not only ignored Freud's belief in universal latent bisexuality but also denied his assumption that genital sexuality was a creation of civilization. Nongenital sex was the product of culture and Reich's conception of sexuality was quite direct and simple. Everyone yearned for the "genital embrace" with the opposite sex. Orgasm was the ultimate goal of the sex act, and in Reich's later theories, of life itself. He barely tolerated homosexuality.[34] He abhorred pornography.

Thus Reich never assumed the posture of dilettante in regard to sex. Although he was quite willing to advocate "sexological agencies" to promote his cause, he never considered a sexual bureaucracy of the Fourierist sort. Sex was necessary and pleasurable; on his terms it is hard to call it fun. In any case, it was too important to leave available to forces of reaction and their agent, the family.

MARCUSE: SEX AND CAPITALISM

Marcuse's work represents a more sustained effort to synthesize Freud and Marx. His general position, as we indicated, is remarkably similar to Reich's. Therefore, our analysis is already well under way. We can concentrate our efforts on the differences between the two.

Marcuse's achievement rests upon his attempt to carry an interpreptation of Freud and Marx to an extremely high level of abstraction. This may appear to be an odd assessment for a writer who forms his indictment of advanced capitalism upon its closed and automatic character. But Marcuse's complaint against Reich, which takes up only a single paragraph in *Eros and Civilization,* is based upon Reich's literalism.

The most important revision in this direction is Marcuse's contention that the family has already been extinguished as an economic and psychological institution in capitalist society. There is a certain wistfulness over the passing of the family. The transmission of values and the creating of individuals through Oedipal conflict was an intensely personal experience and life under the performance principle "still retained a sphere of private nonconformity."[35]

But the repressive organization of the instincts is now collectivized and "the ego seems to be prematurely socialized by a whole system of extrafamilial agents and agencies."[36] The mass media now transmit social values: they offer "perfect training in efficiency, toughness, personality, dreams and romance."[37]

This is a major revision not only of Reich's model of the family as the remaining source of instinctual repression but also of the classical Marxian interpretation. For Marx assumed that as the economic system disintegrated so would the family. Marcuse does not tell us the opposite; he proposes an even more novel interpretation. As the family disintegrates the grip of late capitalism becomes even tighter. "Obsolescent paternal forms" have been replaced by central administration. Freud's reality principle loses its quality as a concession to pleasure. The personalized father figure as representative of the superego generated hatred, fear, and respect. He presented "a living object for the impulses and for the conscious efforts to satisfy them."[38] Now even the generalized superego has been depersonalized. The "sadistic principals" of early capitalism have been displaced by salaried members of the bureaucracy. Hate encounters "smiling colleagues, busy competitors, obedient officials, helpful social workers."[39]

> Sex is even liberated and integrated into work: This is one of the unique achievements of industrial society — rendered possible by the reduction of dirty and heavy physical labor; by the availability of cheap, attractive clothing, beauty culture, and physical hygiene....[40]

Thus Marcuse is forced to reject one of the major tenets of Marxist and Freudian analysis, that modern society rests upon a puritanical repression of the sexual instincts. But sex in late capitalism is of a marketed, socially harmless variety and Marcuse is forced to invent a new word for it, "repressive desublimation." There is an extended treatment of this phenomenon in several of his works but what it comes to is this: Sexual freedom under modern conditions still restrains instinctual energy and, in fact, intensifies domination. A mechanized bureaucratic environment blocks the transcendence of the libido while intensifying localized sexuality. As a result, the reality principle *appears* to merge with the pleasure principle: "The individual must adapt himself to a world which does not seem to demand the denial of his innermost needs — a world which is not essentially hostile."[41] The liberation of sexual pleasure "generates submission and weakens the rationality of protest."[42]

Eros and Utopia

Let us briefly recapitulate Marcuse's argument before we continue. Capitalism has completely narcotized protest. In fact, in this respect this new order seems to possess all the characteristics of Marx's oriental depotism. But it has extended administrative domination throughout society by guaranteeing a rising standard of living, leisure time, and sexual freedom. It has reduced the family to a shell for direct manipulation, thus reducing the agony of the Oedipal complex, and it has even flattened out class distinctions. A theorist with a different perspective would speak of the promise of capitalism fulfilled.

Marcuse is thus faced with the unpleasant alternative of searching for an avenue of revolution that extends beyond both Marx and Reich. For this he reaches back to Freud. All the major categories of psychoanalysis are accepted: the reality principle, the pleasure principle, the death instinct, the primal crime. Marcuse revises these categories in two directions. First, he attempts to mold Freudian concepts into Marxian ones. The primal father is presented as the first captain of industry. Freud is criticized for ignoring the significance of the primal crime as a "'social' protest against the unequal division of pleasure."[43] The reality principle is reformulated as the performance principle. The latter is the "prevailing historical form of the reality principle."[44] The concept of instinctual repression is split in two as basic repression, the necessary modification of human instincts for civilization, and surplus repression, "restrictions made necessary by social domination."[45]

But Marcuse's real innovation of both Freud and Marx is his treatment of sex. Sex becomes the key to "nonrepressive" civilization. "If work pleasure and libidinal pleasure usually coincide, then the very concept of the reality principle becomes meaningless and superfluous. . . ."[46] Marcuse offers his own version of sex-economy. He calls it the "self-sublimation of sexuality." But the striking feature of his treatment of sex is its abstracted quality. Dyadic formations are forgotten; child sexual development is passed over. Sex is not private; it spills over and is not sublimated into work. The entire body becomes an instrument of pleasure. In utopia, the body would be "resexualized" and returned to its original "pregenital polymorphous" state. But Marcuse warns us that instinctual liberation would not lead to "a society of sex maniacs." The Fourierist fantasy is itself overcome by a dream of even greater possibilities. Polymorphic sexuality would reach beyond physical pleasure and *"minimize* the manifestations of *mere* sexuality by integrating them into a far larger order, including the order of work."[47] Sexuality would finally produce its own sublimation. An undeflected instinct would find gratification in "activities and relations that are not sexual in the sense of 'organized genital activity' and yet are libidinal and erotic."[48]

We noted that Fourier saw friendship as emerging from promiscuous sex. Marcuse shortcuts that route by contending that the fusion of desublimated sex and work transforms the former to Eros and the latter to play. Aesthetics replaces morality as it did for Fourier. But Fourier's fascination with color and pomp in the organization of orgies is replaced by the "Form" in Marcuse's motif. Unity is Marcuse's motif and the most important feature of his theory of aesthetics:

> In the aesthetic Form, the content (matter) is assembled, defined, and arranged to obtain a condition in which the immediate, unmastered forces of the matter, of the 'material,' are mastered,

'ordered.' Form is the negation, the mastery of disorder, violence, suffering. . . . [49]

When aesthetics finally characterizes all of society, it is the Form that becomes the organizing principle. In the following passage we can see why Marcuse capitalizes the word:

> The Form of freedom is not merely self-determination and self-realization, but rather the determination and realization of goals which enhance, protect, and unite life on earth. And this autonomy would find expression not only in the mode of production and production relations but also in the individual relations among men, in their language and in their silence, in their gestures and their looks, in their sensitivity, in their love and hate. The beautiful world would be an essential quality of their freedom. [50]

One critic has complained that there is no notion of what people will do in the world of desublimated sex. [51] The answer to that criticism is not that Marcuse is unable to fill in the details of a utopian dream but that sex has finally been liberated from the body and emerges socialized and spiritualized as Eros. The replacement of sexuality by the generalized concept of Eros means that the "biological drive becomes a cultured drive." Sex as Eros ends the disruptive character of ordinary sex; it is now directly a life instinct (shades of Reich again) "which associates individuals to 'greater unities.'" [52] The libido is now a universal "*social* phenomenon" and Marcuse admiringly cites Plato on the joy of spiritual procreation. [53]

Thus the family is now placed even further in the background than in Marx and Engels. The bourgeois family may have rested on money and boredom but now the dyad, as its desirable remainder, is extinguished. "Individual sex love" has no place in Marcuse's vision. Unalienated work eliminates dyadic sex; the latter still represents an estrangement from libidinal work relations. But Eros has always attempted to "eternalize itself in a permanent *order*." [54] This striving has until now been frustrated in the realm of necessity. Individuals furtively sought happiness in dyadic libidinal relations outside society and work. But now this striving can produce *lasting* gratification in "an enlarged order of libidinal relations ('community')": "The pleasure principle extends to consciousness. Eros redefines reason in his own terms. Reasonable is what sustains the order of gratification." [55] Since gratification is defined in terms of work in the collective order, Marcuse's image of the aesthetic Form is frighteningly complete. By contrast, Reich's belief that if only individuals could freely bring themselves to orgasm they could create manageable lives for themselves seems a positively simple, or in Marcuse's words an "arrested," insight.

Thus Marcuse achieves the complete negation both of Freud's views on sex and civilization and of the ultimate goals of Marxism. Sexuality had been "contained" in the family and therefore made "safe." The "repressive desublimation" of sex under capitalism is a temporary phenomenon. What Marcuse assures us again and again is that sex in utopia is not only liberating but safe. By uniting sex to work, sex is contained in a fashion that could never be achieved within the family. It is a solidifying force that unites individuals in structures far larger and more complete than small groups. The transformation of sex into Eros takes on a direct and general unification. Utopia is now "eternal" and "permanent" because these are the characteristics of Eros. Marx contended that the so-called bourgeois thinker constantly attempts to keep sex securely within the family. Marcuse discovered that in late capitalism sex could be safe as long as it was separated from work and hence genitally focused. But now sex is made safe again. Ironically, the only real threat to Marcuse's utopia rests with lovers who might refuse to extend their libido to their work and reserve their satisfactions for each other. By refusing to allow sexuality to ease into Eros, these two lovers still assume the role Freud outlined for them — traitors to the social order.

PART III

no use to make any philosophies here:
I see no
god in the holly, hear no song from
the snowbroken weeds: Hegel is not the winter
yellow in the pines: the sunlight has never
heard of trees: surrendered self among
unwelcoming forms: stranger
hoist your burdens, get on down the road.

–A. R. Ammons, from "Gravelly Run"

13

SPECIAL RELATIONSHIPS

Our review of recent political thought on the family shows a continuing and intensified effort to destroy the family in the name of broader social and political goals. Several trends stand out. First, the dyad, always approached with ambivalence in modern thought, comes under direct attack. In rational individualism it is seen as a disguised form of patriarchy; in the permutations of romantic thought it is seen as an obstacle to individual liberation. Thus in one form of individualism dyadic sentiment interferes with rational goals, in another with emotive ones. The infusion of Marxism with a Freudian radicalism opened up the possibilities of sex as a force for broad-scale social cohesion. Under these conditions likewise, the dyad had to be eliminated.

Second, the parental bond, which had always challenged the natural enclosure of the dyad anyway, is attacked for the first time in individualist thought. In fact, the child now openly takes on a new social role. Particularly in Hobbes, but also in Locke, the child was seen in terms separate from other individuals. It is true that Hobbes insisted that the parental bond be seen in terms of consent, a paradigm which placed the child on the same standing as adults. But the entire relationship of child and adult was based upon the parents' ability to kill him. This is a premise that we saw taken to frightening conclusions in our discussion of the new philosophy's treatment of abortion. Locke, of course, had already made the most damning discovery about children that can be made in the context of rational individualsim: Children are beyond reason and hence lacking in the most important definition of humanity. But Locke made socialization into adulthood and reason a natural right of the child. In fact, this is almost the justification and function of the dyad. But as the dyad has lost its attractiveness as the basis for the family, the child's position naturally has become precarious. It is fair to say that in rational individualist thought the child has now been placed in what we can call the social category of the incompetent. We are told by family historians that childhood as a separate stage of development is a relatively new concept. But the uniqueness of childhood was placed in the context of the social unit of the family. When the child is looked at as a separate and isolated entity it should not be surprising that he assumes all the characteristics of the incompetent: dependent, capable of only limited reason, unable to defend himself. Locke's category of madmen and lunatics was designed to mark off the general human capacity of reason. Children were only temporarily without it.

The new view, of course, is unable to challenge this position but it does emphasize the great burden childhood imposes and reaches the conclusion that is the fate of all those declared incompetent: They must be separated from the rest of the community. In the language of Mary Ann Warren, they may be part of the "genetic" community but certainly not the "moral" one. Children are placed in the same category as the insane, the comatose, and the retarded. As such they are the *collective* responsibility of society. The liberal promotion of children's rights and the radical proposals for the state's responsibility for childrearing converge when we see them both as attempts to deal with the problem of incompetency. Thus one recent commentator has complained that "each woman finds that she, rather than the state, is the primary protector of her child's right to life" and concludes that the community should take over the responsibility for the physical and emotional welfare of her children.[1]

In rational collectivism, the isolation of the child from the parental bond had already been postulated by Marx. Now childhood is seen in independent terms and not just as a portion of life that would naturally be collectivized in utopia. For childhood in capitalist society becomes a separate category and, of course, one of potential liberation. What the rational individualist sees as incompetency, the rational collectivist sees as a new rationality. Childhood becomes the new proletariat. As such it has all the characteristics which Marx assigned to that class. It is romanticized as representing a new moral force. Reich speaks of the "godlike" qualities of the child. Marcuse, always the better Marxist, prefers to emphasize the dark side of the development of a new morality. The subverting force of the new sensibility lies in its "disorderly, uncivil and farcical" qualities. Childhood and adolescence are the most alienated categories of existence in capitalist society. The youth crisis is "insoluble in the context of the framework of the social order"; youth represents a "new working class."[2]

Thus the modern family, even its most truncated forms, is finally abandoned in political thought. As one would expect, new concepts have replaced the ones that formed its basis. The dyad disappears in favor of "nonbinding commitment" and the parental bond dissolves into a general social problem.

THE CONCEPT OF SPECIAL RELATIONSHIPS

Throughout this book I have not attempted to hide from the reader my distaste for the treatment of the family in modern and recent political thought. Each chapter contained a critique of the presentation of the family, its relation to the political order, and the alternatives posed for it. Therefore it is not necessary to repeat each objection here. A few words can put our next effort in perspective.

The one characteristic that stands out most clearly in the treatment of the modern family is its gross incompatibility with the demands of the political order. Each writer who has attempted to devise a relationship between the two has attempted to alter the family to make it fit requirements. Indeed, the transformation of the family into the form that we know was the result of a general effort to find a model of the family acceptable to new conceptions of politics. But even among Locke and Rousseau, those writers who were most responsible for creating the modern family, there were nagging doubts over the validity of this new family form. Locke gave the modern family its individualized and nidal character and Rousseau its emotional basis, but the theories of each threatened to pull these contributions in other directions.

Thus the modern family seems to have become a problem precisely because it could not be made to fit the new requirements of politics. An example from individualist thought can make our point.

Locke's general premise seems to have been that if the family and the polity could achieve as close a structural resemblance as possible, at least in respect to the dyad, the family would be a useful but limited support for the polity. Children were, of course, prepolitical creatures and the major political function of the Lockean man was to socialize youth into the world of the free and rational. We saw how Mill, in adding the concept of individual development as a replacement for the natural and automatic character of Locke's thought, placed the family in a more central position and also one more subject to criticism. The family was no longer a simple, mechanized enclosure that housed the free and rational but a school of individual development. The departure from the automatic character of familial socialization is revealed in Mill's admonition that the state has a direct interest in family forms.

Parsonian theory attempted to put a brake on liberal doubts by reintroducing an automatic Lockean character to the value-resemblance dimension. But this was achieved by the incantation of "basic irreducible" family functions and by inserting the rules of the political system into the family in the form of the father's role as an instrumental leader. Rawls carries liberal doubts to schizophrenic proportions by first questioning whether structural resemblance can guarantee political goals and then making familial socialization the cornerstone of his system.

The collectivist element of rational individualism has always been directly antagonistic to the family. Hobbes' attempt to achieve structural resemblance between the family and polity was designed to strip both patriarchy and any other form of its moral symbolism. The clutch of philosophers we examined on the abortion question never even bothered to attempt a Hobbesian process of demystification. The extreme situation is presented as a given.

The reason that the modern family appears so unable to perform the functions assigned to it — or worse, appears to obstinately combat political goals — is that it is an institution able to promote a value which has been nearly universally rejected in political theory. If we look at all the theories presented, the family is judged in terms of its ability to prepare individuals for participation in a monistic society. This criterion is not so immediately apparent in some theories as it is in others. But we saw how total the world of Locke's free and rational or Fourier's polygenes can be. Moreover, the values which the modern polity is designed to promote are directly antithetical to what the modern family can offer. Equality, autonomy, fraternity — each of these are offered in various formulations by the theories we have presented. When the family cannot sustain these values in its structural makeup or in its socialization function, it is eventually seen as an obstacle to justice. And finally, what exacerbates this entire situation is that the image which so fascinates the modern theorist is the image of a political community. The structure of the modern political community — sovereignty, territorialization, bureaucracy, prescriptive law and rights, citizenship — all run counter to the family as an institution.[3] In liberal societies the professionalized service state stands above the family and threatens to "help" it out of its very existence — while the romantic ethos of its citizens, although it seems to challenge it, only adds to its power. The rational collectivist's utopia envisions a political community so complete, and recently so deep in its psychic basis, that the family can never be made to fit.

What functions then can the family perform and what sort of political order will permit it to flourish? If we look closely at the modern family, we can suggest that it is an institution uniquely designed to promote "special relationships." Let us attempt to explain what a special relationship is and how the family is crucial in promoting it.

The concept of the special relationship is not coterminous with the relationships of the modern family. We can think of other relationships which do not possess a kinship dimension. But all these other forms can probably be fitted into one single category, that of the close friendship. Here under five headings are what appear to be the major characteristics of the special relationship. They are not set in any order of precedence but the fact that all of the characteristics are necessary for a relationship to be called a special one permits us to suggest that we are presenting a phenomeno-logical analysis of the relationship.

1. *Intimacy.* There is a close, personal bond in many ways different in each case.

2. *Emotional basis.* The primary state of consciousness of the parties has an emotional affective character as distinguished from a cognitive or volitional one. Naturally, the special relationship is not bereft of the later forms of consciousness. Love, hate, and sorrow are not the only elements in these relationships at any particular moment.

3. *Indeterminate time.* The concept of time in the special relationship is neither unilinear or discrete. Very often this relationship has a clearly remembered founding in a shared experience. But once begun, the special relationship pursues no goal. This quality is prefigured by its emotional basis. Our current belief that such relationships are by nature temporary is probably the result of a mix of cynicism and overintellectualization. We all know that they often reach a turning point that ends in their termination. When our consciousness of this probability becomes central, we tend to deny the formation of the special relationship itself. This denial gives the appearance that genuine relationships between individuals are sup-ramoral because their permanence is to be assured politically or because they are by nature ephemeral. The lasting relationship reintroduces morality. Concepts of fidelity and commitment form the moral background of the special relationship. It is, of course, a much more complicated moral dimension than is found either in systems based upon connections on the basis of rights and contract or in those based upon connections derived from a general libidinal cohesion.

4. *Object diffusion.* It is difficult to establish a special relationship solely upon one facet of human existence. Any relationship that is highly seg-mented and involves only a particular shared aspect of life (sex, work), a particular shared event (a death of a mutual friend), or shared political beliefs will be lacking in the inclusiveness necessary to produce a special relationship. To anticipate our argument a bit, special relationships chal-lenge the modern compartmentalization of everyday life into friends at work, friends in the neighborhood, friends for parties. The distinctiveness of the special relationship lies in its demand for a wide range of shared objects. The range, of course, need not be complete. For example, special relationships can be, in Freud's terminology, aim inhibited.

5. *Dyadic structure*. Although we shall discuss alternatives, we will contend that the basic unit of the special relationship is the dyadic bond. A family or group of friends may exhibit a more complicated pattern, but the entire structure can still be seen as a set of dayds.

Let us first consider some associated definitional problems of the concept of the special relationship. It should be mentioned as a guiding point that no characterization of any human relationship can be precise and free of variation. For instance, if we can ask whether the special relationship is by definition psychologically and morally always a healthy one, our answer must be no. Special relationships can be psychologically crippling — indeed neurotic. Life and literature can supply us with more than enough examples: the parent and the guilt-ridden child, troubled spouses, overbearing friends. But our case need only establish that special relationships are not by nature morally repugnant or not more so than other relationships. This, I would contend, has not been convincingly demonstrated by any of the writers we have examined. Even Freud, whose work accomplished the great demythologizing mission of modern thought and whose therapy was focused upon the disastrous consequences that special relationships can produce, did not draw a picture of other relationships in any better light. But more on this point in a moment. The saving grace of the special relationship as a social form lies in the range and depth that intimacy can take. Its pathological forms may be the result of an unfortunate complex of unique experiences as well as interaction with antagonistic forms.

If we take a moment to compare briefly the way the special relationship is treated in modern political thought, we can further clarify the concept. Rational individualism and collectivism can never really develop a conception of special relationships. Locke's free and rational individuals can barely contain the marriage dyad; it needs to be solidified by a commitment to parenthood. That commitment is seen to rest upon a natural principle that exists outside the world of the free and rational. Engels' treatment of "individual love" has many of the basic features of the special relationship — exclusivity, emotion, possession — but it is represented as an evanescence (as serial monogamy in the language of modern sociology). In the socialist critique it is property-based relationships that give permanence to civil society. Marx showed in his discussion of crude communism that the dialectic demanded that all special relationships be destroyed in order to collapse the distinction between civil and political society. One floats in and out of dyads while the permanent and thus social primary relationships are to be found in the communalized work order.

Romantic thought exhibits a much more complicated relationship to the special bond. No modern writer explored the concept of special relationships more deeply or with more passion than Rousseau. But from our point of view Rousseau committed two errors. First, he conceived of the special relationship solely in the context of self-actualization. Second, he insisted that the special relationship stood radically apart from the rest of society. Thus the special relationship was seen as a way to check and avoid the dreaded *amour propre*. But the distinction between self-love and selfishness was maintained in the context of self-actualization. On Rousseau's own terms self-actualization was such a difficult state to achieve that even he began to see its pursuit outside special relationships — in the isolated self or in the isolated polity, not the isolated family. We saw that recent thought settled firmly on the search for the self and left all other concerns to a bureaucratic order. In this sense, Fourier set an easier task for himself. Self-actualization was left to the instincts and Fourier settled on the idea of acquaintances as a substitute for special relationships.

It is especially difficult to review in a brief space the Freudian view on the point under discussion. This much can be repeated. As we indicated, psychoanalysis represents an unusual brand of conservatism in that its demythologizing elements are so prominent. Thus when Freud voices his skepticism of radical ideologies he is forced to base his doubts upon the most speculative portion of his work, the death instinct. But most importantly, special relationships are seen as the mutilated results of instinctual drives. The very frustration that results from instinctual repression forms the basis of the instinctual bond. To give the most prominent examples, the father-son bond was in large part determined by the son's unconscious sense of a lost battle in the sexual rivalry for the mother. Thus, as we have seen, it was really a small step to portray the special relationship as an inherently pathological form.

That particular amalgam of rational and romantic collectivism that we find in Reich and Marcuse insists upon making all social relationships intimate. But when intimacy is treated as an inflated currency, it loses its original purpose. Marcuse must transform the sexual bond into Eros in order to give it a rational and permanent basis.

FAMILY FORMS AS SPECIAL RELATIONSHIPS

We must establish one more link before we can attempt a reconstruction of modern political thought. What is the relationship between the family as an institution and the concept of the special relationship? We have already said that the family is not the only conceivable cluster of special relationships.

I have been unable to find an alternative that accepts the idea of the special relationship and still seeks to find its expression in forms other than the modern family. The closest approximations are to be found in the idea of the dyad sans children and the idea of the commune or "intentional family." We have already discussed both of these options but it may be useful to review them again in light of the question at hand.

Unfortunately, when the dyad is presented as the basic structure of special relationship in society, it is its impermanence that is seen as the basis for its attractiveness. Would it be possible to envision a society of permanent dyads (thus allowing for special relationships) while leaving the task of raising children to the community in a nondyadic and nonspecial manner? This is probably not possible and our negative response tells us something about the unique features of the modern family as an institution for special relationships. The answer is not necessarily that the dyad itself is inherently unstable without the parental bond. On the contrary, the arrival of children into the home of two lovers can indeed represent a challenge to the dyadic stability. Rather the answer lies in the fact that the dyad alone is a truncated version of the special relationship. It has no way of assuring that future generations will be able to enter into dyadic union. A child whose world is structured by groups of authorities or a series of individual caretakers will find it extremely difficult to be able to conceive of a special relationship. There is nothing mysteriously conservative in this statement. It need not conjure up theories of instinctual or biological necessities. In fact, if anything, it assumes a cultural priority to human affairs. Without an intimate knowledge of certain kinds of relationships, individuals will be unable to reproduce them or, stated more conservatively, they will be unable to reproduce them on any basis other than a hit or miss system. The latter is hardly a reasonable alternative for one to take if he or she is attempting to fashion a society that gives precedence to special relationships.

The instability of the dyad rests with its inability to offer an intergenerational linkage. The alternative suggested by some writers in our discussion of the new romanticism in Chapter 10 is not much of an advance. The idea of the professional parent, the modern equivalent of the nanny, does represent an attempt to capture dyadic permanence. But it is a woefully inadequate substitute. The nanny was hardly the professional that the new middle-class social worker would be as a surrogate parent. But even in that system the child would not fail to see the professional character of his relationship to the nanny. Her abrupt dismissal at the required age is, after all, the essence of the professional approach to a job task. It may well be that the curious mixture of intimacy and professionalism in the nanny system, which we are again forced to point out is not likely to be repeated in a twentieth-century revival, further traumatized generations of upper-class children.[4] Needless to say, the class discrepancy between the nanny and the natural mother seems to have aggravated rather than lessened oedipal conflict. In summary then, we can say that the dyad fails as a model of special relationships because it must professionalize the raising of children, thus effectively ending the future production of the dyad in the next generation.

A far more comprehensive alternative is the intentional family. Here the dyad is rejected but so is the resort to the insitution of bureaucratic and professional elements into society. In fact, the intentional family is conceived as a nondyadic institution of special relationships. Hermann Schmalenbach's typology of this form as a "Bund" makes this point clear.[5] The origin of the Bund is the identification of a common value and mutual solidarity from members who had no past joint interests. As a social structure it has the following characteristics: unreserved devotion of the individual to the group, relative neglect of economic and organizational spheres of society, complete sacrifice not only of material goods but also of one's self. Schmalenbach describes the Bund generally as being a state of "emotional ecstasy" and concludes that this is the reason for the communes' instability. Emotion is an extremely unstable structure and eventually disintegrates to more conventional forms of Gemeinschaft or to Gesellschaft.

But is the emotional base the cause of instability or is it the form that the intentional family takes? We will focus our attention on one example, the nineteenth-century Oneida communities, with scattered references to other experiments.

The Oneida communities were aggressively opposed to the dyad. Monogamy was seen as both a tyrannical and blasphemous institution. Two people ought not to "worship and idolize each other." As one member phrased it, "The heart should be free to love all the true and worthy." The form of marriage that the commune eventually adopted replaced the dyadic relationships with a system of complex marriage. The leader, John Humphrey Noyes, developed a system of lovemaking that forbade male ejaculation. Sexual partners changed frequently, as often as several times a month. Age segregation was discouraged. The young were to associate sexually with persons of "mature character" and "sound sense." Here is Maren Lockwood Carden's description of sex in Oneida utopia:

> In the early years the amenities preceding a sexual encounter were simple. A man approached the woman of his choice, and she was supposedly free to accept or refuse his addresses. Beginning in the early 1880s, the request was made through a "third party" who was usually an older woman and a central member. The intermediary's function was in part to preserve the Community women from embarrassment, but it was also to check on the members' activities. The Community recorded all encounters. Each "interview" required a separate request. If one partner had a single room, as was often the case in later years, the couple could go there. Alter-

> natively, certain rooms were set aside for "social" purposes (the Community euphemism for sexual purposes). At first a couple could remain together all night ... later this was forbidden ... probably ... to prevent the long private conversations that might lead to exclusive love.

In the case of couples who fell in love and were unable to rid themselves of "selfish" feelings, one of the pair was exiled to a neighboring settlement. Sometimes the individuals were denied sexual privileges altogether. Meetings at Oneida were filled with public confessions of clandestine dyadic encounters. Charles Nordhoff, the peripatetic recorder of the nineteenth-century commune, has preserved for us a verbatim account of Noyes' summary remarks at a "mutual criticism" session with a young man named Charles:

> He said that Charles had some serious faults; that he had watched him with some care; and that he thought the young man was earnestly trying to cure himself.... "In the course of what we call stirpiculture," said Noyes, "Charles, as you know, is in the situation of one who is by and by to become a father. Under these circumstances, he has fallen under the too common temptation of selfish love, and a desire to wait upon and cultivate intimacy with a woman who was to bear a child through him. This is an insidious temptation, very apt to attack people under the circumstances; but it must nevertheless be struggled against."[7]

Noyes went on to note that Charles had agreed that he "isolate himself entirely from the woman, and let another man take his place at her side." Charles was praised for his attempt to "rid himself of all selfish faults."

In the 1860s Noyes introduced a system which he called "stirpiculture." Parents would be selected by a committee. Thus conception as well as parenthood became a community function. Stirpiculture children were separated from their mothers when they were weaned and placed in a wing of the mansion called the Children's House. In the 1870s, there were 48 children in the wing. They were cared for by 3 men and 15 women, impressive figures by today's child-care standards.

Oneida functioned successfully as an intentional family for nearly a generation. This span of time gives us a key to the stability of the commune. More than one writer has noted that relationships in the commune are felt to be familial ones. This being the case, one would expect the commune to develop equivalents to the incest taboo. The system of complex marriage was one such arrangement. If the Oneidans were to function as a family they had to devise a system that met the demands of exogamy. They always did in fact prefer celibacy as the ideal sexual life. But complex marriage, with its avowed purpose of eliminating sexuality as a basis for special relationships, met this requirement. In the words of one participant: "Naturally our relation became more intimate, but I avoided any avowal of special love that, if reciprocated, would estrange her from the central love in the community."[8] It is as if the Oneidans said: "We are a large family, therefore you ought not to have a sexual relationship with your sisters and brothers. If you must have this relationship it will be bereft of any exclusivity and thus brothers and sisters will maintain their more general special relationship to one another." The Oneidans seem to have suffered psychologically under this arrangement just as individuals (as Freud tells us) suffer under the restrictions of the incest taboo. Lockwood even reports that "there was an ever-present awareness of sex" at Oneida.[9] In the context of the high level of sexual activity in the community this is testimony to the community's climate of repressed sexuality.

Since children of the commune are to be regarded as everyone's offspring, the natural bond of parenthood violates the intentional family's norms. To regard one of one's own children as special is equivalent in the intentional family to the grossest form of favoritism within the conventional family. It was one of the achievements of the modern family to insist that each child be valued as nearly equally as possible. This was reflected first in the elimination of primogeniture and much later in the equal treatment of male and female children. If the family was to be an emotional institution, it could not afford to favor one child over another in significant degree. (This is not to say that children need to be treated equally in our modern political sense, but emotional equality within the special relationship can be quite demanding.)

Nevertheless, natural parents of the commune could not be expected to treat their own children and other children with complete equality. Thus communal childrearing is the most likely alternative. Even here children tended to call their communal teachers "papa" and "mama"; rotation was initiated as a means of avoiding even this favoritism. At Oneida, and in the kibbutzim also as we shall see, visiting hours with natural parents are a concession from the model of the commune as a family. In both cases the concession seems to have occasioned intense conflict between parents and authorities.[10] The amount of time, the days available, the location of the meetings with natural children were frequent matters of complaint at Oneida.

But the most striking feature of the Oneida commune, and one now glossed over by its new sympathizers, is the position of the leader.[11] John Noyes, the founder, had nearly all the prerogatives of Freud's primal father. Noyes did not demand sexual abstinence on the part of his "sons" but his position in the sexual life of the community was unchallenged. The best evidence for his position is to quote from a set of resolutions signed by women in their early forties and younger:

> 1. That we do not belong to *ourselves* in any respect, but that we *do* belong first to *God,* and second to Mr. Noyes as God's true representative.
> 2. That we have no rights or personal feelings in regard to child-bearing which shall in the least degree oppose or embarrass him in his choice of scientific combinations.
> 3. That we will put aside all envy, childishness and self-seeking, and rejoice with those who are chosen candidates; that we will, if necessary, become martyrs to science, and cheerfully resign all desire to become mothers, if for any reason Mr. Noyes deem us unfit material for propagation. Above all, we offer ourselves [as] "living sacrifices" to God and true communism. [12]

Noyes routinely assumed the responsibility for initiating young girls to their first sexual experience. These women allegedly "continued to love him for years."[13] During the stirpiculture experiment Noyes sired ten of the fifty-eight children; his eldest son sired three, the next eldest two. We saw earlier the powerful patriarchal figure who scolded the young male at a "mutual criticism" session. It is as if Noyes was accusing the son of sexual trangressions against his mother or sister. It terms of our analysis, he was indeed making this accusation. One need not accept the entire psychoanalytic system to see the utility of the relationship that Freud posited between the primal father and his "family."

All of this leads us to see the commune in a much closer relationship to the modern family than is generally accepted. Variant sexual practices, communal childrearing, and a patriarchal leader are less plausibly seen as alternative forms to the family than as the forms the modern family will take when it is applied to the idea of a nondyadic institution of special relationships. The current generation of romantics must significantly change the nineteenth-century commune in order to make it fit their model of a voluntary organization. There was little that was voluntary about the commune. The reason is obvious — it intended to function as the modern family did, with all the institutional structures it could imagine.

We are now in a position to determine the reason for the instability of the commune. Rosabeth Moss Kanter, in her sensitive account of communes, offers three basic reasons for the decline and failure of the commune: the impact of a changing environment, the inability to maintain the attachment of a second generation, and the antagonism between work methods and the general social life. [14]

Let us look at her reasons in the light of our interpretation of the commune as a family form. Kanter indirectly blames the encroachments of industrialized America for the commune's problems. But she notes that the commune seemed especially unable to cope with this new environment. The Shakers, for instance, eventually divided into three camps based on the degree of separation from the world that they favored. The brittleness of the commune on this point can be traced to its original total lack of connection to the outside world. Industrialization was one change, albeit an enormously significant one, that challenged this isolation. But other changes would have produced the same results. The commune is unlikely to have weathered the impact of war or general political upheaval. As an institution of special relationships, the commune posits a nearly complete isolation from other social institutions. In fact, one of the determinants of its success is its ability to insulate itself from the surrounding community — a rational measure only in terms of its immediate survival.

The modern family is often accused of the same kind of isolation. The results here are likely to be the same: frustration on the part of its members, ad hoc and/or individual relationships to the community and finally disintegration of the institution. But the isolation of the modern family from the social order is not a necessary part of its existence internally as a unit. Unfortunately, this necessity holds for the commune. The very size of communal experiment and the nature of the ties of its members force extreme measures to promote its solidarity. Any systematic intrusion of the outside world breaks the commune into ideological groupings or natural families.

With only a few exceptions, the inability of the commune to maintain the allegiance of the second generation is striking. Despite tremendous attempts to socialize members' children, the Shakers could never keep more than a fraction of them. Harmony was so reduced by egress that by the 1870s there were not enough people to run its factories. At Oneida, by 1880 half the population was forty or older. The death or absence of the first leader spelled the decline of scores of communes. Kanter attributes this failure to the commune's voluntary basis: "In many communities ... children are not automatically admitted to full membership status when they reach adulthood but must indicate a firm commitment of their own."[15]

We can go even a bit farther. In a discussion a few pages back on the idea of the dyad as society's basic special relationship we suggested that unless the child be tied to the parental dyad it is unlikely that such relationships can be replicated intergenerationally. The commune model illustrates the more general point that extreme instability is likely to follow any modification in dyadic relationships. Two points can be made in this case. If relationships within the commune are indeed familial (though not dyadic), one would expect a rebellion on the part of the growing child against the parent. In the context of the conventional modern family, this rebellion, while it can take on ferocious proportions, is eventually lessened when a new set of dyadic relationships is finally approved for the next generation. This ability of the modern family to contain the very rebellion it creates is what so angered Reich. When this rebellion occurs within the commune, what form can it take but egress that is likely to be permanent? Commune youth cannot withdraw into their own subculture; that escape is not permissible. And they certainly cannot withdraw into a dyadic relationship. The latter is permitted only with trepidation by parents in the modern family, and in the commune any dyad is treated with suspicion. It is true that youth rebellion is likely to be less intense against the background of communal childrearing, but when it does appear there seem to be no measures to cope with it.

But there is another reason for the inability of the commune to retain its same character across generations. For an example helpful to our argument let us turn to the Israeli kibbutz. The kibbutz is an intriguing case. It is not fanatically opposed to dyadic relationships but it was founded, according to Stanley Diamond upon whose work we will rely, on the denial of the profoundly nidal climate of family in the East European shtetls.[16] The Vatikim were moved by a desire to create a new generation, "free," "normal," and "manly," unburdened by the "insecure" and "parasitic" environment of the shtetl family. In doing so by setting up communal and peer-group childrearing, the kibbutz parents severed the "psychic link betweeen generations" and produced an "inner uniformity of personality," "a genuine modal type."[17] Here is part of Diamond's argument:

> This primary emphasis on the peer group in the socialization of the Sabra, beginning in the earliest weeks of life, functioned, of course, as the most effective way to break the psychic link between the generations, thus attaining the ideological ends adhered to by the parents. At the same time, however, it substantially deprived the child of profound and complexly ramifying affective-intellectual contact with one or more significant adults, concerned primarily with him, through whom the child first feels his way into the world, and ultimately comes to reflect on it, to think about it, to *conceive* it. Put another way, the conceptual capacity, the capacity to relate things and events, to symbolize, to abstract, and the desire to do so, although a latent, phylogenetically determined, distinctive human capacity, seems to germinate in the soil of personal contacts. That is, concrete personal relationships, and in the growing psyche these can only be *affectively* apprehended, serve as the prototype for the relational or conceptual capacity in general. This abstractive-conceptual capacity is, apparently, a

function of the quality and nature of concrete affective relationships as these accumulate and ramify through the various phases of the culturally determined life-cycle.[18]

Thus the Sabra, the children of the kibbutz, by being "prematurely socialized," assume a "mechanical character." They are certainly freed of the neurotic character of which Reich spoke, but beneath the "collective surface the Sabra emerges as an isolated man."[19] The typical remark of the Sabra captures his personality: "If we can think, why must we feel?"[20] Moreover, this overrational personality has a definite "realistic," pragmatic cast, so much so that parents have complained that their children behave like goyim (gentiles). Diamond notes that within the parents' frame of reference a goy was considered a "physically competent, physically dangerous, rather cold, insensitive person, a person to be feared, envied, and condemned at the same time."[21] It is not likely that such a personality will submit to the authority of a primal father image.

It is indeed ironic that the character of the mass man should be produced from the emotional environment of the commune. Individuals who are apparently "normal" but icily rational and calculating and devoid of any sense of the sacred have horrified political thinkers from Reissman to Arendt. But here we have a passive reason for the instability of the commune as a basis for special relationships. In order to function as a "family" its method of childrearing must be collective and hence professional, thereby destroying in the second generation the intimate tie that defines communal life itself.

Kanter's third dynamic can serve to focus upon the above point from another angle. Her point about the antagonism between work methods and communal life rests upon the assertion that "the kinds of organization that are functional for production and business operations may often conflict with the commitment mechanisms that serve to maintain community feeling."[22] Those communes that did not completely break up survived as corporate enterprises. Oneida is an excellent example: it dissolved into a "family" silverware manufacturing joint-stock company and quickly assumed a benevolent but staunchly middle-class character.

For the commune, material success seems to be a deadly reward. At Oneida, prosperity was clearly a contributing factor to its decline as a commune.[23] Outside people were employed; by the 1860s the less attractive work was being done by employees from the surrounding area. Here again the commune as "family" provides us with an answer. Since in the communal structure work relationships are part of the family structure, any movement toward rationalization directly affects the stability of the family as a set of special relationships. As in the other two cases we have examined, the commune absorbs the world of work straight into its familial structure. When work is rationalized there can be no retreat to the solidifying special relationships of the family since the "family" in the communal sense has been carefully defined as to be part of work.

The fragility of the commune as a nondyadic institution of special relationships suggests that different links between family and society need to be explored.

14

TOWARD A NEW PLURALISM

There is a tradition in modern political thought that is available to us in our attempt to find a reconciliation between the modern family and the political order. In many ways it represents an undercurrent in the predominant trends of modern politics. Moreover, it needs to undergo significant revision to make room for the modern family. Nevertheless, this tradition offers the only hope for preserving the institution of the modern family and — if we are correct — for attaining a political order that is capable of offering a safe, decent, and reasonably just life for its citizens.

The tradition of which I speak is the political theory of pluralism.[1] Admittedly, pluralism is a protean word; but it has been given concrete expression by every major modern ideology. Regrettably, the general model of pluralism has been almost totally defeated in each one of its different formulations. Locke's political thought does have genuinely pluralist elements but they are submerged by his central commitment to rational individualism. John Stuart Mill nearly formed a modern pluralist alternative, but again the necessary political implications of the idea of individual development warred with his goal. Contemporary liberalism is now very much committed to the idea of the Service State and increasingly it seems to be finding that rational individualism is no obstacle to its attainment. Revolutionary pluralism was decisively defeated with the First International; and guild socialism, the most carefully fashioned model of pluralism in the modern era, lost its battle to a centralized democratic socialism. Classical conservatism now has only a ghostly presence in modern politics. It seems never to have recovered from its commitments to the old regime.

But let us pursue the pluralist model in its major forms in order to reconstruct a new pluralist vision, one that not only has room for the modern family but can also comfortably accommodate it.

Robert Nisbet has done much to show pluralism's wide historical foundation. We can safely begin with him. Here are the six dominant features that he offers us:

> 1. *Plurality.* "The plural community is not founded upon a single objective or pursuit—whether kinship, religion, or politics—but upon a plurality of communities."
>
> 2. *Autonomy.* "...each group or community within the larger community should be endowed with the greatest possible autonomy *and* with performance by other groups and communities of the functions embedded in them by tradition or plan."
>
> 3. *Decentralization.* "Authority in society — in the larger system of authority and structure of authority within each of the component communities and associations — should be as far as possible from centralization in one single body or individual."
>
> 4. *Hierarchy.* "Wherever two or more people associate more or less regularly, there is bound to be some form of stratification or hierarchy, no matter how fleeting and minor."
>
> 5. *Tradition.* "The plural community ... is characterized overwhelmingly by tradition in contrast to law, that is, formal calculated, and prescriptive regulations."
>
> 6. *Localism.* "Most alienation (as seen by pluralists) is the consequence of human beings having been uprooted from place, from accustomed habitat."[2]

Pluralism should be able to permit the existence of special relationships along with the necessary commitments to constitutional mechanisms. The family need not be required to be structurally similar to other institutions in society. Pluralism assumes, even celebrates, a diversity of values and thus the family should be able to stand side by side with institutions based on different premises without being attacked for its failure to provide appropriately "socialized" human beings. Social and political conflict are supposed to be accommodated and not suppressed in a pluralist society. That citizens are citizens is not because they hold to certain universal beliefs.

But this general description has not come even close to fruition in political thought, let alone in actual societies. Pluralist models have not paid much attention to the modern family.

LIBERAL PLURALISM

Liberalism, even when committed to the principles of pluralism, has not looked kindly upon items 4 and 5 on Nisbet's list. After all, liberals historically struggled against the conservative model of pluralism, which did indeed rest upon tradition and hierarchy. The function of custom would be replaced by constitutionalism. Hierarchy would be abandoned altogether. Eventually the idea of the voluntary organization would become the basis for a theory of pluralism without hierarchy. The free association fitted well with the premises of constitutionalism. The state could assume a protective and secondary role. If the individual could be assured of movement across organizations or form new ones, the liberal could keep his individualist premises and still recognize the premise of all forms of pluralism, the centrality of life in associations. Even when liberal pluralism — American style — was to be criticized, it was attacked on conventional pluralist premises. Theodore Lowi would complain that associational life in America was in the grasp of a few moribund groups that choked off any newcomers.[3] A rigid adherence to civil liberties would meaningfully protect freedom of association and enlarge the pluralist universe at the same time.

But Tocqueville, the liberal pluralist with conservative sensibilities, could see that this new theory of politics involved significant changes. In contrasting associational activity in America with that of aristocratic societies, he noted the lack of permanence and compulsion in liberal societies:

> Among democratic peoples new families continually rise from nothing while others fall, and nobody's position is quite stable. The woof of time is ever being broken and the track of past generations lost. Those who have gone are easily forgotten, and no one gives a thought to those who follow. All a man's interests are limited to those near himself.[4]

Thus, if association is to flourish, it must be on some other basis than the "natural sentiments" of family and class. In America the family in its aristocratic sense no longer existed and Tocqueville did not see the family as part of the firmament of American pluralism. In aristocratic societies, the father is the "natural and necessary link between the past and the present, the link where these two chains meet and join."[5] But it is a link maintained by fear and economic interest. Tocqueville was much impressed with the eighteenth-century American family. He admired the familiarity and tenderness in it. But he saw the best basis for association in the principle of "enlightened self-interest." This would be the basis for group formation in the new liberal society. While it might not "inspire great sacrifices" nor make a man virtuous," it would produce "orderly, temperate, moderate, carefree, and self-controlled citizens."[6] Thus self-interest was to be the basis of group cohesion. Tocqueville was almost sanguine about the family. It was, of course, based on other sentiments, but it would still continue to bring "kindred together."

Liberal pluralism continued to pursue its commitment to self-interest as the basis for all group ties. David Truman presented a model which saw all groups composed of similar "interests" and Robert Dahl, in a recent book that does much to refurbish pluralism, still conceives of groups as grounded in rational self-interest.[7] Members of groups in a liberal society will remain in them so long as their interests are served. "Naturally," Dahl reminds us, it would be "rational to withdraw my adherence if I expect that the loss would exceed the gain."[8]

For a long time no one would ask why family loyalties did not operate in this fashion. When the question was raised, only one option seemed appropriate: the family *ought* to look more like a voluntary association based on self-interest. If it doesn't, its members must be being coerced to such an extent that they cannot safely cut their losses. Movement in and out of the groups is essential to liberal pluralism. Interests do, after all, change. Therefore the family must be reconstructed. We saw in an earlier chapter how vulnerable liberal pluralism is to an attack from this perspective. The conventional family must be replaced in favor of more kinds of family forms and forms more fitting a model of voluntary association. There is, of course, a sense in which all pluralist models are open to the challenge that they are not pluralist enough. Whether the issue is the rights of political groups or new "life styles," it is extremely difficult for a pluralist of any sort to be able to provide a theoretical response that says in effect, "No *more* pluralism!"

The pluralist universe is a very delicate one but pluralism based on a single mode, that of self-interest, is especially unsuitable for the protection and promotion of the modern family. We will look later at proposals for "saving" the family in a liberal society. But we can note here that even when the liberal looks at the family as an institution *sympathetically,* he devises plans in terms of inducements.[9] The self-interest model then is used in support of the family. Economic incentives are offered to keep it intact. Thus the family is still seen as a voluntary association held together by a bond of self-interest.

Radical Pluralism

Liberal pluralism has taken self-interest as its basis because it permits a convenient connection between the individual and the group. Nothing need be sacrificed to the principle of individualism if groups are formed and maintained by the interests of autonomous persons. Socialist pluralism faces different problems. Its commitment is to the group itself.

Thus it is not so uncomfortable with preserving individual attachment to the group. The problem that the socialist pluralist faces lies in insuring equality, especially in economic life. Pierre Joseph Proudhon offered the slogan "Multiply your associations and be free" and he insisted that his system provided relative equality for all. But when Marx caustically noted that Proudhon could not understand the dialectic, he was really saying that a dialectic which conceived of society as a dynamic balance of forces could not guarantee an equalitarian order. Here, I think, was the basic vulnerability in this form of pluralism when it faced its sister ideological forms.

The doctrine that ties individuals to groups and groups to one another in this model is a form of the social contract. Proudhon called his theory "mutualism"; Peter Kropotkin "mutual aid." Proudhon searched for a principle that was "a synthesis of private property and collective ownership." It must not be found "in utopia or blind routine." Here is his "equation":

> Two men encounter each other, recognize their dignity, ascertain the increased benefit which would result for both working in concert, and consequently guarantee each other equality, which amounts to saying, economy. There is the entire social system: an equation, and there a power of collectivity.[10]

In a similar fashion Kropotkin insisted that social bonds arise only from "social habits and the necessity, which everyone feels, of finding cooperation, support, sympathy among his neighbors."[11] Individuality is protected by the principles of cooperation and reciprocity. The economic and social relationships built on such foundations then take on a life of their own.

Marx once referred to Benthamite utilitarianism as a theory based upon the motives of the English shopkeeper. He made the same criticism against Proudhon and Kropotkin. One difference, however, is that neither of these writers disguised their theories in general terms. Proudhon openly championed the complaints of the petty bourgeois and the peasant. Kropotkin fell in love with the Jura Swiss, with their domestic industry and small landholdings. These loyalties were appropriate. The skilled craftsman, farmer, and shopowner represented a form of economic activity that was locally based and partially cushioned by custom. In short, these activities provided for a community within a pluralist framework. Proudhon's and Kropotkin's concept of alienation was quite different from Marx's, or for that matter, from most contemporary socialists.[12] Cottage industry and farming were unalienated forms of work because they were self-producing activities surrounded by Gemeinschaft. This selection from Kropotkin's criticism of modern industry illustrates our point:

Skilled artisanship is being swept away as a survival of a past condemned to disappear. For the artist who formerly found aesthetic enjoyment in the work of his hands is substituted the human slave of an iron slave. Nay, even the agricultural laborer, who used to find a relief from the hardships of his life in the home of his ancestors — the future home of his children — in his love of the field, and in a keen intercourse with nature, even he has been doomed to disappear for the sake of the division of labor. He is an anachronism, we are told; he must be substituted, in a Bonanza farm, by an occasional servant hired for the summer, and discharged as autumn comes, a tramp who will never again see the field he has harvested once in his life. [13]

Thus we could say that the doctrines of mutual aid and mutualism were indeed a combination of the idea of the social contract in its Lockean and Rousseauan formulations. Interdependence between individuals and groups characterized the socialist and pluralist vision. Mutualism implied a more permanent and historically concrete version of the contract than the rational individualist conceived. Nor did it have any of the features of universal and indivisible acceptance that Rousseau's model required. Proudhon had attacked Rousseau for giving the social contract a "central majesty" that guaranteed only an "abstract sovereignty of the people." [14]

What was the relationship between the family and the mutualist idea? Unfortunately, Proudhon's ideas on the family are severely marred by his commitment to the same romantic patriarchal form as Rousseau's. Men represented power and women grace:

> ... society does no injustice to woman by refusing her equality before the law. Woman really has no place in the world of politics and economics. Her function begins beyond these spheres.... By the ideal nature of her being, woman is, so to speak, of priceless value. [15]

But we can look beyond Proudhon's romanticization of the peasant family and see that the family was conceived foremost as an institution to forge special relationships throughout a pluralist society:

> Every time that men with their wives and children assemble in one place, live and till the soil side by side, develop in their midst different industries, create neighborly relations among themselves, establish a state of solidarity, they form what I call a natural group which soon sets itself up as a political organism. ... [16]

If we note Kropotkin's views on education, we can see the relaxed and confident attitudes he had toward the family. Children would be educated at home, in private schools, or in public ones. The state would provide help in each case. Thus there is none of the anxiety one finds in Rousseau, where children must be educated at home and shut off from the outside world or thrust resolutely into Spartan schools. Kropotkin also showed the ease with which the family could be fitted into a pluralist society. Place "the factory and the workshop at the gates of your fields and gardens and work in them," he urged. Keep them small and numerous and "very soon you will yourselves feel interested in that work, and you will have occasion to admire in your children their eager desire to become acquainted with Nature and its forces, their inquiries as to the powers of machinery, and their rapidly developing inventive genius."[17] Both Kropotkin and Marx were horrified by the conditions of child labor under early industrial capitalism. But Marx applauded the erosion of the family and the gradual assumption of state responsibility under this system. Kropotkin attempted to find a mode of industrial production that would guarantee family autonomy.

What happened to the model of socialist pluralism we have set forth? One must remember that the theories of Proudhon and Kropotkin represented only a thin slice of the anarchosocialist tradition. Writers who were more individualistic would not hold the family in much esteem. William Godwin and Max Stirner were positively hostile to the family. The former interpreted the male-female bond in an extremely cavalier fashion: "I shall assiduously cultivate the intercourse of that woman, whose moral and intellectual accomplishments strike me in the most powerful manner. But it may happen that other men will feel for her the same preference that I do. This will create no difficulty. We may all enjoy her. . . ."[18] Stirner traced violence to intimacy. Eliminate the dyad and opposition between persons would "vanish in complete severance or singleness."[19]

On the other side, the Bakuninists, who formed the mantle of anarchist opposition to Marx after the collapse of Proudhonism, were much too bloodthirsty ever to accept even the basic tenets of pluralism. Barricade equality looked like a decentralization of power but the Bakuninists' cry of "solidarity" would be the decisive organizational factor.

Battered by individualists on one side and opportunist revolutionaries on the other, this form of pluralism would succumb to the commune as the appropriate model for special relationships. One cannot deny that the commune has a particular attraction for this theory. It is an exact structural fit to the economic unit. If work needs to reflect the pluralist universe and if work needs to be brought right to the gates of the home, why not collapse economic and familial roles? Several families, brought together on the basis of mutualist principles, would represent the quintescence of decentralized socialism.

CONSERVATIVE PLURALISM

If radical pluralism seems an efflorescence in modern political thought, the conservative variant is a ghost. Edmund Burke had indeed supplied a view that saw the family as the source of all special relationships. The "ties of nature" were "much better, surer, safer and pleasanter than any which we make for ourselves, politically, as members of parties or states, or in the intercourse of common life as friendships." "The love of the whole is not extinguished by . . . subordinate partiality."[20] In fact, it is promoted by it:

> To be attached to the subdivision, to love the little platoon we belong to in society, is the first principle (as it were) of public affections. It is the first link in the series by which we proceed towards a love of our country, and of mankind.[21]

The "little" platoons surrounded by numerous supporting structures connected the individual with the "great primeval contract of eternal society." For Burke, the family gave structure to human emotion that carried human beings beyond their own life above "the gross animal existence of a temporary and perishable nature."[22]

But it must be remembered that for Burke the inequalities in the family between husband and wife and between parents and children sufficiently resembled the political order itself to make the family an integrated part of the polity. Similarly, the value which the family is seen to be promoting, loyalty based upon kinship, became a model for the nature of authority and obligation in society at large. Burke had no difficulty justifying a political system managed by "great families" since authority was essentially family based. This was a gentle patriarchalism; it has little resemblance to the theories of Filmer and Hobbes. Burke, after all, advocated a pluralist order and a prudent morality, one which could best reflect a largely hidden but benevolent Providence.

Yet when modern conservatism confronts the family it necessarily faces two problems. First, the background to Burke's thought, the belief that held together his pluralist vision, is gone. Burke closed his famous attack on the French revolutionaries with the warning about resisting the "decrees of Providence itself." But there was no ugly underbelly to Burke's determinist base. The moral order could be corrupted by arrogant reform but a just political order would "beautify and soften private society." Providence provided a cover for man's natural defects.

Modern conservatism relies on a much more ambivalent base. The same caution and the same fear of disintegration is there but the new bulwark is the amoral determinism of psychoanalysis or biology. George Gilder bases his case for the family on the "natural" shiftlessness of the unattached male.[23] Lionel Tiger and Robin Fox based their male-bonding theories on a computer analogy:

> It is not instincts in any old-fashioned sense that are at issue here. ... They emerge from the biology of an animal programmed to produce them, once it is given the appropriate stimuli.... The human organism is like a computer that is set up or "wired" in a particular way.... Once this information is received, the computer stores it and goes on to the next task. If the system is confused — if, for example, adult programs are fed to adolescent computers — then the fuses blow and there is risk of breakdown.

Our "wiring" has not changed over millions of years. "We are wired for hunting."[25]

Even so sensible and careful a writer as Selma Fraiberg feels compelled to base her critique of day-care centers on Konrad Lorenz's generalization on the greylag goose.[26] This despite the fact that she has a wealth of clinical studies (many of which are her own) and empirical reports to easily make her case.

But, as we saw with Freud's theories, the amorality of arguments from nature makes them especially susceptible to their own inversion. If man is programed as a hunting animal, then deprogram him. If civilization requires repression of instinct, then abandon civilization and start over. This is what Marcuse and Reich have already urged. These kinds of argument from nature are probably the worst weapon for a conservative use. In the words of Benjamin Barber, they are only "descriptive propositions" with a "moral aura" that permits them to pass as ethical:

> Thus, while to say 'if you want to take the *best* way downtown, then you *ought* to take a train' has normative overtones and an imperative mien, it is in fact a disguised indicative with purely descriptive content....[27]

But that is not the only difficulty the conservative has with the family. In truth, he has never come to terms with the features of the modern family itself. He has never liked its intensity of emotion, its relative equality, or its inward looking character. Conservatism has always found that its support of the middle class and its values is a bitter pill to swallow. To the extent to which the modern family seems to be a bourgeois invention, it often appears to reject conservative values as much as to embrace them.

This ambivalence can be easily seen in Ariès' account of the transition to the modern family:

> The evolution of the last few centuries has often been presented as the triumph of individualism over social constraints, with the family counted among the latter. But where is the individualism in these modern lives, in which all the energy of the couple is directed to serving the interests of a deliberately restricted posterity? Was there not greater individualism in the gay indifference of the prolific fathers of the *ancien régime*?[28]

Thus the new family is entirely too rational. Birth control involved calculations that were literally impossible for those in earlier times: "This power of objective, reasonable calculation, at the heart even of sexual frenzy, had no place in the mental and physical structure of the populations still close to the instincts."[29] It sent the servants out of the house and "degraded" the idea of service by destroying the familiarity between servants, child, and masters. It closed off the home to the outside world, set up business outside the house, and divided up the home (especially the bedroom) into tiny inviolable spheres of privacy. It refused to continue to send its infants out to nurse and its children to apprenticeship. In short, it destroyed a "hierarchical" and "rigid polymorphous social body." And it replaced this by "a host of little societies related to one another by their moral resemblance and by the identity of their way of life, whereas the old unique social body embraced the greatest possible variety of ages and classes."[30]

For Ariès the modern family stands opposed to pluralism, at least the pluralism of the *ancien régime*, and indeed was a major agent in the new "insistence on uniformity." Like so many conservatives, Ariès can only see one kind of pluralism, the pluralism of family lines and estates. The "gay indifference" of the aristocrat certainly represents an instance of uniformity and a dismal one at that. But the real question is this: When the hierarchies and traditions have been swept away, what should our attitude be toward the last remnants of a pluralist world?

This brings us to another and somewhat contradictory stance toward the modern family. Ariès applauded the nonchalance of the premodern fathers who set up a few of their children and neglected the others. At least they had not "moulded the bodies and souls" of their children. Order would come from the depth and strictness of hierarchical communal life. Conservatives who face modern society have no apprenticeship system nor a system of inequalities to view as "something perfectly natural." Thus the family is looked upon as the last bastion of authority and it seems to be failing in this role. Christopher Lasch in his new book takes precisely this position. For Lasch, parents face a crisis of confidence. Uncertain of their roles as authority figures, parents overemphasize their affectional roles.

Children are unable to directly confront the oedipal crisis and become stuck in a narcissistic stage:

> The child who scorns his parents as weak and indecisive — who forms the most tenuous ties to his parents, and pushes them without much difficulty into the background of his mind — conjures up another set of parents in his fantasies. Since those other parents so largely represent the creation of the child's unconscious thought-projections of his unconscious wishes and the fears that go with them, they appear to be as vengeful and punitive, as terrifyingly arbitrary and unjust, as the real-life parents are helpless, reasonable, and bland. The remoteness of the older generation does not mean that children form no vivid impressions of their parents; it only means that those ideas will seldom be tested against everyday experience. The child's fantasies go unchecked; he invents a supremely seductive, castrating mother and a fantasy-father who is remote, vindictive and all-powerful.[31]

Lasch insists that in its heyday the bourgeois family had a clearly defined father figure whom the child could acknowledge and turn his aggression outward against. The more mild family structure fails to instill a work ethic from the intense struggle to replace the father. Lasch quotes approvingly: "These young people can conceive of no competition that [does] not result in someone's annihilation."[32] Even the new ideas of the sexual revolution — "the celebration of oral sex, masturbation, and homosexuality" — spring from a "narcissistic withdrawal of interest from the external world," brought on by a weak father.[33] The psychoanalytic image of a terrifying mother with a vagina full of teeth haunts our social and sex lives.

Lasch's account is not without an element of truth. The modern family is indeed penetrated by the prudential morality of late capitalism. But the real point lies in the overall similarity to Freud's political theories. Affection is a mask in front of instinctual drive, whether the family uses emotion "successfully" or not. Lasch's support of the family does as much to undermine it as to protect it. How can the family be seen as a "haven" when all emotion is the result of the twists and turns of instinct as it batters against the social order?

The idea of authority presented in *Haven in a Heartless World* is derived from the Freudian image of the primal father. Unless authority is internalized on the basis of the psychic drama which the primal father represents it is not authority at all. Hence the modern father and his surrogates in the social and political order must be seen as either "incompetent" or secretly "malevolent." Without the primal father, all-powerful and cool and distant, "the child experiences authority as pure force." No "internalization" of authority can occur.

Pluralism as an aid to the reconstruction of political thought and the family provides us with an image that is at once deep and broad, yet still largely untouched. There are great differences among the three varieties we have reviewed. In each there is a hestitation in using the family as a major institution in society. Nevertheless, an image of an pluralism based upon special relationships, one that welcomes decentralization and indirect administration as a means for fostering them, holds out the possibility for a revitalized social and political order. The withdrawal of the modern family from society may be the result of the inhospitable climate that threatened to surround it rather than the nature of the family itself.

15

AN EPILOGUE
ON
FAMILY POLICY

Picture a typical family in a typical suburb or city. They live in a comfortable house. The husband and father works eight hours a day, five days a week, miles away. The wife and mother works two or three days a week as a nurse, again in the city. One child is of school age; the other spends three days a week in a nursery school. Groceries are bought at a chain store; a large shopping center provides other needs. Breakfasts are hurried affairs. At lunch the family is dispersed. Frequently, the children's dinner is made by the first spouse home. Parents eat later together, when the children are in bed. Our typical family has loving and dutiful parents. Saturdays are spent on the family boat, Sundays about the house. The parents listen attentively to the teachers' assessement of their children's progress. Twice a month husband and wife go to a movie or entertain another couple. Once a week grandparents are called.

For centuries this description was regarded as utopia for millions of people. What is wrong with this picture? Why does it so frequently change to one in which the father and mother are divorced, the children turn to drugs, the grandparents are marched off to old-age homes? Why is it regarded by men and women of learning as a pathological social state? We have argued that the bases of the attack on the family by modern political theorists are wrong. But the social sphere of modern life does need expansion. With that expansion family life can assume an added dimension. One of the most difficult problems the family has faced recently is the disjunction between itself and other social institutions. Parsons attempted a connection between the two with his concept of the father's cardinal role.

But even with the new version of dual roles the family is at best seen as an institution allegedly based on emotional sentiment whose major function is to produce individuals who can function unsentimentally in the outside world. Joseph Schumpeter observed the anomaly of the father and husband who acts mercilessly in the marketplace only to overflow with sentiment and altruism when he arrives home to the bosom of the family.[1] Novelists and scriptwriters have been fascinated with this acceptable form of schizophrenia for some time. But such a state could not hold for very long. Was the family expected to teach the value of special relationships or was it expected to teach placement in the world of the free and rational? Many supporters of the family insist that we must have both. But having both will not work for a variety of reasons. If the family is the only basis of special relationships in society, then family members must treat each other in a most careful manner.[2] Special relationships become muted in the frantic attempt to maintain them. As Lyman Wynne has shown, many families show a desperate preoccupation with harmony in an attempt to prevent role changes in any of their members.[3] Wynne called this behavior "pseudo-mutuality" and it does not surprise me that the theory was devised to explain schizophrenia. Such a reaction may indeed be family-based and the mental aberrations of such children could be the result of the schizophrenic climate in which family members have been forced to live.

Even if the modern family is able to avoid pseudo-mutuality, it must still cope with the fact that if special relationships are indeed genuinely formed they are positively dysfunctional for survival outside the family. Special relationships do indeed form under modern conditions of work and leisure. To a limited extent they will always continue to do so. Even in concentration camps, inmates manage to develop bonds of mutual support. But increasingly they are forged against and in spite of the efforts of the institutions in which they appear. Social workers are admonished to remain "professionally" committed to their clients. Anyone who has visited a doctor's office notices the lack of eye contact and the brutal refusal to listen to the person who is the patient. Long ago industries were designed on the principle of the interchangeability of workers and their submission to a bureaucratic world view. Schools have become notoriously closed institutions. The bevy of professionals they now employ to deal with emotional problems of children serve to further isolate families.

None of what we have just said is meant to deprecate the proposals which attempt to deal with the causes of family disintegration that are the result of poverty. Full employment, income-maintenance programs, and systems of medical care are extremely important and ought not to be rejected. But it is questionable whether the family can be saved through the Service State. Every principle that gives the Service State its momentum — professionalism, equality of opportunity and services, rational management of scarce resources — runs against the values of the family as an institution of special relationships. To simply rely upon the natural tendency of people to continue to cultivate family ties and family feelings in the face of a society dedicated to these antipathetic principles is very naive.[4] The Service State does not *need* the family to function. In fact, its internal dynamic would have us do away with the family altogether. A pluralist vision can certainly accommodate some large-scale services. But it can do so only when they are counterbalanced by institutions that give concrete expression to other world views.

I hesitate to offer a list of proposals designed to "save" the modern family. This book, if it has established any of its contentions, should have made it obvious that if the family is to survive as an institution of special relationships the major thrust of modern politics must be altered. While I think there are remnants of the liberal tradition from which a new vision of politics can be built, this vision is not going to be achieved through a few programs no matter how carefully they are conceived and executed. The consolidation of political and economic forces has proceeded extremely rapidly over the last hundred years in the United States. In many instances, there is simply no way to turn back.

Yet the general model of pluralism points us in the right direction. Here are a few proposals which are extremely limited, although I imagine still not easy to achieve. They are offered only as illustrations.

Some historians have placed a heavy emphasis upon the school as an important influence in the loss of family autonomy.[5] Actually, the movement demanding formal education arose as much as a result of dissatisfaction or "loss of nerve" over familial education. The centrality of the child in the modern family provoked attempts to find appropriate ways of providing him or her with the means to survive and even rise in the outside world. But particulary in the United States the school was an adjunct of the community itself. Schools were locally planned and built and great efforts — efforts which today we would find too confining — were made to assure the propriety of teachers and their integration into the community. School schedules were even arranged to accommodate the work routines of families.

Today schools still hold onto a significant portion of this heritage. In fact, school systems in America are among the few institutions that are truly decentralized. But, on the whole, the school is remarkably isolated from the families who send their children to it. Yet there is no reason why it need be, or why, in the words of social scientists, the school need be an independent socializing agency to which families "give up" their children. Three developments have contributed to the isolation. First, the neccessities of modern life have carried parents' attention away from the school. The recent mass entry of women into the labor force has completed this state of affairs. During most of the day, parents are away from the home and, more often than not, from the neighborhood. Second, school personnel are highly professionalized and have come to regard their autonomy in the education of children as a right. Teachers' unions have become an additional institutional layer between the school and children. Finally, federal and state regulations increasingly limit the scope of local autonomy. As a consequence, although the elementary school and high school may be only a block away from families, the parents might almost as well be sending their children off to boarding school in the fashion of the English aristocracy.

The revitalization of local government may go far toward correcting this situation. We will discuss this in a moment. School reform should move in the direction of making education an adjunct institution for the family. Attempts to open up the closed nature of modern educational systems by emphasizing "children's rights," a tack taken with vigor by the recent Carnegie Council on Children report, will serve only to further alienate the family from the school. Children will need advocates to protect their rights and one can be certain that these advocates will come from the professional middle class. As is nearly always the case, and we noted earlier how perceptive Marx was on this point in his analysis of the Factory Acts, any concerted attempt to guarantee the rights of alleged incompetents by surrogates will only serve the interests of those groups anxious to further the administrative consolidation of society.

Students of the family often note the decline of the family as an economic unit. They generally assume that this is the root cause of the modern fragility of the family as an institution. This assumption was, of course, the basic premise of Marx's analysis. I find this contention a disturbing one for a variety of reasons. It is based on the premise that institutions are held together by an economic bond. Both rational individualism and collectivism make this unwarranted assumption. For centuries the family ties arose from sheer economic need. Farmers and businessmen needed wives and children to help them survive. Now we are told that no one "needs" children or spouses any longer and thus the family will die a natural death. Although it is not fashionable to say so, it was capitalism that in its earlier stages gave birth to the modern family by gradually increasing the standard of living and allowing people to focus upon their children and spouses in an emotional context. The full record of capitalism in this regard is obviously mixed. The rise of the Service State with its economic and political consolidation would indeed make the family superfluous.

There is a real irony in the criticism of the family, first as an economic institution and then, when it has shed its economic function, as an institution of sentiment. To deny that institutions based upon a purely affective tie can be stable ones is actually a most pessimistic assessment of the human condition. In Chapter 13 we tried to suggest that special relationships can form the most enduring bonds. They ought to be all the more applauded because they are based upon motivations that transcend economic need. The assertion that the family cannot survive as an affective institution is really an assertion that affective institutions are not valuable ones, that they must be stamped out in favor of surer bonds.

The loss of the family's economic function is less a problem than the modern organization of work itself. It may be that the radical separation of work and family life, not the constraining ties of economic need on the family, is the basis of our problem. After all, if economic need is *too* demanding, the family will disintegrate as well.

The earlier integration of economic and familial function actually had a twofold affect. First, it did serve to hold the family together through the father's authority as a holder of economic power. In addition, it furthered the family's stewardship role in acquainting its children with economic life. In the Middle Ages, the family had often abdicated this function by farming its children out as apprentices. Under industrialization, this practice underwent grotesque variations. To the extent to which societies assumed bourgeois values, the child was spared this casting out: first, by working within the family's economic sphere until adulthood and later, as parents attempted to free the child of economic burdens altogether, by delaying integration into the adult community through a long educational route. Thus today the child of the middle-class family sees the family's economic base only in the most vague terms and then largely in terms of the benefits it confers. How does one tell a child about one's work as a patent attorney or a personnel director? How does the factory line worker convey to her children the frustration that she experiences? Thus the family seems to stand outside the economic sphere, functions as a leisure/consumption unit, and more frequently than not is itself blamed for the often mindless acquisitiveness that characterizes modern life.

We have already suggested that the collapsing of family life into the sphere of work is not the answer to this problem. Nor is the woman's entry into the working force much of a help. Her departure from the daily life of the family is still on individualistic terms. She works separately from her husband and her absence is justified in terms of "helping" the family with more money or "making mommy a more interesting person." Attempts to provide families with more social services only increase the weight of the Service State by employing other and more men and women to care for the children that are now being left at home.

Thus there is no easy way to give the family back its role as an economic steward to its children or to indicate to them that they are needed in ways other than as affective objects. Closer proximity of work and the home might help. So might more flexible working hours, shared jobs, and a relaxation of nepotism regulations. But nothing comes close to the kind of introduction to economic life that occurs when a parent has a child help in a family business or farm or introduces him early to the mysteries and struggles of a profession or skill. The only real help can be a general devolution of economic life in society to smaller limits. Advocates of the axiom "small is beautiful" need to apply their beliefs to the creation of an interface between family and economics.

Nothing prepared the family for its much-discussed withdrawal from social and political life more effectively than the decline of local government and of the neighborhood. One cannot say that the modern family behaved in an unblemished fashion during the periods of economic and political convulsions from which our cities have suffered. Indeed, city families moved away by the thousands; or when they did not, they tended to form tiny barricades between each other and also between their neighborhoods. Yet what can one expect of an institution so brutally subjected to the chaos of modern life? Even Richard Sennett, a writer not given to idealization of the modern family, writes thus in his study of Chicago in the 1880s: "The context of life for these middle-class people was a sort of great if inarticulate battle, between the forces of fear centered in the intimate, isolated family and the chaotic, ruthless vigor of the industrial and bureaucratic work order of this new metropolis."[6] The family lost its fight to maintain itself in this new environment. Like guerillas fleeing a far superior force, they left for the wilds of suburbia and made daily forays back for their survival. Both those who stayed and those who left bear the same moral scars that any war inflicts on its combatants.

If we just glance at the recent history of cities, without ignoring the role of blatant racism and greed and corruption, the one feature that stands out — more than the loss of the old tax base, more than crime, more than housing blight — is the decline of the neighborhood. Urban neighborhoods rarely had a legally recognized existence. In some cities they formed the basis of machine politics. More often they interlaced more formal boundaries. Neighborhoods underwent transformations and alterations long before massive industrialization and immigration patterns caused wild fluctuations. Thernstrom's study of Newburyport, Massachusetts, showed striking patterns of property mobility among workers.[7] But the changing nature of neighborhoods is different from their obliteration. Many people of the last generation cannot find their old neighborhood to show to their children. The old neighborhood is gone. In its place are parking lots, high-rise apartments, corporation headquarters. Some of the most poignant and indeed, the best contemporary social-science research has recorded this tragedy.[8] Yet the neighborhood was once a center of emotional and material support that was not created and not maintained by the state.

The idea of making neighborhoods administrative and political units extends back to Thomas Jefferson's plan for a ward system. The premise behind neighborhood government or "community control" is simple and persuasive: People care about where they live, work, marry, and die. We would speak of the concept of piety if the word had not already become so alien. Yet there is today often an inverse relationship between political control and the social space essential to policy formation and those which are closest emotionally and physically.

Neighborhood revitalization faces many problems, not the least of which are the questions of economy of scale and the agonizing issues associated with racism. But the neighborhood government is the ideal political form for the rejuvenation of families as more public entities. So far as it exists such government illustrates that the modern family itself does not somehow inherently foster antipolitical privatistic sentiments but rather that the forms of political activity available produce such attitudes.

Admittedly there are very small starts toward changes. But we must remember that we are dealing with a social institution that is based upon different premises and meets different needs from those that large-scale political transformation is designed to produce.

These changes — the humanization of work, the democratization of school, the revitalization of local government — are both limited and radical. They are radical in the sense that they require significant alterations in our conceptions of economic and social institutions. But they are limited in that like all changes that focus upon structural recommendations they lack a visionary element. Let us take time in these remaining few pages to offer a few glimpses into a world with a vision different from that offered by modern political thinkers. The attempt to present these is a very hazardous one. It is best that it take the form of cautions and reservations.

First, when pluralist theory pays attention to its origins it may find that there are necessary limitations to the promotion of pluralism in society. Radical pluralists have discovered this in their efforts to promote the value of equality as have liberal pluralists when they have sought to examine the limits of self-interest. In fact, as we saw in Chapter 11, the more dedicated the attempt to pluralize society, the more likely the result is to be precisely the opposite. For not only do such measures require enforcement at a center but in addition a blueprinted pluralism presupposes a hidden monistic standard. The attempt to encourage many kinds of families is really an attempt to produce only the basic family form on the model of the voluntary organization.

It is also necessary to admit, however, that a new pluralism based upon the concept of special relationships requires a certain underlying pattern. Certainly, the hope is that the individual who emerges from such relationships will have not only the capacity to form new ones but also the independence to seek new forms as well. Thus the existence of special relationships — dyadic, intimate, emotional, and object-diffused — and the confidence of a society to promote them suggests that there are indeed boundaries in this form of pluralism. But they are boundaries that are likely to be naturally flexible. The concept of special relationships probably admits of a much greater variety than now seems available. We must remember that what still passes for pluralism in American society is a very cramped version. Today it seems to be caught in a vise. On one side is pressure from the values inherited from America's early modern and peculiarly parochial past. On the other is pressure from the bureaucratic growth of the industrial Service State.

But our focus upon existing social institutions (school, work, and neighborhood) may not prove to be imaginative enough, given the conditions of modern society. Robert Nisbet has approached this problem in more general terms and introduced the idea of "social inventions" as an answer. He contends that there is a history of social invention in the West just as there is a history of material, technological, and cultural invention. The parish, the guild, the university are social inventions. I would argue that the modern family itself is a social invention as well, one of the few that modernity has produced. Perhaps what we really need is something more than the refurbishment of social institutions in support of the family. Perhaps the obsession with inventing new family forms could be directed toward inventing new social institutions that can nurture the modern family.

In the twilight of the protest movements in the 1960s, some efforts were made in this direction. Remember that no matter how poorly conceived its attempt, the New Left had sought to humanize the American university by ripping it away from its status as an agent of the Service State and giving it a new autonomy. Finally, however, a nasty realism emerged from all these efforts, one that had not been openly stated before: What was the university for if not to train youth for entrance into the Service State? Belatedly, portions of the New Left looked beyond the university itself, not in terms of an infatuation with revolution or personal liberation, but in an inchoate effort to invent new social institutions around the professions. One pamphlet pleaded that "for people out of school and into jobs, maybe with a profession to which we are emotionally committed, maybe with dependents or habits of comfort or interest to support — we *must* work out alternative jobs, alternative ways of living in the society, alternative ways of bringing up and educating children."[9] Here was an invigorating realism, not often found in the brief history of the New Left. The obsession with the commune is absent, as is antinomian posturing. If people want families, professions, and some material comfort, how can the movement avoid the charge that it has produced "neurotic 25-year-olds who feel their politics have only disabled them — made it harder for them to make friends, to communicate with others, to raise their children, to live with their consciences, to endure...?"[10]

Of course, this effort to find alternatives failed miserably. There are no counterinstitutions today. In fact, the slogans of the New Left have been institutionalized as bureaucratic access points in the frantic struggle for entrance into the service professions. The family has suffered accordingly. Not only are there no communes but now we are treated to the sociologist's euphemism, the variant family.

We are left with our final challenge: Can we describe a process of radical change toward a reconstructed pluralism? Unfortunately, there is no pluralist theory — radical, conservative, liberal — that can provide us with a model. Pluralist theorists have spent most of their energies in defense of what they see as an existing pluralism or in a plea for a devolution of power away from the center. Thus we lack available models of change that are founded in theories of incremental reform or revolution. Perhaps we should have no models; a genuine pluralist ought to speak of social change as efflorescence. But we can still speak in general terms about the forms in which change will occur. The bureaucratization of social and economic life in America and the ideological formulations that support it are at such an advanced stage that I feel progress toward a pluralism of special relationships must take the form of mass movements. Recall for a moment Judith Lorber's futuristic scenario of families and childrearing in America. At one point she flirted with the notion of a parenting class as the appropriate structure for dealing with the problems of children in the future. Note that she regarded this class as a somewhat backward one. This "select" group would be inclined (or relegated) to small-scale economic activity — farming, handicrafts, cottage industry. She also worried about what their belief systems were likely to be. Since the existence of these primitives would "probably not be compatible with a unified society," Ms. Lorber replaced her proposal with a "world system of child exchange." For all its obvious faults, this analysis does manage to suggest a "deep social division" between the model of the ideal citizen of the Service State and its allegedly outmoded counterpart. There is indeed a direct conflict between the Service State, even one liberal in form, and a pluralism of special relationships. The conflict is so great that Ms. Lorber is probably correct in an obtuse way. A new pluralist order requires mass political action.

Most of this action must of necessity take the form of resistance, resistance to the extension of the Service State, resistance to the pseudo-pluralism it promotes. There is a danger, of course, that a mass-movement pluralism, once articulate and organized, will take the form of some new orthodoxy. Thus it must take on two tasks simultaneously. It must make demands in the negative, and it has the history of the liberal tradition to draw upon in doing so. The creation of a social space is the first creative act of a new pluralism. But it must also begin the task of inventing new social institutions.

These are not easy tasks. For all its inefficiency, the Service State holds out the promise of a comfortable existence. Moreover, individualism, rational and romantic, is now finally the most acceptable and realistic ethos because now at last political and economic institutions promote it. There is certain awkwardness to special relationships today — whether one looks at the family, as we have done in this book, or whether one looks at other social institutions. The promotion and nurturance of special relationships require a special effort. The common realization of this need is the first step toward a new pluralism.

Admittedly this last chapter is a tentative start toward reconstruction of the family and the political order. But as we noted earlier, we are dealing with a social institution that is based upon needs different from those which large-scale political transformation is designed to produce. Perhaps it is time we rejoice in this difference rather than lament it.

NOTES

CHAPTER 1: pages 1–13

1. Numa Denis Fustel de Coulanges, *The Ancient City* (Garden City: Doubleday, 1955), p. 89.

2. See: Lawrence Stone, *The Family, Sex and Marriage in England 1500–1800* (New York: Harper and Row, 1977), pp. 653–654; and Gordon J. Schochet, *Patriarchalism in Political Thought* (New York: Basic Books, 1975).

3. Bronislaw Malinowski, "Parenthood, the Basis of Social Structure" in *The New Generation*, V. E. Calverton and S. D. Schmalhausen, eds. (New York: Macaulay Company, 1930), p. 113.

4. Edward Shorter, *The Making of the Modern Family* (New York: Basic Books, 1975), p. 78.

5. Cited in Shorter, ibid., p. 326.

6. Philippe Ariès, *Centuries of Childhood* (New York: Vintage Books, 1962), p. 353. Also see: J. H. Plumb, "Children: The Victims of Time," in J. H. Plumb, ed., *The Light of History* (London: Allen Lane, 1972).

7. Ibid., p. 355.

CHAPTER 2: pages 14–27

1. Robert Filmer, "Observations concerning the Originall of Government" in Peter Laslett, ed., *Patriarcha and Other Works* (Oxford: Oxford University Press, 1949), p. 241.

2. Gordon J. Schochet, "Thomas Hobbes on the Family and the State of Nature," *Political Science Quarterly* 82 (September 1967). Similar views which see Hobbes as presenting a consistent patriarchalism can be found in Richard Chapman, "Leviathan Writ Small," *American Political Science Review* 69 (March 1975), pp. 76–90; and Preston King, *The Ideology of Order* (London: Allen and Unwin, 1974), pp. 178–221.

3. Bertrand De Jouvenel, *Sovereignty: An Inquiry into the Political Good* (Chicago: University of Chicago Press, 1957), p. 244.

4. Thomas Hobbes, *Leviathan*, C. B. Macpherson, ed. (Baltimore: Penguin, 1968), p. 254.

5. Most relevant here is the new family economics which assesses children as "producer durables" or "consumer durables." For a helpful critique see Judith Blake, "Are Babies Consumer Durables?" *Population Studies* 22 (March 1968), pp. 5–25.

6. Hobbes, *Leviathan*, p. 255.

7. Ibid., p. 345.

8. Ibid., p. 254. Even sympathetic interpreters have difficulty connecting this passage with Hobbes' remarks about children's standing in regard to contracts. Thus Warrender writes: "...the propriety on Hobbes' part of applying the notion of tacit convenant to the child-parent relationship is very doubtful." *The Political Philosophy of Hobbes* (Oxford: Oxford University Press, 1957), p. 124; also see p. 256, note 1.

9. Ibid., p. 209.

10. Ibid.

11. Ibid.

12. Thomas Hobbes, *Man and Citizen: Thomas Hobbes's De Homine and DeCive,* Bernard Gert, ed. (Garden City: Doubleday, 1972), p. 215.

13. Ibid.

14. Ibid.

15. Ibid. Note that the son is placed in the same category as all those freed from subjection, "whether he be servant, son, or some colony."

16. Ibid.

17. For a brief analysis of Hobbes' use of gratitude and contract in regard to common-wealth by acquisition in general see my *The Shotgun behind the Door: Liberalism and the Problem of Political Obligation* (Athens: University of Georgia Press, 1976), pp. 109–114.

18. Sigmund Freud, *Totem and Taboo,* A. A. Brill, trans. (New York: Random House, 1946), p. 146. For further discussion of the primal crime, see Chapter 7.

19. Hobbes, *Man and Citizen,* p. 117. This passage challenges the interpretation by Schochet that the logical discrepancy of Hobbes "would be removed if the tacit compacts of children were equivalent to the consents that would be forthcoming as soon as each child came of age and became master of his own reason" (p. 435).

20. Hobbes, *Leviathan,* p. 257. Yet even this description ultimately assumes a certain ambivalence. For a few lines later, Hobbes is comparing this great family to a small group of soldiers who, when surprised by an army, may each "use his own reason" to save himself "as he shall think best." How secure are the patriarch's rights in the state of nature?

21. William J. Goode, "Family Disorganization," in *Contemporary Social Problems,* Robert K. Merton and Robert Nisbet, eds. (New York: Harcourt Brace Jovanovich, 1976), p. 543.

22. Hobbes, *Man and Citizen,* pp. 112–113.

23. Hobbes, *Leviathan,* p. 253.

24. Ibid.

25. Ibid. Had Hobbes been willing to develop his argument along the lines later offered by Freud, he might have been able to resolve the inconsistency of the patriarchal family.

26. Ibid.

27. Ibid., p. 250.

28. Hobbes, *Man and Citizen,* p. 219.

29. Schochet, "Thomas Hobbes on the Family and the State of Nature," p. 435.

30. Hobbes, *Leviathan,* p. 254.

31. Frederick Engels, *The Origin of the Family, Private Property and the State* (New York: International Publishers, 1972). For futher discussion, see Chapter 6.

32. Hobbes, *Leviathan,* p. 185.

33. Engels, *The Origin of the Family, Private Property and the State,* p. 109.

34. Sigmund Freud, *Civilization and Its Discontents,* James Strachey, trans. (New York: Norton, 1961), p. 46.

35. Hobbes, *Leviathan,* p. 253. Compare Hobbes' treatment of mother right discussed above to that of Engels (p. 106).

36. Bruno Bettelheim, *The Empty Fortress: Infantile Autism and the Birth of the Self* (New York: Free Press, 1967), pp. 63–67; 77–78.

37. *The Political Philosophy of Thomas Hobbes* (Chicago: University of Chicago Press, 1952), p. 66. For an extended treatment of the limitation of the extreme condition as a basis for political philosophy, see Chapter 9.

38. Colin Turnbull, *The Mountain People* (New York: Simon and Schuster, 1972), pp. 135–136. Children who survived, lived among other youths in roving bands.

39. Ibid., p. 253.

40. Ibid., p. 290.

41. This approach is not limited to a Hobbesian analysis. But see Beverly Jones, "The Dynamics of Marriage and Motherhood" in Robin Morgan, ed., *Sisterhood Is Powerful* (New York: Random House, 1970); Jones argues that the "open weapon that a man uses to control his wife is the threat of force or force itself." Adrienne Rich, *Of Woman Born* (New York: Norton, 1976) suggests that infanticide has its rational basis as a form of liberation from the family. Susan Brownmiller, *Against Our Will* (New York: Simon and Schuster, 1975) has described the relations between man and woman in terms of rape.

42. See Chapman's conclusion to his analysis (note 2 above) of Hobbes' treatment of the family.

CHAPTER 3: pages 28–38

1. John Locke, *Two Treatises of Government,* Peter Laslett, ed. (New York: Mentor Books, 1965), p. 309.

2. Ibid., pp. 374–375.

3. Cited in Richard Ashcraft, "Locke's State of Nature: Historical Fact or Moral Fiction?" *American Political Science Review* 62 (September 1968), p. 907.

4. Ibid., p. 316.

5. Ibid.

6. Ibid., p. 317.

7. Ibid., p. 323. The "Appeal to Heaven," the unifying motif of the *Second Treatise,* is mentioned no less than thirteen times.

8. Ibid., p. 323.

9. Ibid., p. 378.

10. *Judges* 21:25.

11. Locke, *Two Treatises,* II, pp. 386–387.

12. Ibid., p. 433.

13. Ibid., pp. 383–384.

14. Ibid., pp. 387–388.

15. Ibid., I, p. 219.

16. Ibid., pp. 380–381.

17. Ibid., I, p. 215.

18. Ibid., p. 208.

19. Ibid., II, pp. 346–347.

20. Ibid., I, p. 216.

21. Ibid., I, p. 214.

22. See especially John Dunn, *The Political Thought of John Locke: An Historical Account of the Argument of the Two Treatises of Government* (Cambridge: Cambridge University Press, 1966).

23. See *Two Treatises,* II, pp. 363–365.

24. Ibid., II, p. 364.

25. Ibid., p. 363.

26. Ibid., p. 350.

27. Ibid., p. 352.

28. Ibid., p. 357.

29. Ibid., p. 348.

30. Ibid., p. 364.

31. Ibid., p. 365.

32. Ibid., p. 386.

33. Ibid., p. 383.

34. Ibid., p. 334.

35. Ibid., p. 343.

36. Ibid.

37. Ibid., pp. 387–88.

38. Ibid., p. 391.

39. Ibid.

40. Talcott Parsons and Robert F. Bales, *Family, Socialization and Interaction Process* (New York: Free Press, 1955), p. 9. For further analysis of Parsons, see Chapter 9.

41. Ibid., p. 16.
42. Ibid.
43. Locke, *Two Treatises,* I, p. 244. Also: p. 216, p. 217.
44. Ibid.
45. Ibid., p. 220.
46. Ibid., p. 218.
47. Ibid., p. 219.

CHAPTER 4: pages 39–58

1. Robert Nisbet, *The Social Philosophers* (New York: T. Y. Crowell, 1973), pp. 267–268.
2. "Introduction: How to Read Rousseau's *Government of Poland,*" in Jean-Jacques Rousseau, *The Government of Poland,* Wilmore Kendal, ed. (Indianapolis: Bobbs-Merrill, 1972), p. xxviii.
3. Jean-Jacques Rousseau, *The First and Second Discourses,* Roger D. Masters, ed. (New York: St. Martin's Press, 1964), pp. 146–147.
4. Ibid., p. 149.
5. Jean-Jacques Rousseau, *Emile* (London: Dent, 1911), pp. 8, 322.
6. See: Mabel Lewis Sahakian and William S. Sahakian, *Rousseau as Educator* (New York: Twayne Publishers, 1974); Sylvia W. Patterson, *Rousseau's Emile and Early Children's Literature* (Metuchen, N.J.: Scarecrow Press, 1971).
7. Rousseau, *The First and Second Discourses,* pp. 57–58.
8. Ibid., pp. 180–181.
9. Ibid., p. 134.
10. Ibid., p. 135.
11. Ibid.
12. Ibid., p. 215.
13. Ibid., p. 216.
14. Ibid., p. 143.
15. Ibid., p. 146.
16. Ibid., p. 146.
17. Ibid., p. 146–147.
18. Ibid., p. 148.
19. Ibid., p. 147.
20. Ibid.
21. Ibid., p. 117.
22. Rousseau, *Emile,* p. 352.
23. Ibid., p. 325.
24. Ibid., p. 16.
25. Jean-Jacques Rousseau, *On the Social Contract with Geneva Manuscript* and *Political Economy,* Roger D. Masters, ed. (New York: St. Martin's Press, 1978), p. 169.
26. *Emile,* p. 59.
27. Ibid., p. 158.
28. Ibid., p. 160.
29. Ibid., p. 163.
30. Ibid., p. 147.
31. Ibid., p. 150.
32. Ibid.
33. Ibid., p. 175.
34. Ibid., p. 180.
35. Ibid.
36. Ibid., p. 179.
37. Ibid.
38. Ibid., p. 204.
39. Ibid., p. 359.
40. Ibid., p. 357.
41. Ibid., p. 348.
42. Ibid., p. 339.

43. Ibid., p. 325.
44. Ibid., p. 330.
45. Ibid., p. 362.
46. Ibid., p. 326.
47. Ibid., p. 327.
48. Ibid., p. 440.
49. Ibid., p. 443.
50. Ibid., p. 440.
51. Ibid.
52. Ibid., p. 208. See also pp. 180; 181; 189; 205; 295; 296; 368.
53. Rousseau, *First and Second Discourses*, pp. 134–135.
54. Rousseau, *Emile*, p. 322.
55. Ibid., p. 323.
56. Ibid.
57. Ibid., p. 322.
58. Ibid., p. 323.
59. Ibid.
60. Ibid.
61. Ibid., p. 324.
62. Ibid., p. 348.
63. Ibid., p. 349.
64. Ibid., p. 324.
65. Ibid., p. 325.
66. Ibid., p. 332.
67. Ibid., p. 7.
68. Ibid., p. 9.
69. Rousseau, *The Government of Poland*, p. 7.
70. Rousseau, *The Social Contract and Discourses*, G. D. H. Cole, ed. (New York: Dutton, 1950), p. 108. (This edition also includes *Political Economy*.).
71. Ibid., p. 19.
72. Ibid., p. 103.
73. Rousseau, *The Government of Poland*, p. 19.
74. Ibid., p. 22.
75. Ibid., p. 87.
76. Ibid.
77. Rousseau, *Emile*, p. 326.
78. Rousseau, *Political Economy*, p. 308.
79. Ibid., p. 309.
80. Ibid.
81. Ibid.
82. Ibid., p. 310.
83. Ibid., p. 286.
84. Ibid., p. 287.
85. Ibid., p. 286.
86. Ibid., p. 307.
87. Ibid., p. 308.
88. Ibid., p. 296.
89. Ibid., p. 298.

CHAPTER 5: pages 59–71

1. Jonathan Beecher and Richard Bienvenu, eds., *The Utopian Vision of Charles Fourier* (Boston: Beacon Press, 1971), p. 348. Fourier was an incredibly prolific writer, most of whose works are still not readily accessible. I have used two very capable anthologies in English translation.
2. Ibid., p. 350.
3. Cited in Frank E. Manuel, *The Prophets of Paris* (Cambridge, Mass.: Harvard University Press, 1962), p. 234.

4. For an analysis of the commune as a familial form see Chapter 12. For Sorel's comments: *From Georges Sorel,* John C. Stanley, ed. (New York: Oxford University Press, 1976), pp. 96–97, 103–104.

5. Mark Poster, ed., *Harmonian Man: Selected Writings of Charles Fourier* (Garden City: doubleday, 1971), p. 282.

6. Ibid., p. 283.

7. Ibid., p. 238.

8. Ibid., p. 259.

9. Ibid., p. 244.

10. Ibid., p. 224.

11. Beecher and Bienvenu, eds., *The Utopian Vision,* p. 377.

12. Ibid., p. 373.

13. Ibid., p. 374.

14. Ibid.

15. Ibid., p. 377.

16. Ibid.

17. Ibid.

18. Ibid., p. 213.

19. Mark Poster, ed., *Harmonian Man,* p. 235.

20. Ibid., p. 224.

21. Ibid., p. 226.

22. Ibid., p. 234–235.

23. Beecher and Bienvenu, eds., *The Utopian Vision,* p. 275.

24. Ibid., p. 338.

25. Ibid., p. 340.

26. Ibid., p. 337.

27. Ibid., p. 340.

28. Ibid., p. 386.

29. Mark Poster, ed., *Harmonian Man,* p. 229.

30. Ibid., p. 230.

31. Ibid., p. 225.

32. Ibid., p. 230.

33. Ibid., p. 276.

34. Beecher and Bienvenu, ed., *The Utopian Vision,* p. 371.

CHAPTER 6: pages 72–85

1. Karl Marx and Frederick Engels, "The German Ideology" in *Karl Marx: On Education, Women and Children,* Saul K. Padover, ed. (New York: McGraw-Hill, 1975), p. 61.

2. Karl Marx and Frederick Engels, "Manifesto of the Communist Party" in *The Marx-Engels Reader,* Robert C. Tucker, ed. (New York: Norton, 1978), p. 487.

3. Karl Marx, "Economic and Philosophic Manuscripts of 1844," in *The Marx-Engels Reader,* p. 83.

4. Ibid.

5. Frederick Engels, *The Origin of the Family, Private Property and the State* (New York: International Publishers, 1972), pp. 71–72.

6. Ibid., p. 72.

7. Ibid., p. 97.

8. Ibid., p. 100.

9. Ibid., p. 111.

10. Ibid.

11. Ibid.

12. Ibid., p. 113.

13. Ibid.

14. Ibid., p. 117.

15. Ibid., p. 75.

16. Ibid., p. 119.

17. Ibid., pp. 119–120.

18. Ibid., pp. 120–121.
19. Ibid., p. 128.
20. "In the vast majority of cases . . . marriage remained up to the Middle Ages what it had been from the start. . . ." Ibid., p. 139.
21. Ibid., pp. 121–122.
22. Ibid., p. 142.
23. Ibid., p. 193.
24. Ibid.
25. Marx and Engels, "The Manifesto of the Communist Party," in *The Marx-Engels Reader*, p. 488.
26. Ibid., pp. 487–488.
27. Karl Marx, *Capital: A Critique of Political Economy* (New York: Modern Library, 1936) p. 532.
28. Ibid.
29. Ibid., p. 534.
30. Marx, *The German Ideology*, p. 61.
31. Marx, *Capital*, p. 513.
32. Ibid.
33. Ibid.
34. Ibid., p. 530.
35. Ibid., p. 535.
36. Ibid.
37. Ibid., Final Report of the Children's Employment Commission of 1866 as cited by Marx.
38. Ibid., p. 536.
39. Ibid.
40. Ibid., p. 537.
41. Engels, *The Origin of the Family*, p. 137.
42. Ibid.
43. Marx, *Capital*, p. 440.
44. Engels, *The Origin of the Family*, p. 139.
45. Marx, "Economic and Philosophical Manuscripts," p. 82.
46. Ibid., p. 83.
47. Ibid.
48. Ibid., p. 82, note 7.
49. Ibid.
50. Ibid., p. 83.
51. The status of crude communism in the transformation is the subject of some dispute. Shlomo Avinieri has argued that the description in the *Manuscripts* is Marx's depiction of theories other than his own. "Marx's Vision of the Future," *Dissent* (Summer, 1973), pp. 323–331). This seems to me to be an especially weak argument. For a rebuttal see David Resnick, "Crude Communism and Revolution," *American Political Science Review* 70 (December, 1967), pp. 1136–1145.
52. See H. Kent Geiger's discussion of young communists' views on sexuality immediately after the 1917 revolution. *The Family in Soviet Russia* (Cambridge, Mass.: Harvard University Press, 1968), Chapter 2.
53. In fact, one would think that on the basis of Engels' own theory, it would be the woman who would represent the sexually aggressive force in crude communism. See Engels, *The Origin of the Family*, p. 125; p. 138.
54. Marx, "Economic and Philosophical Manuscripts," p. 82.
55. It is worth noting that Hegel's formulation of the family included both a strongly emotive as well as propertied basis. *Hegel's Philosophy of Right*, T. M. Knox, ed. (New York: Oxford University Press, 1952), pp. 110–122. For a fascinating and highly controversial interpretation of Marx as an unreconstructed Hegelian, see Robert Tucker, *Philosophy and Myth in Karl Marx* (Cambridge: Cambridge University Press, 1964).
56. Engels, *The Origin of the Family*, p. 141.
57. Ibid., p. 144.

58. Ibid., p. 139.

59. Ibid., p. 140.

60. Ibid., p. 139.

61. Marx, "Critique of the Gotha Program," in *Marx-Engels Reader,* p. 541.

62. Marx, *Capital,* p. 536.

63. Engels, *The Origin of the Family,* pp. 138, 139, 140, 144.

CHAPTER 7: pages 86–101

1. Eva Figes, *Patriarchal Attitudes* (New York: Fawcett, 1970), p. 136. The issue of Freud and women was first brought into prominence with Deutsch and Horney. The more recent attack on Freud in the 1960s has, of course, been more vehement and owes more to the left-wing critique of the 1930s. On this point see Paul A. Robinson's fine study, *The Freudian Left* (New York: Harper and Row, 1969) and our discussion in Chapter 11.

2. Juliet Mitchell, *Feminism and Psychoanalysis* (New York: Vintage Books, 1974), p. 409.

3. Sigmund Freud, "Three Contributions to the Theory of Sex" in *The Basic Writings of Sigmund Freud,* A. A. Brill, ed. (New York: Modern Library, 1938), p. 617, note 1.

4. Ibid.

5. Sigmund Freud, *Civilization and Its Discontents* (New York: Norton, 1961) pp. 50–51.

6. Ibid., p. 46.

7. Sigmund Freud, *Totem and Taboo* (New York: Random House, 1918), p. 182. Freud was not at all averse to the use of the fantastic hypothesis as a basis for scientific investigation. For an insightful discussion of this point, see Ernest Jones, *The Life and Work of Sigmund Freud* (New York: Basic Books, 1957), vol. 2, pp. 353 ff.

8. Freud, *Totem and Taboo,* p. 47.

9. Ibid., p. 80.

10. Ibid., p. 89.

11. Ibid., p. 161.

12. Ibid., p. 165. See Freud's own case study of a five-year-old boy's fear of horses: "Analysis of a Phobia in a Five-Year-Old Boy," *Standard Edition of the Complete Psychological Works of Sigmund Freud,* ed. James Strachey (London: Hogarth Press, 1955–1964), vol. 10, p. 86.

13. Ibid., p. 183.

14. Ibid., p. 182.

15. Ibid., p. 186.

16. Sigmund Freud, *Group Psychology and the Analysis of the Ego* (New York: Liveright, 1949), p. 114. Although Freud does not mention it, there is the obvious similarity to the Adam and Eve story.

17. Freud, *Totem and Taboo,* p. 204. In his last work, Freud admitted that the "present attitude of biological science" would reject his formulation, but still instisted that he could not "picture biological development" without the concept of inheritance of acquired dispositions. *Moses and Monotheism* (New York: Knopf, 1947), p. 158.

18. Freud, *Group Psychology,* p. 93.

19. Ibid., p. 91.

20. Ibid., p. 92.

21. Ibid., pp. 114–115.

22. Freud, *Moses and Monotheism,* p. 142.

23. Sigmund Freud, *Civilization and Its Discontents,* p. 50.

24. Sigmund Freud, "Female Sexuality" in *Sexuality and the Psychology of Love,* Philip Rieff, ed. (New York: Collier, 1963), pp. 194–211.

25. Sigmund Freud, "'Civilized' Sexual Morality and Modern Nervousness," in *Sexuality and the Psychology of Love,* p. 25.

26. Sigmund Freud, *New Introductory Lectures on Psychoanalysis* in *Standard Edition,* vol. 22, p. 101.

27. Attempts to demystify Freud himself on this and related points have proved difficult. Note the irony from a psychoanalytic perspective in Firestone's rejection of the emotional aspects of pregnancy: "Like shitting a pumpkin, a friend told me when I inquired about the

'Great Experience you're missing.'" *The Dialectic of Sex* (New York: Bantam Books, 1971), p. 199.

28. Sigmund Freud, "Notes upon a Case of Obsessional Neurosis" in *Three Case Histories,* (New York: Collier, 1963), p. 62.

29. Freud, *Moses and Monotheism,* p. 190.

30. Ibid., p. 192.

31. Philip Rieff, *The Triumph of the Therapeutic* (New York: Harper and Row, 1966).

32. Freud, *Civilization and Its Discontents,* pp. 60–61.

33. Ibid., p. 56.

34. Ibid.

35. Ibid., p. 59.

36. Ibid., p. 71.

37. Freud, *Moses and Monotheism,* p. 172.

38. Ibid., p. 108.

39. Freud, *Civilization and Its Discontents,* pp. 62–63.

40. Ibid., p. 88.

CHAPTER 8: pages 105–120

1. John Locke, *Two Treatises on Government,* Peter Laslett, ed. (New York: Mentor Books, 1965), II, p. 309.

2. Ibid., p. 356.

3. Ibid., pp. 346–347.

4. Jean-Jacques Rousseau, *Emile* (London: Dent, 1911), pp. 5, 179.

5. John Locke, "Some Thoughts Concerning Education" in *The Educational Writings of John Locke,* James L. Axtell, ed. (Cambridge: Cambridge University Press, 1968), p. 201.

6. Ibid., p. 311.

7. Ibid., p. 205.

8. See: Samuel T. Radbill, "A History of Child Abuse and Infanticide" in *The Battered Child,* Ray E. Helfer and Henry Kempe, eds. (Chicago: Univeristy of Chicago Press, 1968), pp. 3–17.

9. Cotton Mather, "Some Special Points Relating to the Education of My Children" in *The Puritans,* Perry Miller and Thomas H. Johnson, eds. (New York: Peter Smith, 1963), II, pp. 724–727.

10. Locke, "Some Thoughts Concerning Education," p. 158.

11. Ibid., p. 185.

12. Ibid.

13. Ibid., p. 179.

14. Ibid., p. 176.

15. Rousseau, *Emile,* p. 53.

16. Ibid., p. 86.

17. Cited in Bernard Wishy, *The Child and the Republic* (Philadelphia: University of Pennsylvania Press, 1968), pp. 46–47.

18. Ibid., p. 47.

19. Thomas Gordon, *P.E.T. Parent Effectiveness Training* (New York: Peter H. Wyden, 1970), p. 3.

20. Ibid., pp. 224–230.

21. Joan Beck, *Effective Parenting* (New York: Simon and Schuster, 1976), p. 251.

22. David G. Gil, "Violence against Children" *Journal of Marriage and the Family* 33 (November, 1971), p. 645.

23. Richard J. Gelles, "Child Abuse as Psychopathology: A Sociological Critique and Reformation" in *Violence in the Family,* Suzanne Steinmetz and Murray A. Straus, eds. (New York: Dodd, Mead, 1974).

24. John Holt, *Escape from Childhood* (New York: Dutton, 1974), p. 18. We will concentrate our efforts on Holt and Farson (listed below). For additional presentations of children's rights see: "The Rights of Children," *Harvard Educational Review* 43 (November, 1973); Patricia A. Vardin and Ilene N. Brody, eds., *Children's Rights: Contemporary Perspectives* (New York: Teachers College Press, 1979); Paul Adams, ed. *Children's Rights: Toward the*

Liberation of the Child (New York: Praeger, 1971); David Gottlieb, ed., *Children's Liberation* (Englewood Cliffs: Prentice-Hall, 1973).

25. Richard Farson, *Birthrights* (New York: Macmillan, 1974), p. 27.

26. Holt, *Escape from Childhood*, p. 110.

27. Farson, *Birthrights*, p. vii.

28. Arlene Skolnick, "Introduction" in *Rethinking Childhood,* Arlene Skolnick, ed. (Boston: Little, Brown, 1976), p. 9.

29. Holt, *Escape from Childhood*, p. 47.

30. Ibid., p. 155.

31. Farson, *Birthrights*, p. 15.

32. Ibid., p. 1.

33. Holt, *Escape from Childhood*, p. 57.

34. Ibid.

35. Ibid.

36. Farson, *Birthrights*, p. 11.

37. Ibid., p. 8.

38. Ibid., p. 173.

39. Holt, *Escape from Childhood*, p. 182.

40. Ibid., p. 213.

41. Ibid., p. 215.

42. Farson, *Birthrights*, p. 59.

43. Ibid., p. 147.

44. Ibid.

45. Ibid., p. 149.

CHAPTER 9: pages 121–132

1. See the queries of John Kenneth Galbraith, *Economics and the Public Purpose* (Boston: Houghton Mifflin, 1973), pp. 234–235.

2. See the historical accounts of John Demos, *A Little Commonwealth* and Philip Greven, *The Protestant Temperament*.

3. For a fuller account of forms of liberalism, see my *Furious Fancies: American Political Thought in the Post-Liberal Era* (Westport, Conn.: Greenwood Press, 1980), Chapter 1.

4. John Stuart Mill, "The Subjection of Women" in *Essays on Sex Equality,* Alice S. Rossi, ed. (Chicago: Univerity of Chicago Press, 1970), p. 189.

5. Ibid.

6. Ibid., pp. 148–149.

7. *On Liberty,* Gertrude Himmelfarb, ed. (Baltimore: Penguin Books, 1976), p. 157.

8. T. H. Green, *Lectures on the Principles of Political Obligation* (Ann Arbor: University of Michigan Press, 1967), p. 31.

9. Ibid., pp. 32–33.

10. Mill, *On Liberty*, p. 68. The same analogy is employed in *Utilitarianism,* Oscar Priest, ed. (Indianapolis: Bobbs-Merrill, 1957), p. 14.

11. Mill, "The Subjection of Women," p. 125.

12. Ibid., p. 141.

13. Ibid., p. 142.

14. Ibid.

15. Ibid., p. 173.

16. Ibid., p. 174.

17. Ibid., p. 164.

18. Ibid., p. 174.

19. Ibid.

20. Ibid., pp. 174–175.

21. Ibid., p. 175.

22. Talcott Parsons and Robert F. Bales, *Family, Socialization and Interaction Process* (New York: Free Press, 1955), p. 5.

23. Ibid., pp. 9–10.

24. Ibid., p. 16.

25. Ibid., p. 11.
26. Ibid., p. 26.
27. Ibid., p. 104.
28. Ibid., p. 11.
29. John Rawls, *A Theory of Justice* (Cambridge, Mass.: Harvard University Press, 1971), p. 11. Emphasis added.
30. Ibid., p. 74.
31. Ibid., p. 301.
32. Ibid., p. 511.
33. Ibid., p. 74.
34. Robert Nisbet, "The Pursuit of Equality," *Public Interest* (Spring, 1974), pp. 119 ff.
35. Rawls, *A Theory of Justice*, p. 462.
36. Ibid., p. 463.
37. Ibid.

CHAPTER 10: pages 133–146

1. A self-proclaimed professionalism is the only thread that the philosopher uses to connect his policy analysis on issues ranging from abortion to affirmative action to income distribution. "Philosophers Are Back on the Job," *New York Times Magazine* (July 7, 1974). See Peter Singer's "Bioethics: The Case of the Fetus," in which he demands participation of philosophers on national commissions. *New York Review of Books,* August 5, 1976.

2. The Thomson, Tooley, and Wertheimer essays all appeared in *Philosophy and Public Affairs* during 1971 and 1972. They have been collected along with a critique of Thomson by John Finis and are presented as an anthology, *The Rights and Wrongs of Abortion,* Marshall Cohen, Thomas Nagel, and Thomas Scanlon, eds., (Princeton: Princeton University Press, 1974). Citations are from this edition. Warren's essays appeared in the January 1973 issue of the *Monist*. It has been reprinted with her "Postscript on Infanticide" in *Today's Moral Problems,* Richard Wasserstrom, ed. (New York: Macmillan, 1975). Wasserstrom's collection also reprints Thomson's article along with selections from *Roe v. Wade* and Germain Grisez's *Abortion: The Myths, Realities, and the Arguments*.

3. Cohen, et al., *The Rights and Wrongs of Abortion,* preface.

4. Thomson, "A Defense of Abortion," p. 22.

5. Wertheimer, "Understanding the Abortion Argument," p. 41.

6. Warren, "On the Moral and Legal Status of Abortion," p. 131.

7. Tooley, "Abortion and Infanticide," p. 78.

8. Peter Singer, "Embryonic 'Bioethics'," *New York Review of Books,* November 11, 1976, p. 46. The same sentiments are expressed by Warren (p. 133); Tooley (p. 54); Thomson (p. 3).

9. Tooley, "Abortion and Infanticide," pp. 54–55. Tooley chides Wertheimer for his "superficial dismissal of infanticide."

10. This example is taken from Thomson's appropriately entitled essay, "Rights and Deaths," p. 121.

11. Ibid., p. 122.

12. Ibid., p. 123.

13. Tooley, "Abortion and Infanticide," p. 69. Even Martians are in danger here since Tooley suggests that "if their central nervous systems were radically different from ours . . . one would be forced to conclude that one was not justified in ascribing any rights to them."

14. Magda Denes, "Performing Abortion," *Commentary,* October 1976, p. 37. Denes also reports on the anxiety of medical personnel, a fact not unappreciated by administrators who "initiated" physicans and nurses with early abortions. Also see Francis Kane, et al., "Emotional Reactions in Abortion Services Personnel," *Archives of General Psychiatry* 28 (March 1973), and J. F. McDermott, Jr. and E. F. Carr, "Abortion Repeal in Hawaii: An Unexpected Crisis in Patient Care," *American Journal of Orthopsychiatry* 41 (1971). Both studies concern medical personnel suffering from depression and anxiety.

15. In a later piece, Wertheimer is able to drag himself to the boundaries of the philosophical consensus that separates the moral status of a human from the concept of a human. Yet he again reviews pro- and anti-abortion arguments without being able to tell the reader whether the fetus is human. However, animals apparently pose less of a problem for him.

They have no human status, but perhaps they possess a "substantial moral status" ("Philosophy on Humanity" in *Abortion: Pro and Con*, p. 122). In the same volume, Tooley repeats his position and flavors his argument with some soothing social engineering. A society devoted to free abortion without guilt will produce "happy people" and happy people "if not necessarily constructive citizens, are not destructive ones." In addition, proper care for "defective children" is expensive and "will be thought to impose too great a sacrifice upon parents and taxpayers" (Michael Tooley and Laura Purdy, "Is Abortion Murder?" *Abortion: Pro and Con*, pp. 130–132).

16. Lewis Coser, "Greedy Organizations," *European Journal of Sociology* 7 (October 1967), p. 215.

17. Thomson, "A Defense of Abortion," p. 16.

18. Ibid., pp. 17–18.

19. Ibid., p. 11.

20. Warren, "On the Moral and Legal Status of Abortion," p. 125.

21. Ibid., p. 128. Tooley is concerned that he confine the term "human" to "contexts where it is not philosophically dangerous" (p. 58). He much prefers a "self-consciousness" claim: "An organism possesses a serious right to life only if it possesses the concept of a self as a continuing subject of experiences and other mental states and believes that it is itself such a continuing entity" (p. 59).

22. Warren, "On the Moral and Legal Status of Abortion," p. 130.

23. Ibid., p. 131.

24. Ibid., p. 132.

25. Ibid., p. 133.

26. Ibid., p. 135.

27. Ibid., p. 136.

28. For further discussion, see Chapter 13.

CHAPTER 11: pages 147–155

1. See Leo Strauss's brilliant discussion on this point in *Natural Right and History* (Chicago: University of Chicago Press, 1953), p. 291.

2. This general problem is explored eloquently in Elizabeth Hardwick, *Seduction and Betrayal* (New York: Vintage Books, 1975), pp. 217–218.

3. R. D. Laing, *The Politics of the Family and Other Essays* (New York: Vintage Books, 1972), p. 5.

4. R. D. Laing, *The Politics of the Family*, p. 14.

5. Ibid., p. 121.

6. Ibid., p. 124.

7. R. D. Laing, *The Politics of Experience* (New York: Ballantine Books, 1967), p. 126. For a thoughtful examination of Laing on this point see Francis H. Bartlett, "Illusion and Reality in R. D. Laing," *Family Process* 15 (1976), pp. 51–64.

8. Betty E. Cogswell, "Variant Family Forms and Life Styles: Rejection of the Traditional Nuclear Family," *Family Coordinator* 24 (October 1975), p. 394.

9. Teresa Donati Marciano, "Variant Family Forms in a World Perspective," *Family Coordinator* 24 (October 1975), pp. 407–408.

10. Constantina Safilos-Rothschild, *Love, Sex and Sex Roles* (Englewood Cliffs: Prentice-Hall, 1977), p. 137.

11. Teresa Donati Marciano, "Variant Family Forms," pp. 409–410.

12. Ibid., p. 410.

13. Ibid.

14. Ibid., p. 411. On this point, also see Ray L. Birdwhistell, who argues that any study of the modern family which assumes the absence of pathology assumes a "sentimental" model: "The American Family: Some Perspectives," *Psychiatry* 29 (1966), p. 2111.

15. Constantina Safilos-Rothschild, "Dual Linkages between the Occupational and Family Systems: Macrosociological Analysis," *Signs* (Spring 1976), p. 60.

16. Ibid., p. 61.

17. See the argument of Elizabeth Janeway, *Men's World, Women's Place* (New York: Delta, 1971), pp. 300–301.

18. Rosabeth Moss Kanter, "'Getting It All Together': Some Group Issues in Communes," *American Journal of Orthopsychiatry* 42 (July 1972).

19. Ibid.

20. Marciano, "Variant Family Forms," pp. 417–418.

21. John McMartry, "Monogamy: A Critique" in *Philosophy and Sex*, Robert Baker and Frederick Elliston, eds. (Buffalo: Prometheus Books, 1975), p. 172.

22. Juliet Mitchell, *Woman's Estate* (New York: Vintage Books, 1971), p. 114.

23. Here are two typical examples: Peter J. Stein, "Singlehood: An Alternative to Marriage," *Family Coordinator* 24 (October 1975), pp. 489–503; J. E. Veevers, "Voluntary Childless Wives: An Exploratory Study," *Sociology and Social Research* 57 (1973), pp. 356–365.

24. Shulamith Firestone, *The Dialectic of Sex* (New York: Bantam Books, 1971), p. 206; Suzanne Keller, "Does the Family Have a Future?" in Arlene S. Skolnick and Jerome H. Skolnick, eds., *Family in Transition*, second edition (Boston: Little, Brown, 1977), p. 587. The convergence between the romantic view and the efforts of genetic engineers is remarkable. Compare these comments: Robert Morrison — "It is idle to talk of a society of equal opportunity as long as society abandons its newcomers solely to their families for their most impressionable years" (*New York Times*, October 30, 1966). Joshua Lederberg — The "emotional" responses concerning parenthood should not "be confused with objective biological standards by which we can set up principles of social order as criteria for the operation of law" ("Experimental Genetics," *Bulletin of the Atomic Scientists,* October 1966), p. 4. Garret Hardin — "The biological 'ownership' of children by parents has not been defensible for about a century" (*Science* 169, July 31, 1970, p. 427).

25. Keller, "Does the Family Have a Future?", p. 587. The following presentation is taken from Judith Lorber's explicit scenarios.

26. Judith Lorber, "Beyond Equality of the Sexes: The Question of the Children," *Family Coordinator* 24 (October 1975), pp. 468–469. For similar discussion involving the mobility of children see: Firestone, *Dialectic of Sex*, pp. 230–234; and Richard Farson, *Birthrights* (New York: Macmillan, 1974), pp. 58–62.

27. Lorber, p. 469.

28. Ibid., p. 470.

29. Ibid.

30. Carl Levett, "A Parental Presence in Future Family Models" in *The Family in Search of a Future*, Herbert A. Otto, ed. (New York: Appleton-Century-Crofts, 1970), p. 166.

31. Eleanor Maccoby, "Children and Working Mothers," *Children* 5-6 (1958–1959), p. 86.

32. Leon Yarrow, "Conceptualizing the Early Environment," in *Early Child Care: New Perspectives*, Laura L. Dittman, ed. (New York: Atherton, 1968), p. 22.

33. Rosalyn E. Baxandall, "Who Shall Care for Our Children?" in *Women: A Feminist Perspective*, Jo Freeman, ed. (Palo Alto: Mayfield Publishing Co., 1975).

CHAPTER 12: pages 156–168

1. Eli Zaretsky, *Capitalism, The Family and Personal Life* (New York: Harper and Row, 1976), p. 106.

2. Ibid., p. 101.

3. Ibid., p. 141.

4. Ibid.

5. H. Kent Geiger, *The Family in Soviet Russia* (Cambridge, Mass.: Harvard University Press, 1968), p. 61.

6. Sigmund Freud, *Civilization and Its Discontents* (New York: Norton, 1961), p. 55.

7. Wilhelm Reich, *The Function of the Orgasm* (New York: Farrar, Straus and Giroux, 1961), p. 156. Emphasis is in the original.

8. Ibid.

9. Ibid.

10. Wilhelm Reich, *The Mass Psychology of Fascism* (New York: Farrar, Straus and Giroux, 1970), p. xi.

11. Ibid.

12. Ibid.

13. In an essay in 1922 Reich focused upon unusual forms of masturbation undertaken by neurotics and concluded that the "most essential emotional drives are accumulated, expressed and released in masturbation, which serves as the focal point for infantile and pubertal sexuality" ("Concerning Specific Forms of Masturbation" in Wilhelm Reich, *Early Writings* [New York: Farrar, Straus and Giroux, 1975], vol. I, p. 130). The full-blown theory that contained the assertion that no neurotics have a healthy sex life was first offered by Reich in *Die Funktion des Orgasms*. It was dedicated to Freud, who understandably restricted his reaction to a few polite comments.

14. Reich, *The Function of the Orgasm*, pp. 84–85.

15. Wilhelm Reich, "The Genital Character and Neurotic Character" in *Character Analysis* (New York: Farrar, Straus and Giroux, 1963), p. 122.

16. Wilhelm Reich, *The Function of the Orgasm*, p. 165.

17. Ibid., p. 167.

18. Wilhelm Reich, *The Mass Psychology of Fascism*, p. 29.

19. Ibid.

20. Ibid., p. 30.

21. Wilhelm Reich, "The Imposition of Sexual Morality" in *Sex-Pol: Essays, 1929–1934* (New York: Vintage Books, 1972), p. 173.

22. Ibid., pp. 200–201.

23. Ibid., p. 201.

24. Ibid., p. 162.

25. Ibid., p. 160.

26. Ibid., p. 162.

27. Ibid., p. 163.

28. Wilhelm Reich, *Listen, Little Man!* (New York: Farrar, Straus and Giroux, 1948), p. 42. Also: *The Function of the Orgasm*, pp. 204–205.

29. Wilhelm Reich, *The Mass Psychology of Fascism*, p. xx.

30. Ibid., p. xv.

31. Ibid.

32. Wilhelm Reich, *The Sexual Revolution* (New York: Farrar, Straus and Giroux, 1962), p. 89.

33. Ibid., p. 17.

34. See his second wife's anecdote in Ilse Ollendorf Reich, *Wilhelm Reich: A Personal Biography* (New York: St. Martin's Press, 1969), p. 83.

35. Herbert Marcuse, *Eros and Civilization* (New York: Vintage Books, 1962), p. 87. Marcuse's view of the family has not changed since his pronouncements in 1936. See: "A Study of Authority," reprinted in *Studies in Critical Philosophy"* (Boston: Beacon Press, 1972), esp. pp. 106–107.

36. Ibid., p. 88.

37. Ibid.

38. Ibid., p. 89.

39. Ibid., pp. 89–90.

40. Herbert Marcuse, *One-Dimensional Man* (Boston: Beacon Press, 1969), p. 74.

41. Ibid.

42. Ibid., p. 75.

43. Marcuse, *Eros and Civilization*, p. 57.

44. Ibid., p. 32.

45. Ibid.

46. Ibid., p. 200.

47. Ibid., p. 184.

48. Ibid., p. 190.

49. Herbert Marcuse, *An Essay on Liberation* (Boston: Beacon Press, 1969), p. 43.

50. Ibid., p. 46.

51. Alasdair MacIntyre, *Herbert Marcuse: An Exposition and a Polemic* (New York: Viking Press, 1970), p. 50.

52. Marcuse, *Eros and Civilization*, p. 193.

53. Ibid.

54. Ibid.
55. Ibid., p. 194.

CHAPTER 13: pages 171–186
1. Alison Jaggar, "Abortion and a Woman's Right to Decide," *Philosophical Forum* (Fall-Winter 1973–1974), p. 317.
2. Wilhelm Reich, *The Sexual Revolution* (New York: Farrar, Straus and Giroux, 1962), p. 138; Herbert Marcuse, *An Essay on Liberation* (Boston: Beacon Press, 1969), p. 59.
3. See Robert Nisbet's portrayal of the model of the "political community" in Western political thought: *The Social Philosophers* (New York: T. Y. Crowell, 1973), Chapter 2.
4. See the sympathetic account of Jonathan Gathorne-Hardy, *The Unnatural History of the Nanny* (New York: Dial Press, 1973).
5. Hermann Schmalenbach, "The Sociology of the 'Bund'" in *Theories of Society*, Talcott Parsons, et al., eds. (Glencoe, Ill.: Free Press, 1961), pp. 331–347.
6. Maren Lockwood Carden, *Oneida: Utopian Community to Modern Corporation* (Baltimore: Johns Hopkins Press, 1969), p. 53.
7. Charles Nordhoff, *The Communistic Societies of the United States* (New York: Hillary House, 1961), p. 293.
8. Cited in Rosabeth Moss Kanter, *Commitment and Community* (Cambridge, Mass.: Harvard University Press, 1972), p. 12.
9. Carden, *Oneida*, p. 59.
10. Joseph Stephen, "Families in Social Structure: The Case of the Kibbutz," *Journal of Marriage and the Family* 31 (August 1969), p. 53. Spiro and Spiro have reported an interesting phenomenon regarding the commune's norm of an equalitarian response to all children. He notes that nonfamily visitors to schools tend to visit only the younger children. He concludes: "As the children grow older, then, they experience a 'rejection' by the entire kibbutz — a rejection that differs in intensity from that they may have experienced with their parents. Displaced by their (younger) sociological siblings, . . . they too experience rejection by those to whom they 'belong.' This contrast between expectancy (love and attention) and actuality (rejection) is, according to some nurses, one of the most difficult experiences in the life of the kibbutz child." (Melford Spiro and Audrey G. Spiro, *Children of the Kibbutz* [Cambridge, Mass.: Harvard University Press, 1975], rev. ed., p. 71.) Thus sibling rivalry, as a battle for the parents' love, reappears in the allegedly family-free commune.
11. The history of the communal movement in America is, in fact, a history of strong charismatic leaders — a series of Moseses taking their people into the wilderness. Harmony had Father Rapp; Oneida, Noyes; Aurora, William Keil; Jersualem, Jeremiah Wilkinson; Zoar, Joseph Bimeler.
12. Carden, *Oneida*, p. 62.
13. Ibid., p. 98.
14. Kanter, *Commitment and Community*, pp. 139–161.
15. Ibid., p. 146.
16. Stanley Diamond, "Kibbutz and Shtetl: The History of an Idea," *Social Problems* 5 (1957), pp. 71–99.
17. Ibid., p. 89.
18. Ibid., p. 90.
19. Ibid., p. 91.
20. Ibid., p. 92.
21. Ibid.
22. Kanter, *Commitment and Community*, p. 150.
23. The Volga German community in Russia, over its life from the 1760s till it was broken up during World War II, might furnish another instance, qualified and impure, of the dynamics that make a commune unstable over generations — although this community was not strictly communal. See Fred C. Koch, *The Volga Germans in Russia and the Americas from 1763 to the Present* (University Park, Pennsylvania: The Pennsylvania State University Press, 1977). I am grateful to Willis L. Parker for bringing this point to my attention.

CHAPTER 14: pages 187–198

1. One of the best short general reviews of pluralism in Western thought is John W. Chapman, "Voluntary Association and the Political Theory of Pluralism" in *Voluntary Associations,* J. Roland Pennock and John W. Chapman, eds. (New York: Atherton Press, 1969), pp. 87–118. Also see: Bertrand de Jouvenel, *Sovereignty* (Cambridge: Cambridge University Press, 1957) and *The Pure Theory of Politics* (Cambridge: Cambridge University Press, 1963); Frederick Watkins, *The Political Tradition of the West* (Cambridge, Mass.: Harvard University Press, 1948); William Kornhauser, *The Politics of Mass Society* (New York: Free Press, 1959); R. M. MacIver, *The Web of Government* (New York: Macmillan, 1947).

2. Robert Nisbet, *The Social Philosophers* (New York: T. Y. Crowell, 1973), pp. 387–390.

3. Theodore Lowi, *The Politics of Disorder* (New York: Norton, 1971).

4. Alexis de Tocqueville, *Democracy in America,* J. P. Mayer, ed. (Garden City: Doubleday, 1969), p. 507.

5. Ibid., p. 587.

6. Ibid., p. 527.

7. David Truman, *The Process of Government* (New York: Knopf, 1951); Robert Dahl, *After the Revolution: Authority in the Good Society* (New Haven: Yale University Press, 1970).

8. Dahl, *After the Revolution,* p. 12.

9. See: Mary Jo Bane, *Here to Stay: American Families in the Twentieth Century* (New York: Basic Books, 1976), Pt. II.

10. *Selected Writings of P. J. Proudhon,* Stewart Edwards, ed. (Garden City: Doubleday, 1969), pp. 56–57.

11. *The Essential Kropotkin,* Emile Capouya and Keith Thomas, eds. (New York: Liveright, 1975), p. 170.

12. See John Kenneth Galbraith's criticism of the "self-exploitation" of the small businessman and his plans for its elimination. *Economics the Public Purpose* (Boston: Houghton Mifflin, 1973).

13. *The Essential Kropotkin,* pp. 243–244.

14. *Selected Writings of P. J. Proudhon,* p. 100; also pp. 102, 109.

15. Ibid., p. 255.

16. Cited in Robert L. Hoffman, *Revolutionary Justice* (Urbana, Ill.: University of Illinois Press, 1972), p. 253.

17. *The Essential Kropotkin,* p. 291.

18. William Godwin, *An Enquiry Concerning Political Justice,* F. L. Priestly, ed. (Toronto: University of Toronto Press, 1946), vol. 2, p. 511.

19. Max Stirner, *The Ego and His Own* (New York: Liveright, n.d.), p. 327.

20. Edmund Burke, *Reflections on the Revolution in France,* Conor Cruise O'Brien, ed. (New York: Penguin, 1976), p. 124.

21. Ibid., p. 135.

22. Ibid., p. 195.

23. George Gilder, *Sexual Suicide* (New York: Quadrangle Books, 1973).

24. Lionel Tiger and Robin Fox, *The Imperial Animal* (New York: Dell, 1971), p. 15.

25. Ibid.

26. Selma Fraiberg, *In Defense of Mothering* (New York: Basic Books, 1976).

27. Benjamin R. Barber, *Liberating Feminism* (New York: Dell, 1975), p. 106.

28. Philippe Ariès, *Centuries of Childhood* (New York: Knopf, 1965), p. 406.

29. Ariés, *Histoire des Populations Françaises,* cited in David Hunt, *Parent and Children in History* (New York: Basic Books, 1970), p. 43.

30. Ariés, *Centuries of Childhood,* p. 414.

31. Christopher Lasch, *Haven in a Heartless World* (New York: Basic Books, 1977), p. 180.

32. Herbert Hendrin, *Age of Sensation,* cited in Lasch, p. 182.

33. Lasch, p. 183.

CHAPTER 15: pages 199–208

1. Joseph Schumpeter, *Capitalism, Socialism, and Democracy* (New York: Harper, 1942), p. 157.

2. Richard Sennett, *The Fall of Public Man* (New York: Knopf, 1977).

3. Lyman C. Wynne, et al., "Pseudo-Mutuality in the Family Relations of Schizo-phrenics," *Psychiatry* 21 (1958), pp. 210–211.

4. See the Carnegie Council report which calls for public-advocate lawyers for children to be financed through financial contributions of parents (Kenneth Keniston, et al., *All Our Children* [New York: Harcourt Brace Jovanovich, 1977]) and the National Research Council's plan to provide standardized family resource centers supervised by the Office of Child Development (*Toward a National Policy for Children and Families* [Washington, D.C.: National Academy of Sciences, 1976]).

5. Philippe Ariés, *Centuries of Childhood* (New York: Basic Books, 1970); Bernard Bailyn, *Education in the Forming of American Society* (Chapel Hill: University of North Carolina Press, 1970).

6. Richard Sennett, *Families against the City* (Cambridge, Mass.: Harvard University Press, 1970), p. 149.

7. Stephen Thernstrom, *Poverty and Progress* (New York: Atheneum, 1970).

8. See: Herbert Gans' study of the destruction of Boston's West End by federal renewal programs, *The Urban Villagers* (New York: Free Press, 1962); Michael Young's and Peter Wilmot's account of the removal of the inhabitants of Bethnal Green to a new housing complex, *Family and Kinship in East London* (Baltimore: Penguin Books, 1957); Kai T. Erikson's moving description of the disaster at Buffalo Creek (this brought on by private greed), *Everything in Its Path* (New York: Simon and Schuster, 1976).

9. Bob Gottlieb and Marge Piercy, "M.D.S., Beginning to Begin to Begin" in *The New Left: A Documentary History,* ed. Massimo Teodori (Indianapolis: Bobbs-Merrill, 1969), p. 408.

10. Ibid.

INDEX